ADAPTING TO AMERICA

ADAPTING TO AMERICA

Catholics, Jesuits, and Higher Education in the Twentieth Century

William P. Leahy, S.J.
Department of History
Marquette University

Georgetown University Press
WASHINGTON, D.C.

Library of Congress Cataloging-in-Publication Data

Leahy, William P.
    Adapting to America : Catholics, Jesuits, and higher education in
the twentieth century / William P. Leahy.
        p.   cm.
    Includes bibliographical references.
    ISBN 0-87840-504-6. -- ISBN 0-87840-505-4 (pbk.)
    1. Catholic universities and colleges--United States-
-History--20th century. 2. Church and college--United States-
-History--20th century. 3. Catholics--United States--Intellectual
life--20th century. 4. United States--intellectual life--20th
century. 5. Christianity and culture--History--20th century.
I. Title.
    LC501.L34 1991
377--dc20   90-40505
                                                           CIP

To my parents, Ed and Alice Leahy

soc
377.
L434

Contents

Preface

This is a study of how Catholics adapted to the United States and how American culture affected Catholicism during the twentieth century; it is based on an investigation of major developments in Catholic higher education since World War I. Like other academic institutions in this country, Catholic colleges and universities have functioned as both mirrors and agents of change during the twentieth century as they grew in number, size, and academic quality. In 1900, the Catholic higher educational network consisted of sixty-three schools enrolling approximately 4,200 students, the vast majority of them males. Founded by dioceses or religious orders and staffed mainly by priests, brothers, and sisters, these institutions offered a prescriptive, liberal arts curriculum and stressed character formation in an atmosphere permeated by traditional, believing Catholicism. No school was coeducational, and most lacked adequate faculty and facilities.

But in 1990, Catholic colleges and universities number more than 230 institutions and register approximately 550,000 students in a variety of undergraduate, graduate, and professional programs. Catholic higher education currently ranges from small colleges for women to large coeducational, comprehensive universities and from numerous accredited, though academically undistinguished, schools to a few institutions with national academic prestige. Most Catholic postsecondary schools now admit both male and female applicants, and all rely heavily on lay faculty and administrators. Moreover, in contrast to the confidence, religious zeal, and clear objectives particularly evident in Catholic colleges and universities in the 1920s and 1930s, Catholic higher learning currently faces a growing shortage of personnel committed to fostering Catholic spiritual and educational values. Moreover, it lacks a compelling sense of purpose.[1]

The growth of American Catholic higher education in this century reflected in past decades and continues to reflect today the religious values, population increase, rising educational and career goals, and ideological adjustments of Catholics in the United States. Catholic schools also contributed significantly to Catholic social, political, and economic advancement, providing low-cost education and encouraging Catholics to enter the mainstream. Thus, examination of the development of Catholic colleges and universities since 1900 casts light on the response of Catholics to American culture and the influence of wider society on Catholicism.

Yet despite the importance of schools in the American Catholic experience, the written history of Catholic higher learning is curiously meager, consisting mainly of brief essays and narrow histories of institutions and their sponsoring religious orders. There is a special need for monographs which analyze and interpret Catholic higher education in the context of American culture, non-Catholic schools, and the Catholic community. Contemporary understanding of American Catholicism and its educational institutions suffers from the absence of such studies.

Inquiry into the historical significance of events in Catholic higher education must pay attention to two central questions. First, what were the main developments in Catholic postsecondary institutions during the twentieth century and what accounted for them? Second, what do the changes in Catholic colleges and universities reveal about the adaptation of Catholics to American society and the effects of culture on members of the Catholic Church in the United States?

Since Catholic postsecondary education is a vast and complex subject, this work concentrates on colleges and universities conducted under the auspices of the Society of Jesus, a Catholic religious order of men. The centralized government and policy making in Jesuit schools lend themselves to research and analysis. Furthermore, Jesuits have played a prominent role in American Catholic life as they variously initiated or opposed change, and their institutions have generally reflected issues in the rest of Catholic higher education.[2] Other Catholic colleges and universities drew from Jesuit educational theory and practice because Jesuits had articulated a definite philosophy of education and because they had developed a reputation as effective educators since their founding in 1540.[3] In addition, the Jesuit order has had more men involved in Catholic higher education in the United States than any other religious community, and it also continues to conduct the largest number of Catholic colleges and universities. In 1939, the twenty-four institutions directed by Jesuits in sixteen states and the District of Columbia enrolled about 40% of students attending

Catholic colleges and universities. At that time, all ten Catholic medical and dental programs as well as eleven of fourteen accredited Catholic law schools were part of Jesuit higher education. After 1945, Jesuit universities expanded heavily into graduate education; and in 1970, they awarded 56% (467) of the doctorates granted by Catholic schools. The Jesuit higher educational network in 1988 included nine colleges and nineteen universities in eighteen states and the District of Columbia, with an enrollment of 175,000 students.[4]

To provide perspective on major changes in American Catholicism and Catholic higher education since 1900, the opening section of this study reviews the evolution of the Catholic community before World War I, especially in comparison with Jews and Protestants. It also summarizes the administrative and academic reforms which reshaped the American educational scene in the late nineteenth and early twentieth centuries. Chapter 2 focuses on the conflict between the religious beliefs and educational objectives of Catholics and the increasingly competitive, professionalized American academic environment. Chapter 3 investigates the origins and development of coeducation in Catholic schools, a radical break with Catholic tradition. The next chapter discusses the rise of laity in Catholic higher education, and chapter 5 examines the expansion of Catholic postsecondary schools after World War II, seeking to determine why Catholic colleges and universities have not made greater advances in quality and status.

Consideration of these issues reveals much about the growth of American Catholic higher education in the twentieth century, particularly the struggles of Catholic educators to meet the desires of their Catholic clientele and to balance the demands of religious commitment and academic professionalism. Such analysis also enhances understanding of Catholic upward mobility; the increased status of laity, including women and non-Catholics in Catholic circles; and the impact of secular ideas on Catholic social, religious, and educational attitudes.

The history of Catholic colleges and universities after 1900 is a story not only of dedication, grand dreams, and real successes, but also of poor leadership, narrowness, and missed opportunities. Increased knowledge of the Catholic educational past should enhance understanding of Catholic higher education, Catholicism, and contemporary culture in the United States.

Notes

1. James Hennesey, S.J., *American Catholics: A History of the Roman Catholic Community in the United States* (New York: Oxford University Press, 1981), 187; "Report on the Attendance at Catholic Colleges and Universities in the United States," *Catholic Educational Association Bulletin* 12 (August 1916): 7; and *The Official Catholic Directory,* 1989.

2. For observations on the influence of Jesuit higher education in America, see Philip Gleason, "American Catholic Higher Education: A Historical Perspective," in *The Shape of Catholic Higher Education,* ed. Robert Hassenger (Chicago: University of Chicago Press, 1967), 33-35.

3. For a recent study of the origins and early influence of Jesuit education, see Aldo Scaglione, *The Liberal Arts and the Jesuit College System* (Amsterdam/Philadelphia: John Benjamins Publishing Company, 1986).

4. Charles M. O'Hara, S.J., "The Expanse of American Jesuit Education," *Jesuit Educational Quarterly* 2 (June 1939): 14; W. Todd Furniss, ed., *American Universities and Colleges* (Washington, D.C.: American Council on Education, 1973), 1775-83; and *Directory, Association of Jesuit Colleges and Universities,* 1989-90, 7.

Acknowledgments

I want to thank those who contributed so much during the conceptualization, research, and writing of this work. The Wisconsin Province of the Society of Jesus provided greatly appreciated financial assistance, the Jesuit Communities at Santa Clara and Marquette Universities could not have been more supportive of me, and members of the History Department at Marquette University, especially Dr. Thomas Hachey, the chairman, have been most helpful.

The staffs of the various archives and libraries that I visited during my research also deserve special thanks. I am particularly indebted to Leo Cullen, S.J., archivist of the California Province of the Society of Jesus; to Robert Callen, S.J. of Marquette University; and to three people now deceased: Paul FitzGerald, S.J., former archivist of Boston College; John F. Bannon, S.J., a long-time professor of history at St. Louis University; and Paul Distler, S.J., assistant to the provincial of the Missouri Province.

Other individuals also made significant contributions to this study. Leonard Waters, S.J. of Creighton University generously read my entire manuscript and offered comments which helped me to refine my ideas. Professor Lewis B. Mayhew of Stanford unfailingly responded to my questions about the development of American higher education, and he always was a source of encouragement. In addition, I profited from frequent conversations with Michael Buckley, S.J. of the Jesuit School of Theology, Berkeley, California about Catholic higher education, Catholicism, and contemporary culture in the United States. Nicholas Pope, S.J., a staff member of the Computer Services Division of Marquette University, gave generously of his time and energy in helping me through the intricacies of preparing these pages on a computer.

I also want to thank three professors of history at Stanford. Alexander Dallin and David Tyack carefully evaluated my manuscript, making valuable suggestions about argument and content. I owe a special debt to Professor David M. Kennedy. While completing this study, I especially benefited from his patience, high standards, and broad intellectual perspectives. During my years at Stanford, he taught me in countless ways what it means to be a professional historian today.

Finally, I am especially grateful to Father John Breslin and Eleanor Waters of Georgetown University Press for their generous and invaluable assistance with my manuscript.

1

Catholicism and Education in America

Twentieth-century Catholic higher education in the United States unfolded in a context shaped in important ways by massive immigration and educational reform occurring between the 1840s and World War I. During these years, the Catholic Church struggled to help waves of Catholic immigrants overcome poverty and religious prejudice, and numerous American colleges and universities underwent sweeping revisions in curriculum, governance, and purpose. An understanding of these developments and their impact on American Catholicism provides perspective for analyzing major changes in Catholic higher education after 1900.

In 1800, Catholics in America numbered about 50,000, approximately 1% of the total population; and most lived unobtrusively in Maryland and Pennsylvania. But the flood of Catholic immigrants after 1840 transformed American Catholicism and generated conflicts inside and outside it until the early 1920s when Congress imposed quotas on immigration. By 1850, the Catholic Church had grown to 2,000,000 members, who resided mainly in the urban Northeast; it then ranked as the largest denomination in the country. Its numbers reached 6,000,000 in 1880 and 12,000,000 in 1900, due in large part to an estimated 5,000,000 Catholics among the 17,000,000 persons immigrating to the United States between 1850 and 1900. Continued immigration, natural growth, and conversions to the Catholic faith increased the Catholic community to almost 18,000,000 in 1920, making every sixth person and every third church-goer in the nation a Roman Catholic.[1]

The first waves of Catholic immigrants to America consisted mainly of Irish and Germans; but by the 1890s, most came from southern and eastern Europe. Whatever their origins, many were poor, illiterate, and unskilled peasants, victims of social change. For instance, over half the people in Ireland in 1841 could not read or write, and neither could 54.2% of southern Italian adults arriving in the United States between 1899 and 1909. Only 6% of Polish immigrants in the first decade of the twentieth century were classified as skilled workers.[2] The vast majority of Catholic immigrants grew up in cultures stressing family relationships and traditional ways; an atmosphere of simple, believing Catholicism pervaded their lives. Consequently, after reaching American soil, they looked to their relatives and priests to ease the trauma of adapting to often bewildering surroundings and to help them survive frequently appalling living conditions.

Meeting the widely varying spiritual, psychological, and physical needs of immigrants from different countries posed immense challenges for American Catholicism, particularly in cities. The growth and problems of the Catholic Church in Boston typified the pressures on urban Catholicism. In 1820 about 2,100 Catholics resided within the boundaries of the Boston archdiocese, rising to an estimated 32,000 in 1846. Twenty years later the total had reached 200,000, which tripled by 1896. By 1929, the count stood at 990,000. Most of the immigrants coming to Boston were Irish until the 1880s; then in the next forty years, hundreds of French Canadians, Italians, Poles, Lithuanians, Portuguese, and Syrians settled in the Massachusetts area.[3]

Despite meager funds and limited personnel, the Catholic Church in the United States gradually built an extensive network of parishes (124 in 1820, 2,550 in 1860, and 10,339 in 1900), schools, charitable organizations, and recreational facilities to serve its members.[4] It encouraged development of a Catholic subculture to ease economic hardship and to counter an often hostile environment. American Catholicism was a church of immigrants and workers from the 1840s until World War II.[5]

Inadequate skills, language problems, and cultural differences hindered assimilation of all immigrants. But bias against Catholicism complicated the task for Catholics as individuals and the Catholic Church as a corporate body.[6] Protestants and their ideas had dominated American society from its Puritan beginnings, while the status of Catholicism had always been precarious. But rising Catholic immigration after 1820 disrupted the existing social and economic order. It increased competition for jobs, strained welfare programs, and aroused Protestant fears of domination by "popery." Catholics in New York City further upset the status quo in the early 1840s, objecting that textbooks and hiring policies in the city's public schools favored Protestantism. Led by their bishop, John Hughes, they initiated a campaign for tax money to operate a separate school system. Their protests failed but resulted in the secularization of public education in the state and subsequent criticisms from Catholics that the schools were "godless" institutions.[7] Conflict over education exacerbated Protestant-Catholic tensions throughout the nineteenth century. Not surprisingly, the fears and hostility of Protestants, which occasionally flared into violence, fostered intense anti-Catholic feelings that became deeply ingrained into American consciousness. This animosity surfaced periodically in organizations like the Know Nothing Party (1854), the Ku Klux Klan (1865 and 1915), and the American Protective Association (1887).

Immigration and religious discrimination, so central in the Catholic experience in the United States, had long-lasting consequences for the Catholic Church and its members. Catholics, like most immigrants, started at the bottom of the occupational ladder. But by 1865, many Catholics in urban areas had advanced from unskilled labor to positions as skilled craftsmen, small shopkeepers, and city employees.[8] According to the 1900 census, the Irish were overrepresented in the four professional categories of government officials, journalists, actors, and lawyers; and by 1910, women of Irish extraction constituted 20% of the public school teachers in New York, Chicago, Boston, San Francisco, and eight other cities.[9] A small, wealthy Catholic elite had begun to emerge by the late 1890s.[10]

Catholics also sought collegiate training in increasing numbers by the last decades of the nineteenth century, another indication of their improving social and economic circumstances. At least thirty-three Catholics studied at Harvard in 1881, 300 in 1894, nearly 400 (about 12% of the total enrollment) in 1904, and 480 in 1907. Princeton had two Catholic freshmen in 1877 and five in 1889; and by the mid-1920s, about 7% of first-year students at Princeton belonged to the Catholic Church. The Universities of Iowa, Michigan, California, Minnesota, and Wisconsin each enrolled over 225 members of the Catholic Church in 1907. Catholics at Stanford totaled between twenty-five and thirty-five in 1897, 110 in 1902, and seventy-five in 1907.[11]

Especially interesting in light of Jewish-Catholic intellectual achievements after 1918, the fragmentary data available also suggest that before World War I, Catholics had greater access than Jews to such elite institutions as Harvard, Yale, Princeton, and Stanford.[12] For example, of 972 Harvard undergraduates polled in 1881, thirty-three identified themselves as Catholics and ten as Jews. A 1908 survey of 408 Harvard seniors revealed thirty-one Catholics and twenty-three Jews. The three upper classes at Yale in 1911-1912 numbered forty Jews

(5% of total enrollment), compared to thirty Catholics in senior year alone; and freshmen classes at Princeton between 1876 and 1925 included approximately 625 Catholics and 295 Jews.[13]

A study in 1907 estimated that 18,400 Catholics in the United States attended college, 9,800 of them in Catholic institutions. Catholics amounted to approximately 5% of all Americans enrolled in higher education that year. Among specific ethnic groups in the Catholic Church, Irish and Germans ranked at or above the national norm for college attendance by 1910, but Polish, Slavic, and Italian Catholics lagged behind until the 1950s.[14]

Yet despite evidence of upward movement, most Catholics in the nineteenth and early twentieth centuries remained members of the working and lower middle class, and Protestants continued as the social, business, and educational elite.[15] Protestant hegemony manifested itself in various ways. According to a 1949 study, a mere 7% of leading American businessmen active between 1900 and 1910 were Catholics. Though Charles J. Bonaparte, a Catholic and grandson of Napoleon I's brother Jerome, had served as an overseer of Harvard from 1891 to 1903, no Catholic was a member of the more prestigious seven-member Harvard Corporation until 1920. And at that time, A. Lawrence Lowell, Harvard's president, had to defend the election of James Byrne (Harvard '77), a Catholic lawyer in New York, against the protests of John Pierpont Morgan, who preferred to restrict membership to Protestants. The North Central Association of Colleges and Secondary Schools did not elect a representative from a Catholic institution as president until 1936, forty-one years after its founding; and apparently only two Catholics headed the American Medical Association between 1847 and 1947.[16]

Politically, the most apparent effect of the increasing Catholic population was the rise of Catholics to controlling positions in urban political machines and the election of a growing number of Catholics as mayors of major cities. New York chose its first Catholic mayor in 1880 and Boston did so in 1884. Between 1880 and 1895, Catholics also won the mayoral office in St. Louis (1881), New Orleans (1882), Buffalo (1883), Milwaukee (1890), and Pittsburgh (1893).[17] In addition, the Irish, most of them Catholics, dominated municipal governments by the 1890s in such places as Philadelphia, Chicago, Omaha, Kansas City, St. Paul, and San Francisco.[18]

But success in urban politics did not result in corresponding numbers of Catholics attaining prominence in state or national government prior to the New Deal. Between 1789 and 1932, only six Catholics were appointed to cabinet posts and four to the Supreme Court. In 1880, one Catholic served in the Senate and approximately ten in the House, including territorial delegates from Montana and New Mexico.[19] Fifty years later, there were six Catholic senators, while the total of Catholics in the House had risen to thirty-five, an improvement that still left the 20,000,000 Catholics in the United States (about one-sixth of all Americans) greatly underrepresented. With less than half the Catholic population, Methodists had three times the Catholic representation in Congress; and Episcopalians outnumbered Catholics in both Houses five to one, despite having about one-fifteenth the membership of the Catholic Church.[20]

Catholics had equally dismal records in lower levels of government before 1932. Though over 15% of the population in 1925, they held only 4% of federal judgeships. Only about 5% of the 1,500 federal job-holders listed in the *Congressional Directory* during the fourth session of the 67th Congress (1923) were Catholics. Furthermore, in 1930 not a single state governor belonged to the Catholic Church.[21]

The influx of poor Catholic immigrants and the religious prejudice they often encountered clearly restricted Catholic social and political mobility before World War I. Less obvious but longer lasting was the negative intellectual and ideological impact of immigration on American Catholicism, especially Catholic higher education. Abandoning their peasant cultures in Europe, most Catholics immigrating to America, including clergy, lacked a heritage conducive to the intellectual life and educational achievement, unlike most Jewish immigrants or many in the already established Protestant majority in the United States.[22] Priests composed the Catholic educational elite, but the seminary training they received seldom compensated for their intellectually impoverished backgrounds. Bishop John Lancaster Spalding of Peoria, Illinois observed in a sermon at the Third Council of Baltimore in 1884 that "the ecclesiastical seminary is not a school of intellectual culture, either here in America or elsewhere; . . . its methods are not such as one would choose who desires to open the mind, to give it breadth, flexibility, strength, refinement, and grace."[23]

Like most immigrants, Catholics coming to the United States were aware that education could enable them to attain a better life. But many of them wanted schools primarily to teach basic language and technical skills and to communicate ethnic and religious values, not to encourage learning for its own sake or to promote scientific research. Furthermore, some suspected that too much learning undermined loyalty to family and faith. Such thinking contributed to an unsympathetic atmosphere for inquiry and scholarship, effectively discouraging interest in higher learning among many Catholics.[24]

Poverty and its consequences also influenced Catholic attitudes toward intellectual pursuits. The necessity of additional income commonly forced Catholics to remove their children from schools and send them to work.[25] Numerous college age Catholics simply could not afford the cost of tuition. For people struggling to survive, education, particularly after high school, seemed a luxury and less desirable than a cash-paying job. In the decade prior to World War I, 7% of American Catholics in the 17-25 age bracket attended college, while the national average was 17%. During these years Catholics were the least likely of denominations in the United States to continue their education after high school, a difference caused in large part by poverty. Cardinal Richard Cushing of Boston remarked at a Congress of Industrial Organizations convention in 1947 that he did not know a single member of the American Catholic hierarchy whose father or mother was a college graduate, adding that the bishops came from working class backgrounds.[26]

Especially during the years of heavy immigration, constructing schools and churches and meeting the immediate needs of destitute Catholics consumed the limited resources of the institutional church. Consequently, personnel and money could not be spared to support higher learning as it required. Such burdens deprived Catholicism of perspectives and training which could have reduced insecurities and produced a more balanced, sophisticated analysis of American culture and the ways in which Catholics should respond to current issues. In 1889, when Bishop John J. Keane, head of the newly established Catholic University of America, sought teachers, he could not find trained native Catholics to fill the positions and was forced to hire six foreign-born Catholics and two converts to Catholicism for the original faculty. He did so even though he wanted to avoid facing charges by groups like the American Protective Association that foreigners dominated the Catholic Church in the United States.[27] Father Maurice Sheehy, assistant to the president of Catholic University, commented in 1932 that many of the academic and financial weaknesses in contemporary Catholic colleges and universities resulted from "the necessity under which we labored of adhering to the essentials of the faith and of concentrating our financial resources upon elementary schools."[28]

Yet when conditions improved and financial pressures lessened, enrollment problems and lack of scholarship continued to plague Catholic higher education. Seemingly, desires for material possessions and wealth, not schooling and intellectual development, prevailed as the controlling motivation for many in the Catholic Church. Jesuit educators representing nine Midwest institutions partially attributed the low numbers in their colleges in 1917 to the "prevalence of the commercial and money-making spirit" among Catholics.[29]

The majority of Catholics who did attend college chose occupations promising status and financial rewards. They shunned teaching or scholarly work partly because of low salaries and uncertain job prospects but also because little in Catholic culture promoted such commitments, especially by nonclerics. Suggestive of Catholic aspirations and priorities, enrollment in Catholic professional programs rose from approximately 1,000 in 1900 to 7,100 in 1916.[30] A 1923 survey of 2,555 graduates from eight Catholic colleges for males revealed that 56% chose careers in business, law, and medicine but only 10% became teachers.[31]

Catholic intellectual attitudes and educational achievement contrasted sharply with those of Jews. Most Catholic and Jewish immigrants arrived in the United States with little or no money, but Jews possessed two advantages over their Catholic contemporaries. First, many of them were literate, and their cultural traditions stressed the importance of disciplined learning and intellectual accomplishment. While young Catholics often left school because of inadequate motivation or financial need, Jewish parents emphasized the value of education. Second, numerous Jews entered the United States with experience in occupations which prepared them for jobs in a modern industrial economy. Of Jewish immigrants between 1899 and 1909, 67% were classified as skilled workers. For instance, during these years, they constituted 80% of immigrant hat and cap makers, 68% of tailors and bookbinders, and 55% of cigarmakers and tinsmiths. Jews ranked first in the number of printers, bakers, carpenters, blacksmiths, and building trades workers entering the United States during the first decade of the twentieth century.[32]

Because many Jewish fathers and mothers possessed the skills needed to earn enough income to provide for their families, fewer young Jews had to sacrifice schooling for employment. Taking advantage of educational opportunities, Jewish students in 1919 totaled 79% of enrollment at the College of the City of New York, 55% at New York University, 23% at Fordham, 21% at Columbia, and 18.5% at Chicago. The passion for knowledge and scholastic achievement among Jews figured prominently in their rapid advance in American society, while the absence of such an intellectual orientation handicapped Catholics.[33]

The intellectual climate in America, at best aloof and generally unfriendly to Catholic thought, further retarded the development of Catholic academic culture. Lacking sufficient support from within the church and thus especially vulnerable to external forces, Catholic thinkers and their ideas needed a sympathetic reception from the non-Catholic world. But outbreaks of nativism and religious prejudice poisoned the atmosphere, precluding significant interchange between Protestant and Catholic intellectuals.

Hostility and bigotry also heightened the anxiety of Catholic ethnics about loss of faith and promoted an apologetical, defensive approach to American life.[34] Threatened by their environment and conservative by tradition, Catholics in America (except for a tiny minority) retreated from the culture around them into their own secure enclaves. Instead of wrestling with the challenges Darwinism and experimental psychology posed to Christian teachings about the inerrancy of Scripture, creation of the world, original sin, and existence of the soul, they reiterated old formulations. Concerning new scientific and social theories, American Catholicism imitated the uncompromising, isolated stance of the papacy. During his pontificate between 1846 and 1878, Pope Pius IX sought to defend the church against what he perceived to be secularizing trends in society. Perhaps symbolic of Catholic attitudes in the United States, Woodstock College, a Jesuit seminary, was moved from Georgetown in 1869 to rural Maryland, a place less likely to be contaminated by the world. But leading Protestant divinity schools remained in urban settings and became more involved with contemporary issues.

Few American Catholics during the late nineteenth and early twentieth centuries acted in accord with Bishop Spalding's words in a homily at the Third Council of Baltimore in 1884: "When our zeal for intellectual excellence shall have raised up men who will take place among the first writers and thinkers of their day, their very presence will become the most persuasive of arguments to teach the world that no best gift is at war with the spirit of Catholic faith."[35] The Catholic hierarchy in the United States did agree in 1884 to establish the Catholic University of America to provide graduate training in philosophy and theology, mainly for priests. But the school did not open until 1889 and languished until the early twentieth century because it lacked faculty, students, and money. Whether consciously or not, the American Catholic Church essentially subordinated intellectual excellence to denominational concerns about assimilating immigrants and maintaining religious commitments. Seldom did it give priority to academic excellence and scholarship over orthodoxy and moral formation.[36]

The combination of numerical growth and religious prejudice also generated ideological problems for Catholics in the United States concerning their relationship to society. The central conflict was how to be American and Catholic, how to be faithful to family and religion and yet act and be accepted as free, loyal citizens involved in a culture that was changing rapidly because of increasing population, wealth, and scientific discoveries. In particular, starting in the 1880s, controversies erupting over rights of workers, education, and scholarly research disturbed Catholicism. Resolution of these problems, complicated by ethnic rivalries and ecclesiastical politics, had major significance for Catholics in the twentieth century.[37]

The influence of Pope Leo XIII and Cardinal James Gibbons of Baltimore, the social theory enunciated in such papal encyclicals as *Rerum Novarum* (1891), and an awareness of problems stemming from its large lower class membership enabled the Catholic Church in the United States to respond with some effectiveness to contemporary economic issues and the needs of working people. As industrialization advanced in the United States after the Civil War, labor tried to cope with developments by organizing into unions. Because so many Catholics were part of the working class and interested in better conditions and higher wages, large numbers of them became union members.

But some in the Catholic hierarchy grew alarmed about the secrecy, socialist overtones, and sometimes violent tactics of labor organizations.[38] In 1884, the archbishop of Quebec persuaded the Vatican to condemn the Knights of Labor in Canada. A few American bishops sought a similar decree even though Terence Powderly, head of the Knights in the United States, was a Catholic and had publicly disavowed socialism.

In response, Cardinal Gibbons and the large majority of Catholic bishops in the United States defended the right of labor to organize, and they further insisted that Catholic participation in such efforts did not endanger Catholic principles or values.[39] The action of the hierarchy boosted unions at a critical time and prevented possible alienation of Catholic workers from the church. But more important for Catholic ideology, it marked a significant adaptation to American social conditions. Gibbons and other prelates interpreted Catholic traditions and doctrine in terms of existing circumstances and did not allow old fears about the threat of Masonic-like groups and socialism to preclude support for workers.

But the Catholic Church in the United States lacked similar leadership, principles, and unanimity concerning adjustment to the social, political, and intellectual environment of America. By the 1880s, acute disagreements over how to care for immigrants and cope with a changing society were dividing the church into two ideological camps.[40]

Proponents of "Americanization," led by Archbishop John Ireland of St. Paul and to a lesser extent by Cardinal Gibbons, Bishop Spalding, and Bishop Keane, encouraged immigrants to enter into American life; and they minimized anxiety about loss of Catholic faith in a Protestant land. Ireland and a few like-minded churchmen, mostly in the Midwest, recommended that immigrants learn the English language and American customs as soon as possible.[41] Optimistic about Catholic opportunities and ardent nationalists, they deplored Catholic separatism, though never suggesting that the church should modify dogma to gain acceptance.[42]

In contrast, the majority of Catholics, following Archbishop Michael Corrigan of New York City, Bishop Bernard McQuaid of Rochester, New York, and German bishops in the Midwest, urged maintenance of ethnic and Catholic identity at all costs and viewed much of the non-Catholic world with suspicion. The denial of government aid to parochial schools in the 1870s and the founding of the anti-Catholic American Protective Association in 1887 confirmed for them that Catholics were not accepted in America. They distrusted efforts by Gibbons, Ireland, and others to adapt Catholicism to the American scene. Indicative of their mood, Corrigan warned Cardinal Camillo Mazzella, S.J., a senior advisor of Pope Leo XIII, on November 7, 1890 that certain American bishops led by Gibbons, Ireland, Keane, John Foley of Detroit, and Patrick Riordan of San Francisco were organizing "to rule the destinies of the American Church. In the *ultra*-Americanism of these Prelates, I foresee dangers and sound the alarm."[43] Preoccupied that immigrants were losing their Catholic faith, this conservative segment of the church favored preservation of native language and cultural heritage. They advocated a slow approach to assimilation and encouraged isolation from the mainstream.

Ethnic conflicts, especially over retention of foreign languages and cultures, compounded tensions in the church. German-speaking Catholics complained insistently that the Irish-dominated hierarchy neglected immigrant needs. They pressed their views most notably in 1890 and 1891 when Peter Paul Cahensly, a member of the German Reichstag acting as a representative of European Catholic immigrant aid societies, presented petitions to Roman authorities asserting that ten to sixteen million Catholics from Europe had left the church after arriving in the United States. The American bishops, including those of German nationality, rejected the claims as wild exaggerations. But the charge that the Irish controlled the hierarchy could not be refuted. In 1886, thirty-five bishops were of Irish ancestry, fifteen of German origin; and between 1790 and 1960, men of Irish birth or descent made up almost 75% of those chosen to be bishops.[44]

But the most divisive and bitter exchanges occurred over the issue of schools. Different mind-sets among Catholic leaders surfaced repeatedly in the formation of Catholic educational policy after the mid-nineteenth century, especially in the furor over parochial schools and the crisis of "Americanism" during the 1890s.[45] Though Bishop

Hughes had committed New York Catholics in the 1840s to a separate educational system, other sections of the church delayed doing so, still hopeful of cooperating with non-Catholic schooling. But after the Civil War, many Catholics reconsidered their attitudes. The rapid growth of compulsory public education, which was officially nonsectarian but actually Protestant-oriented, alarmed them. Also, German Catholics, arriving in large numbers by the 1870s, wanted their own schools to strengthen faith and ethnicity, much more so than had previous immigrants from Ireland. Continuing anti-Catholic bias led Catholics to operate their own schools as a defense and a way of transmitting Catholic culture. In addition, James McMaster, the lay editor of the *New York Freeman's Journal*, and other vocal opponents of public education succeeded in obtaining a directive from the Vatican in 1875 prescribing that Catholic children should not attend state-supported schools unless dangers to the faith were removed. Under pressure from Rome, the American bishops issued a decree at the Third Council of Baltimore in 1884 calling on every parish to establish an elementary school within two years, though refusing to order excommunication for Catholics sending offspring to the public system.[46]

By 1890, the church operated 3,000 elementary schools enrolling 600,000 students.[47] While Archbishop Ireland did not urge abandonment of the existing Catholic parochial school network, he and others favored reaching some accommodation with public education. They sought not only to lessen the financial burden on the church but also to improve Protestant-Catholic relations and to insure that religion had a place in American schools.

Addressing the National Education Association at its convention in St. Paul on July 10, 1890, Ireland proposed two plans for achieving a union between public and Catholic schools: (1) imitating England and Prussia, the state school could be conducted according to the majority religion with denominational institutions reimbursed by the government for secular instruction provided; or (2) "as Protestants and Catholics in Poughkeepsie and other places in the U.S. have agreed to do," the local school board could rent the parochial facilities, direct and fund the entire operation, and allow religion classes outside official school hours.[48] The following year, he approved requests from two parishes in his archdiocese to implement the Poughkeepsie plan.

Though attracted by the benefits of state aid, the majority of Catholic clergy and lay people objected to compromise efforts, fearing state domination and loss of Catholic identity. They campaigned for retention and expansion of a distinctly Catholic education program. Many non-Catholics also attacked cooperation between Catholic and public schools in Minnesota as an unconstitutional subsidy to the

Catholic Church and a threat to independent public education.[49] Due to the intense opposition, joint public-parochial schooling in Minnesota ended in 1893 and in Poughkeepsie in 1897. But the impact of the "school wars" and the disagreements about how to fit into American culture lingered far longer in Catholic education and life.

Besides increasing suspicion of the liberal minority in the church, the acrimonious dispute over education undercut efforts to improve Protestant-Catholic understanding in the United States. It left Catholics even more concerned about protecting their faith and deepened their aversion to non-Catholic America, especially secular education. In addition, Catholic leaders like Ireland turned away from trying to secure a place for religious instruction in state schools, and the church expanded its commitment to a separate educational system. Bishops and priests focused on constructing elementary schools, believing that early instruction about Catholic doctrine was essential. Their decision also reflected pressure to implement the legislation passed at the 1884 Council of Baltimore mandating each Catholic parish to operate its own school.

Moreover, the dissension and accusations of unorthodoxy in American Catholicism produced a reaction that hampered the growth of a vigorous intellectual element in American Catholicism, one which could have fostered a less defensive, more vibrant Catholic higher education. In the late nineteenth century, few Catholics in the United States knew enough about trends in psychology, philosophy, and the natural sciences to evaluate them intelligently, let alone integrate religious and secular knowledge.[50] Yet by the 1890s, there were signs of an awakening in Catholic intellectual activity. Father Edward Pace of Catholic University, possibly the only American Catholic in the 1890s with a graduate degree in experimental psychology, frequently defended his specialty from its many critics in the church, and John Zahm, C.S.C. of Notre Dame denied in his book *Evolution and Dogma*, printed in 1896, that any real conflict existed between science and religion.[51] Journals like the *Catholic World, American Catholic Quarterly Review,* and *American Ecclesiastical Review* periodically published scholarly articles treating topics in science, history, and theology.

But the promise of such scholarship went largely unfulfilled. Alarmed conservatives in Rome and America forced the dismissals of Monsignor Denis O'Connell, rector of the North American College in Rome, and Bishop Keane, head of Catholic University, in 1895 and 1896, respectively, thus eliminating two leading supporters of Catholic renewal. To prevent a formal condemnation of his ideas, Zahm withdrew his book on evolution in 1898. The next year Pope Leo XIII issued *Testem Benevolentiae,* a warning against erroneous ideas on faith and religious life attributed to Catholics in the United States. This papal encyclical, which some Catholics in the United States and Europe regarded as a reprimand, led to greater scrutiny of Catholic intellectuals for doctrinal purity, making them more cautious in their research. The final blow fell in 1907 when Pope Pius X, in condemning philosophical and theological ideas that he called Modernism, established more limits on scholarship, especially biblical research and efforts to reconcile Scripture and science.

A spirit of repression blew through the church, running counter to Archbishop Ireland's declaration in 1889 that because the contemporary era worshipped intellect, Catholics must always be ready to give reasons for their faith, "meeting objections from whatever source, abreast of the times in their methods of argument. They must be in the foreground of intellectual movements of all kinds. The age will not take kindly to religious knowledge separated from secular knowledge."[52] Frightened by many aspects of modern society, the church set out to control its environment as much as possible. But the price for American Catholic intellectual life was high. The combination of the Americanism and Modernism crises "effectively put an end for the next fifty years to further development of Catholic thought in authentic American dress."[53]

Catholics and their educational institutions struggled for decades after the 1840s against conditions greatly affected by heavy European immigration and Protestant bias. A small denomination in 1820, the Catholic Church ranked as the largest one hundred years later, but it still remained on the periphery of national life, lacking influence comparable to its size. It had made impressive efforts to assimilate millions of immigrants but still was uneasy with its surroundings. Catholics approached the post-1918 world with a mixed legacy from the preceding century: low social status, but potential for acceptance and wealth; strength in urban politics, but political underrepresentation on the national level; strong religious loyalties to a faith with a rich philosophical and theological heritage, but intellectual narrowness; and ideological conservatism, yet an eagerness to be fully American. Reconciling these tensions and adapting Catholicism, especially Catholic higher education, to its circumstances in the United States remained an unfinished task.

Besides the burdens imposed by being part of the heavily immigrant Catholic Church in Protestant America, Catholic colleges and universities faced challenges peculiar to education. In particular, they had to contend with the administrative and academic reforms reshaping the American educational scene after 1865.

Widespread social, political, and ideological changes occurred in post-Civil War America and left their effects on education. The United

States moved from being a rural, unmechanized society to an urban, industrialized nation; and it resumed westward expansion and railroad construction. Demand for workers and capital grew, and technology boosted economic growth. Many in America achieved a higher standard of living, despite periodic economic downturns and labor strife. New wealth appeared as entrepreneurs such as Carnegie, Rockefeller, and Morgan acquired immense fortunes and power. Darwin's theory of biological evolution earned wide support, while religion fumbled for convincing responses to materialism and science. Psychology and sociology emerged as influential disciplines, further challenging Christian faith.

Never immune from their American environment, academic institutions after 1865 faced increasing demands as scientific advances encouraged specialization and industry needed a better trained work force. The spreading network of public elementary and secondary schools looked to higher education to prepare teachers. In providing federal assistance to start agricultural and mechanical schools, the Morrill Act of 1862 promoted practical education, especially application of scientific theory to concrete problems of industrial production and farming. Partially influenced by the example of the national government, individual states, especially in the Midwest, established universities. Also, as more educators became acquainted with the lecture, seminar, and research methods of German universities, and with the stress in these institutions on intellectual achievement over religious concerns, support grew for similar emphases in the United States. Finally, private wealth existed to finance new universities like Johns Hopkins, Chicago, and Stanford, each breaking with past educational ideas.

The new expectations and opportunities generated a clash in intellectual culture between advocates of reform and upholders of traditional education. While antebellum colleges were never as retrogressive, rigid, and short-lived as Hofstadter and Tewksbury thought, most did maintain a strong religious orientation, denominational ties (more than 80%), and commitment to a classical curriculum.[54] Because of their origins, limited resources, and isolation, many of these institutions opposed innovation or could not respond adequately to different social and economic needs. In addition, their largely conservative clientele preferred the traditional curriculum, inhibiting change.

Yet some observers in the 1860s perceived a decline in college influence and insisted that education must discard paternalistic attitudes, rigorous discipline, and anachronistic courses.[55] By 1880, numerous educators from elite private, land-grant, and newly founded institutions like Johns Hopkins campaigned for education that recognized the importance of science and that furnished the specialized skills needed in contemporary society. They placed a lower priority on character training and the liberal arts, disturbing denominational interests.

Such differing perspectives especially provoked controversy over the purpose and control of higher education institutions and ultimately revolutionized American academic life. Traditional humanistic, denominationally controlled education yielded in the industrial era to "a broadly secular higher learning emphasizing preparation for a great variety of specialized and technical occupations."[56] The conflict and ensuing secularization, curriculum reform, accreditation, and standardization in education held particular significance for Catholicism and its schools, especially in the twentieth century.

Secularization in education, a process resulting in the diminution or elimination of previous institutional commitments to religion and to a specific denomination, has been the long-term trend in American educational history.[57] The movement toward secular values did not originate in institutions of higher learning. Rather, it mirrored the growing abandonment by society and some religious groups sponsoring colleges and universities of a single, closed world view centered around Christianity. Gradually, heterogeneity and toleration replaced homogeneity and coercion, and academic culture became characterized by appeals to facts derived from research, not authority or theological doctrine.

Within this environment, a complex interplay of individuals and choices accelerated secularization in American academia. Harvard's selection in 1869 of thirty-five-year-old Charles Eliot as its first nonclergyman president, and his policies until he retired in 1909, reflected the shift in rationale for higher education. Unlike his predecessors, Eliot did not teach, and he further distanced himself from the moral development of students by appointing deans and creating a layer of bureaucracy beneath them. He and his contemporaries, Andrew White of Cornell and Daniel Gilman of Johns Hopkins, not only represented a new generation of college leaders but also stood for educational methods and purposes different from those of the traditional college.[58] They conceived of their institutions as intellectual enterprises first of all and were much less concerned with the earlier collegiate priorities of character building and religious instruction.

Eliot, White, and Gilman repeatedly attacked church-related education as poorly staffed, academically weak, and opposed to higher standards. They attributed these defects to the excessive number of denominational schools and their greater devotion to religious tenets than to the pursuit of truth. Attempts by midwestern denominations to stifle development of secular universities by state governments heightened the antipathy of these three presidents toward sectarian education. In his 1868 inaugural address as Cornell's president, White specifically denied that "'any great university fully worthy of that great name can ever be founded upon the platform of any one sect or combination of sects.'"[59]

Gilman allowed a place for religion but in a diluted form, calling for the university to be "'avowedly Christian—not in a narrow or sectarian sense—but in the broad, open and inspiring sense of the Gospels.'"[60] Whatever the contradictions in Gilman's position, he and others worked successfully to eliminate religion as a controlling element in academic life.

Such educational views reflected growing sentiment in the final decades of the nineteenth century as professional and technical education increased and state-funded universities expanded. A different breed of professors, individuals valuing intellect over piety, rose to faculty prominence. Institutional trustees, predominately clergymen until the 1870s, acquiesced to changes in purpose as they placed educational goals ahead of denominational concerns. The necessity of attracting larger enrollment to fund programs encouraged religious pluralism in education and a blurring of denominational character. As governing boards in the closing decades of the nineteenth century wrestled with mounting financial and administrative problems, they reorganized to add businessmen and alumni. These new trustees usually favored basic changes in educational philosophy and influenced academic institutions to adopt the administrative structures of secular business.[61]

Philanthropic foundations also figured in the secularization of higher education. The Carnegie Foundation before World War I specifically excluded church-related schools from receiving grants, holding that such institutions by definition put limits on intellectual freedom and could not meet the test of a true college or university. In 1905, it offered to fund pensions for faculty but restricted eligibility to nonsectarian higher education. Anxious for financial support, Bowdoin, Wesleyan, Rochester, Drake, Coe, Hanover, Occidental, and other schools cut their already tenuous denominational ties. In the century following the Civil War, several hundred colleges, once strongly Protestant, became officially nonsectarian.[62]

The drift toward secularization did not mean the absence of religion on campus. Individual administrators, faculty, and students still professed strong beliefs in religion and actively supported organizations like the YMCA. Aware of creeping secularism, denominations assigned ministers to work in colleges and universities. The first list of accredited colleges and universities (seventy-three schools) published by the North Central Association in 1913 noted that thirty-one institutions were denominationally controlled.[63]

But religious faith had become privatized and no longer dominated institutional life as before. By 1900, the demise of religion in American education was obvious. In the first decade of the twentieth century, laymen headed most Protestant-founded colleges, not because being a minister was an inherent impediment to institutional leadership but because few clergy possessed the educational background and business skills required in the more secular college world. Arthur Hadly and Woodrow Wilson, the first lay presidents of Yale (1899) and Princeton (1902), respectively, were among the men chosen more for their academic and administrative abilities than for their moral and spiritual qualities. This replacement of clergy as presidents indicated the decline in clerical talent but also the degree of secularization in American higher education. Professional competence now counted for more than continuation of clerical leadership.[64]

Moreover, freedom, pluralism, and toleration increasingly prevailed against former sanctions and orthodoxy. Schools gradually dropped religious qualifications for hiring and retention of faculty, and chapel attendance became optional. Church-sponsored colleges and universities fell in enrollment; their growth rate around 1900 was half that of public higher education. No longer would they prepare the majority of American youth for positions of leadership. Fewer institutions regarded religion as an essential part of their existence or integrated religious issues into academic life. Instead, more schools focused on the educational questions and needs of modern society without reference to Christian beliefs and practices. Fundamentally, religion gradually lost its place as the center of institutional unity, not because of great organized opposition, but because of apathy and changed institutional priorities.[65]

The same forces impelling American education toward secularization also inspired movements for curriculum reform. According to the traditional view, articulated in the Yale Report of 1828, schools should strive primarily to inculcate mental and moral discipline through definite rules and prescribed courses in Greek, Latin, mathematics, and moral philosophy.[66] Discovery of new knowledge and mastery of material represented secondary goals at best. Furthermore, such prominent educators as James McCosh, president of Princeton from 1868 to 1888, and Noah Porter, who headed Yale between 1871 and 1886, argued that academic institutions should foster Christian beliefs and shun religious neutrality. In McCosh's words, "'Religion should burn in the hearts, and shine ... from the faces of teachers. ... And in regard to religious truth, there will be no uncertain sound uttered within these walls.'"[67]

But by the 1870s, defenders of the status quo in academia found themselves under increasing attack from advocates of three competing academic philosophies. One coalition, composed of agricultural and industrial interests and people like Charles Eliot and Andrew White, campaigned for a utilitarian approach. They believed that education should prepare students for useful service and to meet contemporary needs, ideas culminating in the organization of land grant institutions and professional schools. But Thorstein Veblen and others, influenced by German universities, urged a focus on research and encouraged specialization. The third group, a distinct but vocal minority counting Irving Babbitt, George Woodberry, and Josiah Royce as members, could be described as secular humanists. They reacted against the emphases on utility and minute investigation; and much like traditional educators, they sought to maintain a humane, liberal culture. But formal religion was not a constituent part of their academic outlook; Babbitt and Woodberry, for instance, were unbelievers.

The educational debate stemming from these contrasting ideas centered on electivism, that is, whether to discard a narrow, prescriptive curriculum stressing transmission of knowledge, classics, and moral development for one allowing students to choose from a broad spectrum of courses oriented to discovery, science, and practical training.[68] With American culture gradually endorsing technology, social Darwinism, personal freedom, and professionalism, higher education shifted from a prescriptive to an elective curriculum and eventually to a combination of the two types. Responding to pressures for professional training, colleges added schools of law, medicine, dentistry, and engineering, evolving into universities.[69]

Electivism was both a product and promoter of secularization. Its advent signalled the collapse of a system committed to communicating a specific set of required truths. The resulting pluralism struck at the roots of denominational education, undermining its prescribed courses and efforts to maintain orthodoxy. Thus, curriculum reform contributed to the pressures transforming the church-related college into the secular American university. In the process, it also made elective courses, graduate schools, and professional training standard features of higher education in the United States.

By the 1880s, secularization and curriculum reform had thrown the old educational order, which relied heavily on religion and the classics, into confusion. Consequently, American education found it difficult to solve serious structural problems caused by surging enrollment. The high school had emerged as a new division in the educational system, but it varied in quality and scope. As a result, some students received inadequate preparation for college, and officials in postsecondary institutions complained that they could not determine if high school graduates fulfilled admission criteria. Also, the break-up of the classical curriculum and introduction of electivism produced serious disagreement about qualifications for entrance and graduation. Colleges and professional schools operated without either uniform or minimum standards. Finally, the growing size and complexity of academic institutions complicated efforts to administer them.

To remedy such defects, a movement began to standardize curriculum and to set minimum requirements for secondary and higher education.[70] For example, state universities, imitating the University of Michigan, started inspecting high schools and then automatically granting entrance to graduates from approved schools. In 1878, the New York Board of Regents initiated examinations to determine admission to public higher education, establishing a standard for both high schools and colleges in the state. Like other philanthropic organizations, the Carnegie Foundation set conditions before giving grants to institutions, requiring that colleges have at least six full-time professors, a four-year liberal arts course, and department chairmen with doctorates. The 1910 Flexner report on medical education in the United States led to vast improvements in medical schools.

Regional accrediting groups, organized first in New England in 1885 and spreading to the West by 1918, were instrumental in efforts to insure common standards and procedures.[71] Especially in the Midwest where state university personnel took active roles, accreditation teams evaluated faculty, curriculum, facilities, and endowment according to definite criteria. To enforce their demands, they eventually published lists of accredited schools, which became widely accepted as measurements of educational quality.

Besides addressing concerns about standards, colleges and universities needed to rationalize their administrative structures. The president alone could no longer oversee all aspects of the expanded institutions. To replace the shared values which largely unified the traditional small college, schools adopted a bureaucratic model, probably borrowing from business. Cornell and Johns Hopkins organized departments in the 1880s, followed by Harvard, Chicago, and Columbia in the next decade. In 1900, Charles F. Thwing published his book *College Administration*, which he claimed was the first one on the topic.[72]

By World War I, higher education in the United States differed remarkably from its pre-Civil War counterpart. It was increasingly nondenominational, reflecting the decline of clerical power and institutional commitments to religion. Practical education and scientific research received emphasis, not mental and moral training. The curriculum encouraged students to select courses according to their interests, a shift from the previous orientation toward prescription and classics. Colleges had become universities, adding professional and graduate divisions to the traditional liberal arts. Institutions operated less from narrow local concerns and more from regional and national perspectives. They paid greater attention to quality and standards, due in part to the influence of foundations, regional accrediting agencies, and national educational associations.

The revolution in American higher education posed immense problems for Catholic postsecondary institutions. In 1900, almost all Catholic colleges followed the continental model, offering a predominately liberal arts program requiring six to seven years to complete. The curriculum emphasized sequential learning, breadth of knowledge, and a deductive approach, not specialization and induction. Instruction in science was minimal, since many Catholics either regarded it as hostile to the interests of religion or failed to appreciate its importance. Some schools, particularly in the Midwest, offered classes in commercial subjects to satisfy their clientele seeking immediately useful courses. But primarily, Catholic educators stressed the study of classical languages and literature, believing such a focus essential for a truly liberal education and for the moral and religious training of students. Few of them endorsed even a moderate electivism, convinced that permitting it was to admit that they did not know what was worth learning nor the order in which material should be studied.[73]

When measured against new academic ideas and standards, Catholic higher education fared poorly. In an 1899 article published in *The Atlantic Monthly*, Charles Eliot, a consistent champion of electivism, criticized the uniform, prescriptive curriculum in Jesuit colleges. He insisted that only "an unhesitating belief in the Divine Wisdom" could justify such an approach because "no human wisdom is equal to contriving a prescribed course of study equally good for even two children of the same family."[74] A Catholic priest advocating academic improvements in Catholic colleges wrote in 1911 that many Catholic postsecondary schools "'give a course scarcely better than that of an ordinary High School.'" The University of Notre Dame was the sole Catholic institution included when the North Central Association published its first directory of accredited colleges and universities (seventy-three schools) in 1913. That same year, the Association of American Universities recognized 119 institutions throughout the United States as offering college-level instruction; only two Catholic schools made the list, Catholic University and Fordham.[75]

Catholic colleges and universities before World War I commonly suffered from debilitating competition, small enrollments, inferior academic reputations, and the unconcern of many in the Catholic community, problems closely related to one another.[76] Their growth rate between 1890 and 1900 lagged behind the rest of American education, and secular institutions attracted two-thirds of all Catholics attending college in the 1890-1907 period. Charles Eliot allegedly boasted that more Catholics attended Harvard than the combined enrollment of Boston College and Holy Cross, two nearby Catholic schools; and attendance records for 1894 and 1907 validate his claim. Few Catholic schools could match state schools offering free or low tuition, a wide range of courses, proximity to home, and the possibility of valuable friendships and business connections. Nor could they meet the social expectations of upwardly mobile Catholics. Thomas Kernan, son of New York's U.S. Senator Francis Kernan, wrote in 1900 that some wealthy members of the church could not find Catholic colleges with sufficient prestige and comforts; consequently, they chose elite secular schools.[77]

Efforts to adapt Catholic higher education to its new context encountered various obstacles. First, because of overwork, poor training, and faulty judgments of educational trends, an insufficient number of teachers and administrators in Catholic postsecondary institutions grasped the necessity of academic reform. Extensive administrative and pastoral duties burdened many presidents and faculty, leaving them little time or energy for academic affairs. Few of them were scholars or individuals with broad academic vision; they relied mainly on their own educational experience for ideas and procedures.[78]

Most Catholic educators in the late nineteenth and early twentieth centuries kept aloof from developments in American academia or dismissed them as insignificant. Such isolation and arrogance robbed Catholic education of vitality and left many Catholic educators locked into traditional methods. Only one Catholic school sent a representative to the National Educational Association convention in 1900; and fewer than ten Catholics belonged to the NEA in 1906, even though the organization had been founded in 1870. The president of the Catholic University of America supposedly wondered in 1899 if it would be worthwhile to accept an invitation to be one of the fourteen founding members of the Association of American Universities, a prestigious group of research-oriented institutions.[79] Certain Jesuits early in the twentieth century advised their superiors that Ph.D. requirements were so high that no one should be sent for doctorates. Two members of the

Jesuit order from the Midwest assigned to Johns Hopkins in 1903 for doctoral studies in classics reportedly returned after a short stay announcing that the place had nothing to offer them.[80]

Chronic financial problems also restrained the advancement of Catholic colleges and universities. Roughly two-thirds of those started before 1900 failed to survive, often because of money shortages. Few Catholics possessed large fortunes, and those with wealth made gifts for immediately useful churches, hospitals, and orphanages, seldom to educational institutions. No contributions to Catholic institutions compared to the benefactions establishing Johns Hopkins, Stanford, or Chicago. In its first fifty years of existence (1841-1891), Fordham averaged $2,000 a year in gifts, and Catholic University received only ten bequests of $100,000 or more between 1889 and 1955, with none larger than $1,000,000.[81]

Catholic higher education received little financial support from philanthropic organizations or the institutional church. The Rockefeller-funded General Education Board gave money to denominational colleges (unlike the Carnegie Foundation), but it made only one grant between 1902 and 1914 to a Catholic college, $75,000 to the College of St. Thomas in St. Paul, Minnesota.[82] Nor could aid be expected on a regular basis from ecclesiastical sources. Except for a few schools operated by dioceses, Catholic colleges and universities were the direct responsibility of religious orders, not the hierarchy. Consequently, support from local bishops and clergy depended on individual interest. For instance, in 1919, the archdiocese of New York declined a request to help save Fordham's school of medicine because many of the medical students were non-Catholics and the archdiocese had decided to commit its resources to programs in social work. But in response to a similar plea in 1921, the archbishop of Chicago provided assistance to the Loyola University School of Medicine.[83] In contrast, Protestant denominations frequently provided financial subsidies for their higher educational institutions.[84]

Because of money shortages, Catholic colleges and universities could not easily afford costly additions to faculty and facilities urged by academic reformers. Also, more than one Catholic college delayed separating from its prep school (a step urged by proponents of standardization) because it depended on revenue from secondary students to help finance the collegiate division. Financial problems placed Catholic higher education in a quandary: it did not have sufficient revenues to upgrade programs quickly and thus enhance academic standing; but without better faculty, curricula, and facilities, it could not attract students to generate badly needed income.

The personnel and financial deficiencies of Catholic higher education exposed its serious organizational weaknesses. Unlike Presbyterians,

Methodists, Baptists, and Lutherans, Catholics never formed a nation-wide board with a mandate to supervise the growth and quality of Catholic education. Various Catholic educational leaders urged increased cooperation among Catholic schools, and they also sought greater assistance from the Catholic community, especially the bishops. At the initiative of Catholic University, Catholic colleges in 1899 started the Association of Catholic Colleges, which became the Catholic Educational Association in 1904. But Catholic loyalties centering around family, parish, and neighborhood worked against the broad perspectives necessary for regional and national coordination. Even when Catholic educators agreed on the value of greater unity and centralization, they could not overcome the persistent localism among Catholics and the traditional autonomy of Catholic postsecondary institutions. The CEA had no power to limit expansion, raise money, or allocate scarce resources. And the attempts of the CEA and Catholic University after 1912 to enforce standards never succeeded.[85]

In 1907, prominent Catholic college and university officials launched a campaign to convince the Catholic hierarchy to provide '"the same aid and encouragement"' for Catholic higher education as the church did for parochial schools. In particular, they requested that bishops stop committing priests and money to the Newman movement, an effort to care for the religious needs of Catholics on non-Catholic campuses. These Catholic educators argued that acceptance of their proposals would strengthen Catholic higher learning and also reduce the number of Catholics attending non-Catholic institutions.[86]

But representatives of the bishops sought some measure of control or guarantee of academic quality and religious orthodoxy in return for moral and financial support. In addition, the hierarchy felt obligated to minister to all Catholics wherever they attended college, especially after Pope Pius X issued an encyclical in 1905 urging that religious instruction be provided for Catholic students in public institutions. Furthermore, some Catholic administrators worried that accepting help from the bishops would threaten the independence of their institutions, perhaps resulting in domination by the hierarchy or Catholic University. Others involved in Catholic higher education feared that adoption and enforcement of academic standards would compel a number of Catholic colleges to close, thus causing even more Catholics to attend secular schools.

Besides limitations in personnel, finances, and organizational structure, deep ideological differences with trends in secular academic culture frustrated reform in Catholic higher education during the late nineteenth and early twentieth centuries. Catholic educators, reflecting widespread views in the Catholic Church, vigorously opposed the steady displacement of religion occurring in American colleges and universities. They particularly objected to Carnegie Foundation policies which restricted grants to nonsectarian higher educational institutions and thus tempted schools to abandon religious ties for money. Those attending the Catholic Educational Association convention in 1911 passed a resolution criticizing the Foundation "as a private educational agency which . . . aims at dechristianizing American education, which is, therefore, a menace to our intellectual and moral well-being as a people."[87]

Catholics also regarded public higher education as a threat to religious belief. Based on his four years at "a State university in the Mississippi Valley," a Catholic wrote in 1916 that "the young man who expects to go through a secular university with faith unshaken and morals unimpaired, must possess the courage of a saint and the mental training of a Catholic doctor of philosophy." Jesuit provincial superiors at a meeting in 1918 described secular universities as places "where doctrines contrary to the Faith and teaching of the Church are disseminated."[88]

Many involved in Catholic education in the late nineteenth century also opposed government interference in schools. For example, numerous individuals in the Catholic Church strongly protested laws passed in Wisconsin and Illinois in 1889 requiring children to attend approved schools and specifying that certain courses must be taught in English. Catholics of German descent particularly criticized such legislation, maintaining that the preservation of their faith and culture in America required instruction in their native language. Also, possibly influenced by bitter European experiences with national schools and government coercion, some Catholics denied that the state or other agencies had any right to compel school attendance. They insisted that educational matters should be the sole responsibility of families.[89] When Thomas Bouquillon, a priest on the faculty of Catholic University, published a pamphlet in 1891 granting that the state could demand compulsory education, he quickly found himself in a minority position and under sharp attack from fellow Catholics.[90]

Moreover, while acknowledging the necessity of educational standards, segments of Catholic higher education regarded the continual demands by standardizing bodies for additional faculty, laboratories, and endowment as abuses of power and questioned whether they led to corresponding improvements in training.[91] More conservative Catholics specifically insisted that much of academic excellence was an intangible; thus, it could not be produced by conforming to arbitrary standards or measured by objective criteria. Others regarded accrediting groups as biased and inflexible, threats to the faith and independence of Catholic institutions. They argued against accepting requirements established by non-Catholic educators often unsympathetic to the religious purpose and classical traditions of Catholic schools. St. Louis University reportedly vetoed membership in the North Central Association early in the twentieth century because it feared that the organization was contaminated by money from the Carnegie Foundation, regarded by many Catholic educators as an agent of secularization.[92]

Guarding against secularism and erosion of religious belief fostered defensiveness and rigidity, creating major obstacles for those trying to modernize Catholic higher education. Opposition of conservatives within the Holy Cross order forced the replacement of John Zahm, C.S.C. as provincial in 1906, halting his plans to reorient Notre Dame and curtailing assignment of men for graduate studies. James Morrissey, S.J. revitalized Santa Clara College after being named its president in 1913, but conflicts with older Jesuit faculty over his innovations and style of government so disheartened him that he left office three years later.[93]

Yet in spite of obstacles, Catholic higher education made visible progress between 1865 and 1918.[94] It elicited greater support within Catholicism, partly because functioning in American society required schooling and also because Catholics had developed higher intellectual and social aspirations. The Catholic Educational Association provided a much-needed forum to disseminate new ideas and methods and to renew the spirit of Catholic education. Institutions gradually adopted the prevailing pattern of a four-year collegiate program, modernized their curricula to include some electives, and started reducing the number of required courses (especially in classical languages). Colleges responded to desires of Catholics for professional training by adding schools of law, medicine, dentistry, engineering, and pharmacy. More Catholic leaders realized that accrediting demands could not be ignored. For instance, Alexander Burrowes, S.J., provincial of midwestern Jesuits, wrote in 1915 that "The day is not far distant when our College diplomas and High School certificates will be of little value to the owners unless our institutions have the standing recognized by the State. As we cannot set the standard, we shall have to follow."[95]

Perhaps most important of all, leading Catholic educators recognized that they had to rethink their educational approach if their institutions were to survive and to meet the needs of American Catholics. Isolation from American culture and reliance on a European model of education were no longer feasible or desirable. The challenge for Catholic higher education in the United States, once the disruption of World War I had ended, was to formulate and then implement an educational rationale bonding intellectual excellence to religious commitment.

Notes

1. For statistics summarizing the development of American Catholicism, see Edwin S. Gaustad, *Historical Atlas of Religion in America*, rev. ed. (New York: Harper & Row, 1976), 29-36 and 103-12; and James Hennesey, S.J., *American Catholics: A History of the Roman Catholic Community in the United States* (New York: Oxford University Press, 1981), 73-75, 173, 207, and 237; Winthrop S. Hudson, *Religion in America*, 3d ed. (New York: Charles Scribner's Sons, 1981), 249.

2. Philip Gleason, "Immigration and American Catholic Intellectual Life," *Review of Politics* 26 (April 1964): 154-55; and Stephen Steinberg, *The Academic Melting Pot: Catholics and Jews in American Higher Education* (New York: McGraw-Hill Book Company, 1974), 80. For social profiles of immigrant Catholics, see Jay P. Dolan, *The American Catholic Experience* (Garden City, N. Y.: Doubleday and Company, 1985), 127-57; and Delores Liptak, R.S.M., *Immigrants and Their Church* (New York: Macmillan Publishing Company, 1989), 57-75.

3. See Robert H. Lord, John E. Sexton, and Edward T. Harrington, *History of the Archdiocese of Boston, in the Various Stages of Its Development* (New York: Sheed and Ward, 1944), vol. 2, 126 and vol. 3, 189; and *The New Catholic Dictionary*, ed. Conde Pallen and John J. Wynne, S.J. (New York: The Universal Knowledge Foundation, 1929), 134.

4. Gaustad, *Historical Atlas of Religion in America*, 43-44. For an account of nineteenth-century charity efforts among Irish and German Catholics in New York City, see Jay P. Dolan, *The Immigrant Church: New York's Irish and German Catholics, 1815-1865* (Baltimore: Johns Hopkins University Press, 1975), 127-40.

5. David J. O'Brien, *The Renewal of American Catholicism* (New York: Oxford University Press, 1972; paperback ed., Paramus, N.J.: Paulist Press, 1974), 6.

6. Arthur Schlesinger, Sr. remarked to John Tracy Ellis in 1942 that he regarded anti-Catholic bias as the most persistent prejudice in the history of the American people. See John Tracy Ellis, *American Catholics and the Intellectual Life* (Chicago: Heritage Foundation, Inc., 1956), 16-17.

7. Vincent P. Lannie, *Public Money and Parochial Education: Bishop Hughes, Governor Seward, and the New York School Controversy* (Cleveland: Case Western Reserve University Press, 1968); and Richard Shaw, *Dagger John: The Unquiet Life and Times of Archbishop John Hughes of New York* (New York: Paulist Press, 1977), 139-75.

8. Dolan, *The Immigrant Church*, 52-53 and 74-75.

9. Gleason, "American Catholic Higher Education," 27. For additional evidence of Catholic upward mobility, see Stephen Thernstrom, *The Other Bostonians: Poverty and Progress in the American Metropolis, 1880-1970* (Cambridge: Harvard University Press, 1973); Humbert S. Nelli, *The Italians in Chicago 1880-1930: A Study in Ethnic Mobility* (New York: Oxford University Press, 1970); and Thomas Kessner, *The Golden Door: Italian and Jewish Immigrant Mobility in New York City, 1880-1915* (New York: Oxford University Press, 1977).

10. See Stephen Birmingham, *Real Lace, America's Irish Rich* (New York: Harper & Row, 1973).

11. For data on Catholic college attendance, see Laurence R. Veysey, *The Emergence of the American University* (Chicago: University of Chicago Press, 1965; Phoenix Books, 1974), 281, fn. 55; Marcia Graham Synnott, *The Half-Opened Door: Discrimination and Admissions at Harvard, Yale, and Princeton, 1900-1970* (Westport, Conn.: Greenwood Press,

1979), 19, 43, 131, 177-79, and 267, fn. 34; John Whitney Evans, "John LaFarge, AMERICA, and the Newman Movement," *Catholic Historical Review* 65 (October 1978): 618; Armando Trindade, "Roman Catholic Worship at Stanford University: 1891-1971" (Ph.D. dissertation, Stanford University, 1971), 71-73; and John J. Farrell, "The Catholic Chaplain at the Secular University," *Catholic Educational Association Bulletin* 4 (1907): 152-59. On February 5, 1896, J. Havens Richards, S.J., president of Georgetown University, wrote to his superiors in Rome that "'Harvard alone had more than 300 Catholic students three years ago in her *colleges classes*, without counting Law or Medicine. This is double the number of students at that time in the corresponding four years of any Catholic college in the United States'"; see excerpt of letter in C. Joseph Nuesse, "Undergraduate Education at the Catholic University of America: The First Decades, 1889-1930," *U.S. Catholic Historian* 7 (Fall 1988): 430.

12. In contrast, a 1933 survey of people who had graduated from the University of Chicago between 1893 and 1930 showed that Jews represented 11% and Catholics 6%. See Synnott, *The Half-Opened Door*, 267, fn. 34.

13. For data on Jewish-Catholic college attendance at these institutions, see Veysey, *The Emergence of the American University*, 281, fn. 55; Synnott, *The Half-Opened Door*, 19, 43, 131, 177-82; and Trindade, "Roman Catholic Worship at Stanford University: 1891-1971," 71-73.

14. Farrell, "The Catholic Chaplain at the Secular University," 151-52; Seymour E. Harris, *A Statistical Portrait of Higher Education* (New York: McGraw-Hill Book Company, 1972), 926; and Andrew M. Greeley, *The American Catholic: A Social Portrait* (New York: Basic Books, 1977), 40-47.

15. Mel Piehl, *Breaking Bread: The Catholic Worker and the Origins of Catholic Radicalism in America* (Philadelphia: Temple University Press, 1982), 29-31. See also the following analyses of *Who's Who in America*: Ellsworth Huntington and Leon F. Whitney, "Religion and 'Who's Who,'" *American Mercury* 12 (August 1927): 438-43; and William S. Ament, "Religion, Education, and Distinction," *School and Society* 26 (24 September 1927): 399-406.

16. See William Miller, "American Historians and the Business Elite," *Journal of Economic History* 9 (November 1949): 203; Synnott, *The Half-Opened Door*, 10 and 44; Calvin O. Davis, *A History of the North Central Association of Colleges and Secondary Schools, 1895-1945* (Ann Arbor: North Central Association, 1945), 160-62; and Walter L. Bierring, "Biographies of the Presidents of the American Medical Association, 1847-1947," in *A History of the American Medical Association, 1847-1947*, ed. Morris Fishbein (Philadelphia: Saunders Publishing Company, 1947), 569-830.

17. See Melvin G. Holli and Peter d'A. Jones, eds., *Biographical Dictionary of American Mayors, 1820-1980, Big City Mayors* (Westport, Conn.: Greenwood Press, 1981).

18. John P. Bocock detailed the dimensions of Irish political strength in a magazine article published in 1984; see his lament "The Irish Conquest of Our Cities," *The Forum* 17 (April 1894): 186-95; reprinted in James B. Walsh, ed., *The Irish: America's Political Class* (New York: Arno Press, 1976).

19. Felician A. Foy, O.F.M., ed., *1989 Catholic Almanac* (Huntington, Ind.: Our Sunday Visitor, Inc., 1988), 408-9. The number of Catholics in Congress in 1880 was obtained from biographical information gleaned from the *Congressional Directory, Biographical Directory of the American Congress, 1774-1971* (particularly place of burial), and *Dictionary of Catholic Biography*.

20. John F. Moore, *Will America Become Catholic?* (New York: Harper & Brothers, 1931), 232-35.

21. See Samuel Lubell, *The Future of American Politics* (New York: Harper & Row, 1951), 86; and Moore, *Will America Become Catholic?*, 233.

22. For a discussion of the cultural differences between Catholic and Jewish immigrants, see Steinberg, *The Academic Melting Pot*, 59-74.

23. Ellis, *American Catholics and the Intellectual Life*, 21-27 and 35-39; and John Lancaster Spalding, "The Higher Education," in *Means and Ends of Education* (Chicago: A.C. McClurg and Co., 1897), 212.

24. For a study of immigrant attitudes toward education, see Timothy L. Smith, "Immigrant Social Aspirations and American Education, 1880-1930," *American Quarterly* 21 (Fall 1969): 523-43.

25. For instance, see Stephen Thernstrom's findings about Catholics in Newburyport, Mass. in *Poverty and Progress: Social Mobility in a Nineteenth Century City* (Cambridge: Harvard University Press, 1964), 22-25.

26. Greeley, *The American Catholic*, 40; and Ellis, *American Catholics and the Intellectual Life*, 34.

27. Ellis, *American Catholics and the Intellectual Life*, 24-25.

28. Nevertheless, Sheehy thought the earlier priorities were correct since "if we had concentrated our resources upon the university level as the Unitarians did in regard to Harvard or the Baptists in Chicago, we might have about the same situation as prevails in those schools where only a handful of students professing the faith of the institution can be found." See Sheehy to Wilfred Parsons, S.J., editor of *America*, 18 June 1932, "Catholic University," Box 15, Jesuit Educational Association Collection, Archives, Boston College (hereafter cited as ABC).

29. Interestingly, these Jesuits also believed that "diminishing esteem for college education" among Catholics contributed to declining enrollment in their schools; see "Topics to be discussed at the meeting of the presidents of the Jesuit Colleges of the Missouri Province, April 2, 1917," Archives, Jesuit Community, Saint Louis University (hereafter referred to as AJCSLU).

30. Edward Power, *Catholic Higher Education in America: A History* (New York: Appleton-Century Crofts, 1972), 100-8; and "Report on the Attendance at Catholic Colleges and Universities in the United States," *Catholic Educational Association Bulletin* (12 August 1916): 7.

31. The 10% figure included only laymen; 22% of those surveyed entered the priesthood, some of whom undoubtedly spent part of their lives in education. See Francis M. Crowley, compiler, *Why a Catholic College Education?* (Washington, D.C.: Department of Education, National Catholic Welfare Conference, 1926), 17.

32. Steinberg, *The Academic Melting Pot*, 75-96; and Moses Rischin, *The Promised City: New York Jews, 1870-1914* (Cambridge: Harvard University Press, 1962), 59.

33. Leonard Dinnerstein, "Education and the Advancement of American Jews," in *American Education and the European Immigrant: 1840-1940*, ed. Bernard J. Weiss (Urbana: University of Illinois Press, 1982), 44-60; and Synnott, *The Half-Opened Door*, 16.

34. See Ellis, *American Catholics and the Intellectual Life*, 17-18; Thomas F. O'Dea, *American Catholic Dilemma* (New York: Sheed & Ward, 1958; Mentor Omega Books, 1962), 69-83; and idem, "The Role of the Intellectual in the Catholic Tradition," *Daedalus* 101 (Spring 1972): 151-89.

35. Spalding, "The Higher Education," 220.

36. Power, *Catholic Higher Education in America*, 353.

37. For perspective on social, intellectual, and religious challenges facing Catholicism in America during the nineteenth and twentieth centuries and the response of the institutional church, see Aaron I. Abel, *American Catholicism and Social Action: A Search for Social Justice, 1865-1950* (Garden City, N.Y.: Doubleday and Company, 1960); and Thomas T. McAvoy, C.S.C., *The Great Crisis in American Catholic History, 1895-1900* (Chicago: Henry Regnery Company, 1957).

38. For a summary of Catholic reaction to labor organizations, see Hennesey, *American Catholics*, 188-89; and John Tracy Ellis, *American Catholicism*, 2d ed. (Chicago: University of Chicago Press, 1969), 105-7.

39. See Gibbons' letter to the Vatican in February 1887, defending the Knights of Labor, in Henry J. Browne, *The Catholic Church and the Knights of Labor* (Washington, D.C.: Catholic University of America Press, 1949), 365-78.

40. A sense of the issues and their resolution can be obtained from Richard M. Linkh, *American Catholicism and European Immigrants, 1900-1924* (Staten Island, N.Y.: Center for Migration Studies, 1975), 1-17; Robert D. Cross, *The Emergence of Liberal Catholicism in America* (Cambridge, Mass.: Harvard University Press, 1958); Gerald P. Fogarty, S.J., *The Vatican and the American Hierarchy from 1870 to 1965* (Wilmington, Del.: Michael Glazier, Inc., 1985), 9-141; and Liptak, *Immigrants and Their Church*, 76-114.

41. For a recent analysis of Ireland's life and views, see Marvin O'Connell, *John Ireland and the American Catholic Church* (St. Paul: Minnesota Historical Society Press, 1988).

42. Their ideas and desires for engaging contemporary society resembled the Catholic perspective in the 1780s, when Catholic-Protestant relations warmed noticeably after the Revolution, and in the 1950s, when Catholic liberals again turned toward American culture. See Jay P. Dolan, "American Catholicism and Modernity," *Cross Currents* 31 (Summer 1981): 150-62.

43. Corrigan to Cardinal Camillo Mazzella, S.J., 7 November 1890, Archives of the archdiocese of New York, as cited by Emmett R. Curran, S.J., "Conservative Thought and Strategy in the School Controversy, 1891-93," *Notre Dame Journal of Education* 7 (Spring 1976): 44.

44. Hennesey, *American Catholics*, 194-96; and David Noel Doyle, "The Irish and Christian Churches in America," in *America and Ireland, 1776-1976: The American Identity and the Irish Connection*, ed. David Noel Doyle and Owen Dudley Edwards (Westport, Conn.: Greenwood Press, 1980), 178.

45. See Robert D. Cross, "Origins of the Catholic Parochial Schools in America," *American Benedictine Review* 16 (June 1965): 194-209; and Marvin Lazerson, "Understanding Catholic Educational History," *History of Education Quarterly*, 16 (Fall 1977): 297-317.

46. See Harold Buetow, *Of Singular Benefit: The Story of Catholic Education in the United States* (New York: The Macmillan Company, 1970), 151-63; and Thomas T. McAvoy, C.S.C., "Public Schools vs. Catholic Schools and James McMaster," *Review of Politics* 28 (January 1966): 19-46.

47. "The Growth of Catholic Education in America," *School and Society* 20 (20 December 1924): 783.

48. John Ireland, "State Schools and Parish Schools—Is Union between Them Possible?" *The Journal of Proceedings and Addresses of the National Education Association, 1890* (Topeka: Kansas Publishing House, 1890), 179-85. See also O'Connell, *John Ireland*, 322-47.

49. For reaction to the experiments in Minnesota, see Daniel F. Reilly, O.P., *The School Controversy, 1891-1893* (Washington, D.C.: Catholic University of America Press, 1943; reprint ed., New York: Arno Press, 1969); Timothy H. Morrissey, "Archbishop John Ireland and the Faribault-Stillwater School Plan of the 1890s: A Reappraisal" (Ph.D. dissertation, University of Notre Dame, 1975); and Joseph H. Lackner, S.M., "Bishop Ignatius Horstmann and the School Controversy of the 1890s," *Catholic Historical Review* 58 (January 1989): 73-90.

50. For data on the involvement of Catholics in scientific disciplines, see John R. Betts, "Darwinism, Evolution, and American Catholic Thought, 1860-1900," *Catholic Historical Review* 45 (July 1959): 161-85; and Henryk Misiak, "Catholic Participation in the History of Psychology in America," *Historical Records and Studies* 49 (1962): 15-23.

51. For information about Zahm's struggles to link science and religion, see Ralph E. Weber, *Notre Dame's John Zahm: American Catholic Apologist and Educator* (Notre Dame, Ind.: University of Notre Dame Press, 1961), 44-93 and 103-28.

52. John Ireland, "The Mission of Catholics in America," in *The Church and Modern Society* (Chicago: D.H. McBride Co., 1897), 74.

53. Hennesey, *American Catholicism*, 217. For an excellent analysis of American Catholicism between 1899 and 1917, see Thomas T. McAvoy, C.S.C., "The Catholic Minority after the Americanist Controversy, 1899-1917: A Survey," *Review of Politics* 21 (January 1959): 53-82.

54. Richard Hofstadter, *Academic Freedom in the Age of the College* (New York: Columbia University Press, 1955); and Donald G. Tewksbury, *The Founding of American Colleges and Universities before the Civil War* (New York: Columbia University Press, 1932). For a vigorous and convincing argument against the older interpretation of antebellum higher education, see Colin E. Burke, *American Collegiate Populations: A Test of the Traditional View* (New York: New York University Press, 1982).

55. See Veysey, *The Emergence of the American University*, 3-10.

56. John S. Brubacher and Willis Rudy, *Higher Education in Transition: A History of American Colleges and Universities, 1636-1976,* 3d ed. (New York: Harper & Row, 1976), 163.

57. Richard Hofstadter and C. DeWitt Hardy, *The Development and Scope of Higher Education in the United States* (New York: Columbia University, 1952), 3. For a sense of the issues and personalities involved in the trend toward secularization, see Richard Hofstadter and Walter Metzger, *The Development of Academic Freedom in the United States* (New York: Columbia University Press, 1955); Talcott Parsons, *Structure and Process in Modern Societies* (New York: The Free Press, 1960), 295-321; and William C. Ringenberg, *The Christian College: A History of Protestant Higher Education in America* (Grand Rapids, Mich.: Christian University Press, 1984), 114-46.

58. For an excellent analysis of the educational impact of these men and other reforming presidents, see Earl H. Brill, "Religion and the Rise of the University: A Study of the Secularization of American Higher Education, 1870-1910" (Ph.D. dissertation, American University, 1969), chaps. 3, 4, and 14.

59. As cited in Brill, "Religion and the Rise of the University," 152.

60. Veysey, *The Emergence of the American University*, 162.

61. Frederick Rudolph, *The American College and University, A History* (New York: Alfred A. Knopf, 1962), 409-10; Veysey, *The Emergence of the American University*, 11; and Brubacher and Rudy, *Higher Education in Transition*, 363.

62. Henry S. Pritchett, "The Relations of Christian Denominations to Colleges," *Educational Review* 36 (October 1908): 217-41; Rudolph, *The American College and University*, 431-34; and Christopher Jencks and David Riesman, *The Academic Revolution* (Garden City, N.Y.: Doubleday & Company, Inc., 1968), 327.

63. Ringenberg, *The Protestant College*, 147-57; and Charles H. Judd, "List of Approved Colleges and Universities in the North Central Association of Colleges and Secondary Schools for 1913," *School Review Monographs* 4, no. 9 (Chicago: University of Chicago Press, 1913), 7-9.

64. Rudolph, *The American College and University*, 419; and Brill, "Religion and the Rise of the University," 379-80.

65. Brill, "Religion and the Rise of the University," 221-23 and 464-65; John Whitney Evans, *The Newman Movement: Roman Catholics in American Higher Education, 1883-1971* (Notre Dame, Ind.: University of Notre Dame Press, 1980), 3-11.

66. For a lengthy discussion of the reigning academic ideas of the nineteenth century, see Veysey, *The Emergence of the American University*, chaps. 1-4.

67. As cited in Veysey, *The Emergence of the American University*, 25-26.

68. See Brubacher and Rudy, *Higher Education in Transition*, 100-19.

69. For the development of professions in the United States, see Nathan O. Hatch, ed., *The Professions in American History* (Notre Dame, Ind.: University of Notre Dame Press, 1988).

70. For a summary of these efforts, see Brubacher and Rudy, *Higher Education in Transition*, 241-50.

71. See William Cook, "A Comparative Study of Standardizing Agencies," *North Central Association Quarterly* 4 (December 1929): 377-455.

72. Veysey, *The Emergence of the American University*, 302-17.

73. Power, *Catholic Higher Education in America*, 238-66; and Gleason, "American Catholic Higher Education," 45.

74. Charles W. Eliot, "Recent Changes in Secondary Education," *The Atlantic Monthly* 84 (October 1899): 443. See also Timothy Brosnahan, S.J., "President Eliot and Jesuit Colleges" (Boston: Review Publishing Company, n.d.) (pamphlet); and Ruth Everett, "Jesuit Educators and Modern Colleges," *The Arena* 23 (1900): 647-53.

75. James H. Plough, "Catholic Colleges and the Catholic Educational Association: The Foundation and Early Years of the CEA, 1899-1919" (Ph.D. dissertation, University of Notre Dame, 1967), 378; Judd, "List of Approved Colleges and Universities in the North Central Association of Colleges and Secondary Schools for 1913," 7-9; and Association of American Universities, *Journal of Proceedings and Addresses, 15th Annual Conference* (Champaign, Ill.: n.p., 1913), 60-62.

76. For a perceptive analysis of the ills afflicting Catholic higher education, see William J. Bergin, C.S.V., "The Conservation of Our Educational Resources," *Catholic Educational Association Bulletin* 14 (November 1917): 57-70.

77. "Report on the Attendance at Colleges and Universities in the United States," 1916, 9-11; "F.J.R., '89," letter to the editor, *America*, 1 March 1919): 527; and Thomas P. Kernan, "The Catholic Layman in Higher Education," *Catholic World* 71 (June 1900): 381-85.

78. Power, *Catholic Higher Education in America*, 84-86 and 90-111.

79. James P. Fagan, S.J., "Meeting of the N.E.A. at Chicago," *Woodstock Letters* 29 (1900): 128; Plough, "Catholic Colleges and the Catholic Educational Association," 112-14; and Roy J. Deferrari, *Memoirs of the Catholic University of America, 1918-1960* (Boston: Daughters of St. Paul, 1962), 259-60.

80. Minutes of the meeting of the Jesuit Commission on Higher Studies, January 5-7, 1932, New Orleans, 34, Archives, California Province of the Society of Jesus (hereafter cited as ACPSJ); and Samuel Knox Wilson, S.J., "Catholic College Education, 1900-1950," *Catholic School Journal* 51 (April 1951): 121.

81. Edward Power, *A History of Catholic Higher Education in the United States* (Milwaukee: Bruce Publishing Company, 1958), 46-47; Robert I. Gannon, S.J., *The Poor Old Liberal Arts* (New York: Farrar, Straus & Cudahy, 1961), 51; and Ellis, *American Catholics and the Intellectual Life*, 31.

82. Plough, "Catholic Colleges and the Catholic Educational Association," 216-30 and 300.

83. Robert I. Gannon, S.J., *Up to the Present: The Story of Fordham* (Garden City, N.Y.: Doubleday & Company, Inc., 1967), 157; and Edward Kantowicz, *Corporation Sole: Cardinal Mundelein and Chicago Catholicism* (Notre Dame, Ind.: University of Notre Dame Press, 1983), 108-9.

84. Paul Moyer Limbert, *Denominational Policies in the Support and Supervision of Higher Education* (New York: Teachers College, 1929), 115-74; and Charles E. Peterson, Jr., "The Church-Related College: Whence before Whether," in *The Contribution of the Church-Related College to the Public Good*, ed. Samuel H. Magill (Washington, D.C.: Association of American Colleges, 1970), 24-30.

85. Brubacher and Rudy, *Higher Education in Transition*, 71-72; and Plough, "Catholic Colleges and the Catholic Educational Association," 75-78, 175-81, and 316-20.

86. Evans, *The Newman Movement*, 32-36; and Plough, "Catholic Colleges and the Catholic Educational Association," 216-35.

87. "Resolutions of the Catholic Educational Association," *Catholic Educational Association Bulletin* 8 (November 1911): 41. See also Plough, "Catholic Colleges and the Catholic Educational Association," 299-302 and 135-38; Timothy Brosnahan, S.J., "The Carnegie Foundation for the Advancement of Teaching—Its Aims and Tendency," *Catholic Educational Association Bulletin* 8 (November 1911): 119-56; and Matthew Schumacher, C.S.C., "Discussion," ibid., 156-59.

88. "F.L.," "Dangers of Secular Universities," *Catholic Mind* 14 (22 August 1916): 431; and minutes of provincials' meeting, Campion House, New York City, April 10-11, 1918, 4, Archives, Missouri Province of the Society of Jesus (hereafter cited as AMPSJ).

89. For Catholic attitudes toward compulsory education, see James Conway, S.J., letter to editor, *American Ecclesiastical Review* 3 (December 1890): 460-64; [H.J. Heuser], "Compulsory Education in the United States," ibid., 420-35; and Edward A. Higgins, S.J., "The American State and Private School," *Catholic World* 53 (July 1891): 521-27.

90. Thomas Bouquillon, *Education: To Whom Does It Belong?* (Baltimore: John Murphy & Co., 1891). For attacks on Bouquillon's thesis, see Rene I. Holaind, S.J., *The Parent First* (New York: Benziger Brothers, 1891); and James Conway, S.J., *The State Last* (New York: Fr. Pustet & Co., 1892).

91. For a representative statement, see the address at the 1919 Catholic Educational Association meeting by Alexander J. Burrowes, S.J., "Attitude of Catholics towards Higher Education," *Catholic Educational Association Bulletin* 16 (November 1919): 159-74.

92. Joseph J. Labaj, S.J., "The Development of the Department of Education at Saint Louis University, 1900-1942" (M.A. thesis, St. Louis University, 1952), 80-81 and 27, fn. 24.

93. Thomas T. McAvoy, C.S.C., "Notre Dame 1919-1922: The Burns Revolution," *Review of Politics* 25 (October 1963): 432 and 439; and Gerald McKevitt, S.J., *The University of Santa Clara: A History, 1851-1977* (Stanford, Calif.: Stanford University Press, 1979), 174-76.

94. For an in-depth study of changes at Notre Dame, DePaul, and Loyola University of Chicago, three Catholic midwestern schools, during the nineteenth and early twentieth centuries, see Lester F. Goodchild, "The Mission of the Catholic University in the Midwest, 1842-1980: A Comparative Case Study of the Effects of Strategic Policy Decisions upon the Mission of the University of Notre Dame, Loyola University of Chicago, and DePaul University." Ph.D. dissertation, University of Chicago, 1986, 121-404.

95. Alexander J. Burrowes, S.J. to members of the Missouri Province, 9 August 1915, AMPSJ.

2

American Catholicism vs. Academic Professionalism

Higher education in the United States grew to new prominence following World War I. College and university attendance climbed from 600,000 in 1920 to 1,500,000 in 1940.[1] Members of the Catholic Church shared the national enthusiasm for education and the material success and status it conferred. The percentage of college-age Catholics enrolled in postsecondary institutions rose from its pre-1914 figure of 7% to 14% in the 1920s and to 19% during the Depression decade.[2] Plagued by chronic enrollment shortages until 1918, Catholic school officials welcomed the additional students and the evidence of upward mobility among Catholics.

But the rising educational and social expectations of Catholics, a more secular intellectual climate, and the tougher requirements of accrediting agencies during the 1920s and 1930s confronted Catholic higher education with two central challenges. First, to maintain minimum academic standing in an increasingly professionalized and competitive environment, Catholic colleges and universities had to conform to various educational standards commonly accepted in contemporary academic culture. Catholic postsecondary institutions lacking accreditation could not effectively communicate Catholic values and ideas in American society, a long-standing goal of Catholic education in the United States. Second, if Catholic schools were to retain the allegiance of their clientele, they had to meet growing desires for quality training in science, business, and the professions.

These demands conflicted with the protective, traditional orientations of the American Catholic Church and its institutions of higher
learning. Many Catholic educational and religious leaders in the early
decades of the twentieth century believed that staying aloof from
developments in modern society offered the best safeguard to Catholic
faith and culture. They also maintained that Catholic colleges and
universities should continue their long-standing emphasis on humanistic, collegiate education and resist trends toward research, graduate
schools, and professional programs. The pressures on Catholic postsecondary institutions reflected the broader task facing the Catholic
Church in the United States: to adapt to the new aspirations of Catholics and the movements shaping contemporary life without sacrificing
Catholic identity, principles, and objectives. A focus on Jesuit higher
education, especially its policy debates and reforms, illumines the clash
between Catholic and secular cultures during the interwar period. It
also reveals much about the evolution of the Catholic educational
network during these years.

Catholic colleges and universities in the United States functioned
in a wider context formed by the Catholic Church, secular higher education, and American society. Though Catholic postsecondary schools
in 1918 included business and professional training, they clearly
exalted the traditional liberal arts curriculum, particularly philosophy
and classics. As did other denominational educational institutions,
Catholic schools operated with a definite "custodial" orientation,
seeking to defend the teachings of the Catholic Church, inculcate
orthodoxy, and protect the faith of their students.[3] As a representative
of the Jesuit superior general declared while visiting the United States
in 1921, "the primary end of our [Jesuit] colleges is to impart religious
instruction in the most effective manner and to imbue the minds of
boys and young men with solid and manly piety."[4] Such a priority
often resulted in schools giving inadequate attention to the development of critical thinking, research, and intellectual excellence.

But certain experiences during World War I encouraged Catholics
to soften their opposition to secular educational trends and to end their
long-standing isolation from American society. Participation in defense
efforts reduced Protestant-Catholic animosity and left many Catholics
with a deeper sense of cultural belonging, greater self-confidence, and
broader perspectives. After the war, Catholics manifested optimism,
certitude about their religion, belief in progress, and an abiding faith
in traditional American values such as patriotism. They largely
escaped the postwar disillusionment that ravaged many Americans,
especially intellectuals.[5]

In 1919, the Catholic hierarchy displayed an uncharacteristic assertiveness, publishing a program of social reconstruction calling for minimum wage legislation, unemployment insurance, legal enforcement of labor's right to organize, public housing, and a national employment service. The bishops also issued their first national pastoral letter since 1884.[6] The slowing of immigration reduced the need for the Catholic Church to care for newcomers and released resources for advancing the position of Catholics in the United States. Organizations like the Catholic Writers Guild of America (1919), American Catholic Historical Association (1921), Catholic Library Association (1921), and American Catholic Philosophical Association (1926) were formed to promote Catholic cultural and educational activities.[7]

The greater sense of security felt by Catholics allowed them to engage in public self-criticism. In a 1922 article in the *Catholic Mind*, Carleton J. H. Hayes, a convert to Catholicism, urged development of Catholic intellectual leaders and an end to defensive and petty attitudes among Catholics. Both *America* and *Commonweal* provoked controversies in the mid-1920s when they printed negative assessments of Catholic intellectual life.[8]

In the 1920s, Catholic schools found themselves contending with new currents within Catholicism. More prosperous and more interested in education than previously, greater numbers of Catholics enrolled in college, and not all of them went to Catholic schools. Though undergraduate registration doubled and total enrollment tripled in Jesuit colleges and universities between 1920 and 1930, an estimated 40,000 Catholics in 1920 attended non-Catholic colleges and universities, and perhaps as many as 200,000 in 1940.[9]

Like many of their American peers, numerous young Catholics wanted preparation for better-paying jobs in business and the professions. Students in the professional schools of Catholic universities increased by approximately 45% between 1920 and 1928, and constituted nearly one-half of the total enrollment in Catholic higher education during these years. In the late 1920s, business colleges outnumbered any other type of professional school in Catholic higher education. These student preferences clashed with the traditional emphasis on the liberal arts and moral development in Catholic institutions of higher learning.[10]

The changing career goals of Catholics produced higher expectations of the curriculum and teaching methods of Catholic higher education. A letter appearing in *Commonweal* in September 1925, criticizing the overextension and poor performance of Catholic colleges, generated a debate in subsequent issues concerning the merits of

Catholic educational institutions.[11] Reporting on St. Ignatius College in San Francisco to his provincial, a Jesuit commented in 1929 that "we are only in our infancy in regard to what is expected of us for higher Catholic education. Year by year many of our most desirable students are compelled to enter godless universities because we are not yet able to meet their needs in certain higher courses."[12] During the 1920s and early 1930s, certain Jesuits and influential alumni increasingly maintained that the curriculum of Jesuit education was overcrowded, and they judged that philosophy and religion classes were academically weak and poorly taught. Edward Tivnan, S.J., president of Fordham between 1919 and 1924, noted in 1931 that students in Jesuit schools "have a reputation for lack of initiative when they graduate and go to other schools. They have not been trained to face problems squarely and to think for themselves. . . . They have been trained to depend too much on memory and too little on independent thought."[13]

Besides having to adjust to postwar changes within American Catholicism, leaders of Catholic colleges and universities also had to contend with external pressures, especially decisions of secular accrediting agencies. In 1918, the American Medical Association began requiring class A medical schools to accept only students from colleges affiliated with state universities or accredited by the state or regional associations. Responding to such demands, the Catholic Educational Association became a standardizing body for Catholic schools and published a list of members meeting minimum standards. But the AMA refused to accept the evaluations of the CEA, declaring that it recognized only nonsectarian accrediting organizations; the American Council on Education announced a similar decision in 1920. By the 1920s, accreditation groups like the North Central Association of Colleges and Secondary Schools had become widely accepted as judges of academic quality, and failure to satisfy their standards marked institutions as educationally suspect.[14]

The accrediting movement reflected trends in American academic culture toward a more rational, disciplined, and professional approach to education, one in harmony with spreading middle class values of merit and competence.[15] Meeting secular educational standards further burdened Catholic colleges and universities. In 1920, only a small number of them held memberships in accrediting organizations, mainly because of endowment, faculty, and financial deficiencies but also because of philosophical objections to the concept of standardization. Undergraduate programs approved by the AMA in 1920 included only four Jesuit colleges; and of 314 institutions on the accredited list issued by the American Council on Education in 1920, only twenty-six were Catholic schools, about 20% of Catholic higher education.[16]

When graduates of unaccredited Catholic institutions applied for teaching positions, they sometimes learned that states or individual schools refused to accept their degrees. Others were denied admission to graduate and professional schools or found that they were prepared inadequately by their Catholic education. One alumnus of a Catholic university, whose experience had shown him the deficiencies of his education, complained in a letter to the editor of *America* in 1932 that when his alma mater granted his degree, it not only did him "a grave injustice, but it also committed a public fraud." Catholic colleges and universities could ill afford such unhappy alumni and negative publicity.[17]

Yet few Catholic educational and religious leaders in the early 1920s accepted that the viability of their schools required conforming to an academic model largely determined by non-Catholic education, no matter how distasteful or costly it might be. Growing secularism and anti-Catholicism in American society reinforced Catholic insularity. In 1922, Oregon voters approved a referendum requiring children between eight and sixteen to attend public schools. A committee of Jesuit educators warned the following year that "We are daily witnessing the alarming development of an increasingly dangerous and hostile attitude throughout this country toward denominational education in general and toward Catholic education in particular reaching from the grade school to the university." The revival of the Ku Klux Klan after World War I and the religious prejudice marring the 1928 presidential campaign increased Catholic defensiveness and further discouraged interchange between Catholics and the dominant Protestant majority.[18]

The changing social and educational climate posed major challenges to Catholic postsecondary institutions, and Catholic educators struggled during the 1920s to respond effectively. Like most of their fellow Catholics, many Jesuits in the World War I era lived largely isolated from American culture, bound by tradition and defensive attitudes. For instance, Jesuit officials at St. Ignatius College in Cleveland decided in 1918 that Jesuits should not be permitted to attend "'even Shakespearean plays in public theaters.'" In 1923, Richard Tierney, S.J., editor of *America* magazine, told American Jesuit provincials, the major superiors of the Jesuit order in the United States, that he wanted articles from Jesuits; but they "generally speaking, show a great lack of acquaintance with recent books in the fields of literature and philosophy, and for this reason their contributions often fail to meet present needs." Without much knowledge of current trends, the majority of Jesuits in the United States before the early 1920s provided little support for new academic programs and curriculum revisions.[19]

The religious leaders of American Jesuits were more aware of changing circumstances, but too often they failed to translate their concerns into effective action. In October 1918, Jesuit provincials formed "The Association of Jesuit Universities and Colleges in the United States" and appointed Tierney, then head of the *America* staff, to be secretary-general. They indicated that the new organization should particularly concern itself with education bills in Congress and state legislatures, "adaptation of courses to present status of Colleges," and preparation of "specialists" in education.[20] It should also hold yearly meetings with representatives from Jesuit provinces (geographic governing units of the Society of Jesus) to discuss mutual problems. The proposed association represented the first attempt by Jesuit superiors to meet contemporary educational problems by forming a national organization and assigning it specific tasks. Inexplicably, the proposed association never functioned in any appreciable way, despite the stated desires of the provincials.[21]

But a small number of Jesuits, mainly institutional administrators well acquainted with academic matters, initiated efforts which eventually resulted in higher standards and increased enrollment in Jesuit colleges and universities. Jesuit educational renewal in the postwar period originated in an informal meeting of Jesuits at Fordham during the Catholic Educational Association convention in June 1920. During a discussion of common problems, Albert Fox, S.J., president of Campion College in Prairie du Chien, Wisconsin and a vocal advocate of academic reform, proposed that Jesuit provinces unite their efforts to study recent developments in education and then work together to solve difficulties.[22] Those present agreed and urged that the provincials authorize an interprovince meeting to begin the task. Within a few months, Jesuit superiors approved the request, and the first meeting of what became the Inter-Province Committee on Studies (IPCS) was held at Campion College from March 27 to April 2, 1921 at the invitation of Fox.[23]

The IPCS reflected desires within Catholicism to form organizations which could analyze current issues, present Catholic positions, and lobby for specific proposals. In 1919, the Catholic hierarchy established the National Catholic Welfare Council (NCWC), the successor of the National Catholic War Council started in 1917 to coordinate Catholic contributions to the war effort; the NCWC included a department of education to assist all divisions of the church's educational effort. By 1921, the Benedictines, Capuchins, and Franciscans, three Catholic religious orders involved in education, had founded educational conferences.[24]

Endorsed by the provincials and Wlodimir Ledochowski, S.J., superior general of the Society of Jesus, in 1921, the IPCS showed early promise. During the next decade, its members repeatedly stressed in their reports the need for admission to accrediting associations, doctoral studies for Jesuits, and institutional endowments. In addition, they proposed establishment of an association of Jesuit colleges and universities with membership standards (1922-1924), a limitation on expansion (1927), publication of a journal of Jesuit education (1929), and major revisions in the academic training of Jesuits (1931). They generally perceived the defects and opportunities of Jesuit schools and proposed insightful solutions. Persistence, a basic optimism, and awareness of educational trends distinguished their efforts.[25]

Other Jesuits shared the desires of the IPCS to update Jesuit higher education without sacrificing its core values and to inject Catholic ideas into American culture. They especially worked to make Jesuit schools more professional and contemporary in their educational approach. In 1920, Francis X. McMenamy, S.J., provincial of midwestern Jesuits, promulgated a revised collegiate curriculum, which made Greek optional, allowed more electives, and introduced majors and minors as mechanisms of specialization; similar changes occurred among Jesuit schools in the East in 1923.[26] Fox and Alphonse Schwitalla, S.J., graduate school dean and later head of the medical school at St. Louis University, became deeply involved in the national accreditation movement. Columbia University recognized Fox's educational contribution by conferring an honorary doctorate on him in 1928; and in 1936, Schwitalla became the first representative from a Catholic institution to serve as president of the North Central Association.[27]

Various Jesuit schools reorganized administrative structures, initiated fund drives, and paid greater attention to graduate programs in the 1920s. Instead of their traditional practice of giving responsibility to one teacher to instruct a class in a broad range of disciplines, Fordham and St. Louis University adopted the departmental system in 1921 and 1925, respectively.[28] Such Jesuit institutions as Boston College, Santa Clara, St. Louis, and Fordham launched ambitious campaigns to raise money for capital improvements and financial reserves.[29] Jesuit provincials agreed at their annual meeting in 1924 that their schools "were old enough in the field to have their own graduate schools," and they subsequently committed themselves to developing graduate education in Jesuit universities.[30]

The move to professionalize Jesuit higher education especially manifested itself in new attitudes toward degrees and doctoral studies. Before World War I, Jesuits in the United States did not seek degrees for academic work completed during their more than ten years of ascetical, philosophical, and theological training. Jesuit scholasticates (seminaries) operated apart from the prevailing American academic system, and some in the Society of Jesus during the early decades of the twentieth century seemed to regard degrees as worldly honors antithetical to Jesuit asceticism and thus to be avoided.[31]

But the increasing emphasis on professional training and graduate degrees within American education forced a change in attitudes among Jesuit educational and religious leaders. Jesuit provincials agreed at their annual meeting in 1914 that Jesuits merited degrees for their academic work. They added that such recognition should be granted because "laws will require certified teachers in the near future," a view probably influenced by recent legislation passed in such states as Wisconsin, Nebraska, and Ohio requiring teachers to meet new certification standards. These superiors also recommended that Ph.D.s be conferred on Jesuit college and university presidents and those who signed public educational documents such as diplomas and reports. They noted that "without these degrees our institutions are considered inferior to others that possess them, [and] our reputation among educators necessarily suffers."[32] In 1917, Alexander Burrowes, S.J., president of St. Louis University, announced that Ledochowski, the highest superior in the Jesuit order, had granted permission for American Jesuits to receive diplomas "in view of the urgent need of our Professors being equipped with academic degrees." Burrowes urged that Jesuit faculty seek degrees to fulfill state requirements and meet the demands of "powerful educational associations to whose standards we are forced by circumstances to conform more or less."[33]

After World War I, the number of Jesuits in doctoral programs and attending secular schools rose dramatically in comparison with earlier decades. According to records of the Missouri Province, only eleven of its members received Ph.D.s between 1900 and 1919 (one from Johns Hopkins, the rest from Catholic institutions). But in the next decade, twenty-three earned doctorates, thirteen of whom studied at non-Catholic universities (four at Cambridge, three at Johns Hopkins, and one each at California, Michigan, London, Munich, Ohio State, and Chicago). Midwestern Jesuits showed signs of an intellectual awakening and greater involvement with secular education.[34]

The reforms started in Jesuit higher education paralleled similar changes in other segments of the Catholic educational system. During the 1920s, Notre Dame restructured its academic government and established a lay board of trustees to handle endowment money received from the General Education Board. Leaders of the Holy Cross order, which operated Notre Dame, also sent more men for graduate degrees. The Catholic Educational Association urged its members to adopt higher standards and to professionalize in the pattern of non-Catholic education.[35]

Advocates of educational renewal in the Jesuit order concentrated mainly on academic and administrative problems within Jesuit institutions. But some of them also joined in efforts to discredit the Newman apostolate and to dissuade Catholics from attending secular schools. Newman centers on secular campuses represented attempts by the Catholic Church to offer some level of pastoral care for Catholics in non-Catholic schools. By 1926, 134 Newman clubs provided spiritual guidance and social activities for Catholics enrolled in state and private institutions.[36]

Eager for more students but also motivated by concerns about dangers to the faith of Catholics attending non-Catholic institutions, Catholic leaders in the early 1920s began publicizing the merits of Catholic schools.[37] Painfully aware of Catholicism's limited resources, influential figures in Catholic higher education also urged a deemphasis of Newman activities, which they thought encouraged Catholics to attend non-Catholic schools. Their efforts intensified after a survey revealed that while Catholic higher education enrolled 35,000 Catholics in 1924, an estimated 38,000 members of the Catholic Church attended public and other private institutions. Members of the Catholic Educational Association passed a resolution at their 1926 annual meeting declaring that secular colleges could not supply the religious and moral training available in Catholic institutions. Moreover, they insisted that the presence of Catholics in non-Catholic higher education was "not at all desirable but at most in certain circumstances tolerated." Their statement reflected continued suspicion of non-Catholic education and strong preferences for retention of a distinct Catholic subculture.[38]

Through their journals *America, Woodstock Letters,* and *Civiltà Cattolica,* Jesuits became leading critics of the Newman apostolate. *America,* a weekly with a national circulation, printed fifteen articles in 1925 and 1926, discussing the strengths of Catholic education and the defects of Newman clubs. In particular, it attacked the positions of Father John O'Brien, Newman chaplain at the University of Illinois and an advocate of Catholic pastoral centers on non-Catholic campuses.[39] Wilfred Parsons, S.J., editor of *America,* explained to the Jesuit provincials in 1928 that the magazine operated from an editorial policy which condemned the theory that Catholic education consisted merely in the addition of a course in Christian doctrine to the ordinary curriculum.[40] Along with other Catholic officials, certain Jesuits argued that Newman clubs could not substitute for the religious atmosphere of Catholic higher education and suggested that choosing non-Catholic colleges and universities conflicted with the educational ideals and canon law of the Catholic Church.[41]

Efforts to improve Catholic colleges and universities during the 1920s produced mixed results. Enrollment in Catholic higher education tripled between 1920 and 1930, and the number of accredited Catholic postsecondary institutions rose from twenty-six to sixty during these years. But many Catholic schools failed to advance academically. In 1930, approximately 60% of the 162 Catholic colleges and universities still did not qualify for membership in regional accrediting associations, and only sixteen Catholic schools had been recognized as approved institutions by the prestigious Association of American Universities.[42] A national evaluation of doctoral education in 1934 gave approval ratings to only six Ph.D. programs in Catholic universities (chemistry at Notre Dame and classics, history, philosophy, psychology, and sociology at Catholic University).[43]

Like numerous other Catholic colleges and universities, most Jesuit schools faced an unpromising future in the early 1930s, beset by academic mediocrity, low morale, and public criticism. In 1932, the approved list of the Association of American Universities included only six of twenty-five Jesuit postsecondary institutions, and eight of fourteen Jesuit law schools could not satisfy requirements of the American Bar Association.[44] Also in that year, only one member of the California Province, which encompassed the western portion of the United States, had a Ph.D.; a mere six Jesuits in the South possessed doctorates; and officials of the New England and Maryland-New York Provinces reported eleven and fifteen Jesuit Ph.D.s, respectively.[45] A special committee studying Jesuit education in the United States agreed in 1931 that "Everywhere a pall of discouragement hangs over Our [sic] men, at once real and warranted." James B. Macelwane, S.J., chairman of the evaluation group, declared the following year that Jesuits "are on trial before the hierarchy who say we have no outstanding men; that we are mediocre as a class, that we are four flushers."[46]

A complex interplay of various factors retarded Catholic colleges and universities during the 1920s, an interplay which reveals much about the state of Catholicism during these years. First, the mass of Catholics immigrating to America in the nineteenth and early twentieth centuries came from intellectually impoverished Catholic cultures in Europe. Consequently, few of them had much interest in the development of quality Catholic higher education in the United States. Penal laws enacted after the Protestant Reformation restricted Catholic access to schools in Ireland and England, stunting Catholic intellectual life in these two countries for decades. More than half of the people in Ireland in the early 1840s could not read and write, and the illiteracy rate in most of southern Italy in 1901 exceeded 70%.

Furthermore, most Catholic immigrants grew up in peasant societies which did not communicate habits and attitudes fostering intellectual activity. Their environments stressed tradition, family ties, and acceptance of authority, orientations which often conflicted with the independence, critical thinking, and curiosity necessary for sustained intellectual activity.[47]

Most Catholic colleges and universities founded to educate immigrants did not start to address the question of academic standards seriously until shortly before World War I, at least two decades after most secular institutions. Catholics did not begin attending high schools and colleges in large numbers until 1918. James Ryan, president of Catholic University, noted in 1932 that leading Catholics in the United States "have not been 'university-minded.'"[48]

Bigotry also slowed the accommodation of Catholics to American culture. Following World War I, Catholics were less fearful, more open to change and their environment. But the outbreak of anti-Catholic prejudice during the 1920s poisoned the social and intellectual atmosphere. Old anxieties about loss of religious faith surfaced among Catholics, encouraging a return to a previous cultural isolation. Catholic leaders launched fresh efforts to build a separate Catholic educational system, and many bishops reduced their support of the Newman movement. Such circumstances were not conducive to the new ideas and breaks with traditional methods urged by educational reformers.[49]

Anxious about the spread of secularism and atheism in American society, many Catholics in the decade following World War I became greatly concerned about maintaining religious orthodoxy and traditions. Certain American Catholics complained to the Holy See in the mid-1920s that Jesuit higher education, especially its expanding professional schools, lacked a sufficiently Catholic orientation and was becoming secularized. A distressed Ledochowski wrote the American provincials on March 12, 1927 that Cardinal Merry del Val, head of the Holy Office (the Vatican congregation responsible for safeguarding Catholic doctrine on faith and morals), had informed him of four charges made against Jesuit universities in the United States.[50] According to information sent to Rome, these schools could "in no sense of the word be called Catholic Universities"; only Catholic University and Notre Dame merited such status. Second, the professors in Jesuit institutions of higher education were mostly Protestants, Jews, or even atheists. Furthermore, Jesuit presidents had little or no authority over selection of faculty. Finally, Jesuits in the schools exercised "practically no influence over the religious and spiritual welfare of the students."[51]

While confident that most of the claims were false or exaggerated, Ledochowski nevertheless requested that the provincials answer specific questions about the number of non-Catholic students, faculty, and administrators in Jesuit schools and reasons for their presence. He also inquired about the authority of institutional leaders to hire and dismiss teachers as well as about measures to foster a Catholic atmosphere in Jesuit colleges and universities.[52] After analyzing responses to the questionnaires, Ledochowski issued a set of directives the following year revealing his preoccupation with the religious character, not the academic standing, of Jesuit schools in the United States. In particular, though acknowledging the difficulties involved, he called for limits on the number of non-Catholic students and teachers and urged that greater efforts be made to recruit Catholics. Furthermore, "I do now positively ordain that in the future no one who is not a Catholic must under any circumstances be given the office of dean, and I desire that wherever it can be prudently done, present non-Catholic deans be replaced by Catholics."[53]

The criticism of Jesuit universities and Ledochowski's response reflected the deep concerns within Catholicism about secularism. Such feelings reinforced adherence to a narrowly Catholic educational focus and made it difficult to institute curriculum and administrative changes. James Ryan, appointed rector of Catholic University in 1928, encountered heavy opposition to his program of academic reorganization. He was removed from office in 1935 after Archbishop John T. McNicholas of Cincinnati, a member of the university's board of trustees, convinced the Apostolic Delegate that Ryan was secularizing the school.[54]

Besides the limits imposed by history, culture, and religion, educational and financial realities also worked against academic and institutional reform in Catholic higher education during the 1920s. Regional differences in American education frequently frustrated attempts by Catholic educators to promote national perspectives and to agree on common policies. Schools in New England resisted efforts to form an accrediting association until 1952.[55] Support for traditional liberal arts education remained strong in the East, partly because private institutions dominated educational policy making and hindered development of state-funded colleges and universities oriented toward science and technology. Without external pressures from accrediting agencies, many Catholic schools there felt no urgency to relinquish their localism or give priority to curriculum reform and graduate training. They maintained a strong allegiance to classical education.

In contrast, Catholic schools in the Midwest had to contend with the rising academic and endowment requirements of the powerful

North Central Association.[56] They also struggled to compete with expanding state universities and to satisfy a clientele more interested in business and science courses than in learning Latin and Greek. The different educational environments in various sections of the United States fostered opposing attitudes among Catholic educators. For instance, it led Jesuit superiors in the Missouri Province to send more men to doctoral studies during the 1920s and to accept accreditation more quickly than their counterparts in the East and West. Matthew Germing, S.J., head of the Missouri Province, wrote Ledochowski in 1930 that while standardizing groups may impose conditions which Jesuits dislike or which seem unreasonable at times, "it is clear to me that the effect of these agencies on our schools has, on the whole, been salutary. Moreover, our experience in this province is that they are not at all anti-Catholic." But Walter Fitzgerald, S.J., president of Gonzaga University in Spokane between 1921 and 1927, held a contrasting position. Commenting on the 1929 report of the Inter-Province Committee on Studies, he proposed that Jesuits resist pressures for accredited degree programs and suggested that American universities were placing too much stress on accreditation and "neglecting real education." Such varying conditions and attitudes complicated attempts to agree on reforms and promote united efforts, whether by Jesuits for their own schools or the Catholic Educational Association for all of Catholic higher education.[57]

Even when Jesuit or other Catholic educational leaders agreed with recommendations of a group like the Inter-Province Committee on Studies for endowment, better faculty, expanded libraries, and modern laboratories, they lacked the financial resources and manpower needed to make such improvements. Though Jesuit schools like St. Louis, Boston College, Santa Clara, and Fordham conducted fund drives in the decade following World War I, none achieved its goals.[58] While certain Catholic families possessed great wealth, they had yet to develop a tradition of philanthropy to Catholic higher education. By necessity, Catholic colleges and universities in the 1920s operated on a meager financial basis. In 1926, thirty-nine Catholic institutions counted a combined endowment of $17.4 million; seventy-four other schools either had no reserves or reported none. That year, the best-endowed Catholic college or university was Catholic University with $2.9 million, followed by Creighton ($2.3 million), Marquette ($1.9 million), and St. Louis ($1.5 million).[59] In comparison, Columbia in 1927 operated with an endowment of $98 million, Harvard ranked second with $76 million, and Yale held third place with $45 million.[60]

In addition to financial problems, Catholic higher education continually labored to find qualified faculty. Reporting on implementation of Ledochowski's 1928 directives concerning the religious character of Jesuit schools, the provincial of the Missouri Province advised Ledochowski in 1930 that "it remains true that Catholics have not to any extent entered the teaching profession. There is a decided lack of Catholic professors for colleges and professional schools."[61] Though it was discouraged, hiring non-Catholics was sometimes the only option. William Magee, S.J., president of Marquette, represented the views of many administrators when he told his provincial in 1929 that "While it is certainly highly desirable to have only Catholic deans, at the present time this is well-nigh impossible."[62]

Perhaps the most critical factor in the failure of reform in Catholic higher education during the early twentieth century was the intellectually and culturally isolated American Catholic seminary system. To become academically respectable, Catholic colleges and universities after World War I needed leaders with vision, flexibility, intellectual sensitivities, and an awareness of contemporary secular thought. Catholics traditionally expected such leadership from their priests and bishops.

But Catholic seminaries were profoundly inadequate for the task. They emphasized character formation and an apologetical approach, one stressing systematic arguments to defend Catholic beliefs. Instead of fostering habits of inquiry, analysis, and reflection, seminary training frequently left priests rigid, burdened by old categories and definitions, and largely unfamiliar with trends in American culture. It often had a deadening effect on the intellectual lives of priests and ultimately on the Catholic community.[63]

Especially after the papal condemnation of Modernism in 1907, seminary officials sheltered their students from developments in American society and academic culture. In particular, they firmly resisted proposals to reorganize clerical education so that priests could obtain advanced degrees, costing Catholic higher education badly needed faculty.[64] Charles Carroll, a Jesuit active in attempts to reform Catholic colleges and universities, observed to his provincial in 1932 that "If as Father Woods [a veteran member of the California Province] and others have well said, the Society [Jesuit order] has lost much of its old prestige in education and in general scholarship, our ultra-conservative scholasticates are chiefly to blame."[65]

Most clerical leaders in the American Catholic Church during the 1920s and 1930s did not value intellectual excellence. Many of them excelled as pastors and builders, not as writers or scholars.[66] Jesuit administrators and religious superiors typified Catholic officials before World War II. Zealous, full of good will, but more suited to an earlier age, the great majority clung to tradition, orthodoxy, and religious discipline as defenses against a more secular environment. For instance, in January 1925, Laurence J. Kelly, S.J., provincial of the Maryland-New York Province, informed Richard Tierney, S.J., editor of *America*, that he wanted to censor all future articles concerning modern psychology and the theories of Freud written by an Irish Jesuit named E. Boyd Barrett. Despite protests by Tierney and the magazine's staff that Barrett's writings had been approved by competent Jesuit authorities in Ireland, England, and Belgium, and that Kelly had no power to interfere, the provincial prevailed.[67]

Often seminary professors before becoming administrators or superiors, few Jesuits in leadership positions during the interwar period understood contemporary university education, having had minimal exposure to it. Albert Fox, a prominent Jesuit, declared in 1932 that "We [the Jesuit order] have not many Superiors, Provincials, and Rectors, who are sympathetic, forward-looking with the proper educational background. It is from the Rectors that Our [*sic*] men should get their inspiration."[68] When the Inter-Province Committee on Studies recommended in 1923 that Jesuit schools form a national organization headed by a permanent secretary, Jesuit provincials denied approval, judging that such a move might "create antagonism and be regarded by other Catholic educators as a manifestation of Jesuit exclusiveness." But as Charles Carroll, S.J. noted in 1932, Jesuit superiors also feared this association of Jesuit institutions might become a superorganization, interfering with the authority of provincials and humiliating some schools by denying them membership.[69] In subsequent years, the provincials deferred action on IPCS proposals for the founding of a journal of Jesuit education, enforcement of higher standards, limits on expansion, and revamping of Jesuit training to assist in obtaining doctoral degrees.[70]

Unfavorable conditions and attitudes in American Catholicism during the 1920s thwarted most proposals to upgrade Catholic colleges and universities. Yet advocates of reform defined issues and drew attention to problems and opportunities in Catholic postsecondary institutions. Their efforts prepared the way for significant developments in Catholic higher education during the next decade.

The academic standing of Catholic higher education advanced noticeably during the 1930s. By 1938, 76% of Catholic postsecondary institutions qualified for membership in regional accrediting associations, compared to approximately 40% in 1930.[71] The Phi Beta Kappa Society awarded its first chapters to Catholic schools in 1937 (to the College of St. Catherine in St. Paul) and in 1940 (to Catholic University). In 1943, Edward Doisy of St. Louis University shared in the Nobel Prize for physiology and medicine.[72] These improvements stemmed from new perspectives among Catholic educators, and they occurred despite continued financial problems and ideological objections. An examination of academic changes in Jesuit colleges and universities sheds light on factors promoting and hindering Catholic educational reform in the 1930s.

Efforts to upgrade Jesuit colleges and universities during the interwar period advanced significantly after the Jesuit superior general shifted from being an opponent to an advocate of educational reform. During most of the 1920s, Ledochowski had been mainly concerned about the religious and specifically Catholic aspects of Jesuit higher education in the United States, and he essentially ignored key recommendations from members of the Inter-Province Committee on Studies. But apparently, continued reports of weaknesses in American Jesuit schools and conversations with various Jesuits, bishops, and laymen gradually persuaded him that serious problems plagued Jesuit academic institutions in America. In the fall of 1930, Ledochowski summoned certain American Jesuit educators to Rome for consultation. Alphonse Schwitalla, S.J., dean of the medical school at St. Louis University, stressed to Ledochowski that Jesuit schools in the United States must cooperate with accrediting agencies and adopt rigorous standards in graduate programs.[73] Furthermore, in the early 1930s, officials at Catholic University and Notre Dame, the chief Catholic rivals of Jesuit higher education, instituted various academic reforms, including establishment of graduate schools and prescription of higher standards; their moves may also have helped convince Ledochowski that Jesuit schools in this country must make certain improvements to compete in the American educational environment.[74]

Ledochowski formally intervened in late 1930, giving immediate credibility to those urging major changes in Jesuit higher education. Writing to the American provincials on December 8, he noted that "the religious or Catholic aspect of your institutions is not the only one that calls for consideration and study," and he asserted that the Jesuit order "could and should take more influential share in determining the intellectual policy of the country."[75] Though still maintaining that Jesuit schools in America had chosen the "tentative methods and standards of the day" over certain of their educational traditions, he made some startling admissions. First, serious problems within Jesuit higher learning required solution; and instead of remaining aloof from secular education, Jesuits should study the procedures of preeminent colleges and universities. Furthermore, accrediting agencies had "assumed an ascendancy and controlling power which cannot any longer be ignored." Finally, more Jesuits should obtain "higher degrees," a need which might require a restructuring of Jesuit training.

Clearly concerned about the viability of Jesuit education in this country, Ledochowski announced that he was appointing a special commission to evaluate the situation and to make recommendations.[76] Underscoring his interest in the status of Jesuit schools in the United States and suggesting his dissatisfaction with American superiors, he specified that the findings of the special commission should be sent directly to him.[77]

In March 1931, Ledochowski formally constituted the Commission on Higher Studies of the American Assistancy of the Society of Jesus, appointing a representative from each of the six American provinces and naming James B. Macelwane, S.J., dean of the graduate school at St. Louis University and holder of a doctorate in geophysics from the University of California, as chairman.[78] The commission became the center of reform efforts in Jesuit higher education and achieved lasting impact. Through its meetings around the country and surveys sent to Jesuits, it brought hope of badly needed improvements. Second, the deliberations, judgments, and recommendations of its members, recorded in 750 pages of minutes and a final report, further acquainted Ledochowski with the problems restricting American Jesuit colleges and universities, and they also convinced him that reorganization was essential. For instance, Ledochowski's support of the commission seemed to be wavering in March and April 1932 because certain American Jesuits had protested it was unduly interfering with the training of Jesuits. But Macelwane and Hynes, a former seminary professor and currently president of Loyola University in New Orleans, persuaded Ledochowski that Jesuit education in the United States was in a critical state and that sweeping reforms were necessary.[79]

Most important, Macelwane's group formulated concrete proposals to reform Jesuit schools, ideas based on a comprehensive analysis of existing conditions. To overcome academic malaise and what Albert Fox described as an "all-sufficient, cocky spirit among a great many of Ours [which] has done a great deal toward keeping us back from real advanced study, research work and degrees," the commission essentially called for greater professionalism and centralization within Jesuit higher education.[80]

In particular, the *Report of the Commission on Higher Studies*, submitted to Ledochowski in August 1932, specified that the training of Jesuits should be revised to provide for academic specialization and the location of scholasticates "within easy reach of our recognized universities." In addition, the goal of every Jesuit should be to earn a doctorate, reflecting agreement among the Commission members that doctoral degrees "would drag us out of our intellectual lethargy to make us forward looking, alert in the Educational [*sic*] world, capable, confidence-inspiring, ambitious in a good sense." Furthermore, all Jesuit schools and programs should be accredited by the appropriate regional or professional association, a proposal made a decade earlier by the Inter-Province Committee on Studies.

The commission's final report also called for an "Association of Jesuit Universities, Colleges and Secondary Schools of the United States" to unify, supervise, and defend the Jesuit educational apostolate. Because of the many challenges facing Jesuit education, the association's first head should be appointed by the superior general and given the powers of a "commissarius" or commissioner, that is, full authority over Jesuit schools for as long as necessary. If not, "the inertia of local traditions, the inbred opposition of Ours [*sic*] to any change, and the prevailing ignorance of conditions among both inferiors and superiors" will prevent reform, as happened to measures advanced by the IPCS.[81]

The recommendations of the Commission on Higher Studies received a mixed reaction from American Jesuits. A few endorsed the *Report* enthusiastically, and most agreed that a national organization of Jesuit schools was needed. But many objected strongly to the idea of a commissioner, and others thought that Macelwane and his associates were too critical of Jesuit schools and proposed unwise changes in the training of Jesuits. At least some in the East suspected the suggested reforms reflected an attempt by Jesuits from the Midwest and West to dominate Jesuit education in the United States.[82]

The involvement of Ledochowski and the work of the special commission he appointed created a momentum for change, spurring Jesuits to analyze the condition of their schools and to debate how they should respond to developments in contemporary higher education. Initiatives by officials at Catholic University supplied additional impetus to the reform movement in Jesuit higher education.

In the late 1920s and early 1930s, articles appeared in various journals and magazines citing the poor record of Catholics as scholars and leaders in American society.[83] Officials at Catholic University acknowledged the defects in Catholic intellectual life and responded with plans to remedy the situation. Monsignor James Ryan, rector of Catholic University, and Dr. Roy Deferrari, a layman and dean of the graduate school at CU, initiated a public campaign to have the limited resources of Catholic graduate education concentrated at their institution.[84] In promotional literature and financial appeals, they argued that popes and bishops had selected Catholic University to be *the* national Catholic university and reminded that Pope Leo XIII had stipulated in 1889 that no similar Catholic institutions should be started until CU had been fully developed. They also stressed that Catholic University was the only Catholic institution in the prestigious Association of American Universities.[85]

In addition, Catholic University administrators sought to expand their institution beyond Washington, D.C. In 1932, they announced plans to sponsor a summer school devoted exclusively to graduate work at Dominican College in San Rafael, California; and Deferrari proposed establishing branch campuses in San Francisco and St. Louis. Moreover, Maurice Sheehy, assistant to the rector of CU, suggested to numerous bishops and presidents of Catholic universities that degrees from Catholic graduate programs be granted from Catholic University, just as the University of California extended the advantage of its charter to three or four graduate schools.[86]

John Hynes, S.J., a member of the Jesuit Commission on Higher Studies, called the moves by Catholic University "a declaration of war"; and Wilfred Parsons, S.J., editor of *America*, used similar language, warning that CU was "waging a severe war against our [Jesuit] graduate schools."[87] Their reactions stemmed in part from the strained relations that had existed between the Jesuit order and Catholic University for the preceding forty years.[88] Jesuits also wanted to protect their own interests from domination by Catholic University; during the 1932-1933 school year, they operated thirteen of thirty-three Catholic institutions conferring graduate degrees, and their programs enrolled approximately 60% of all graduate students attending Catholic schools.[89]

To thwart Catholic University, supporters of Jesuit universities responded in two ways. First, they raised objections to the proposed concentration on one Catholic graduate school and publicized an alternative vision. Francis Crowley, a layman and dean of St. Louis University's school of education, answered Ryan and Deferrari in articles printed in *America* during May and June 1932 after *Commonweal* had refused to publish them.[90] He argued that a focus on one graduate institution would result in inbreeding, fail to meet regional needs, and destroy the good already being achieved in the various Catholic graduate schools. Moreover, numerous Catholics could not afford to travel to Washington, D.C.; consequently, they would be deprived of Catholic training now available locally. According to Crowley, a better idea than promoting Catholic University exclusively would be to develop six to eight quality universities in strategic locations.[91]

Second, because of the threat posed by Catholic University, Jesuits moved to strengthen their graduate schools. As Edward Tivnan told his fellow members of the Macelwane Commission, "if we do not build up one or several good Graduate Schools, the Catholic University is going to win out." The commission's final report urged formation of a national association of Jesuit schools partly to defend against the "hostile attitude of the Catholic University of America, especially as recently expressed towards our Graduate Schools."[92]

The third key factor in Jesuit educational reform was a proposal for a Catholic standardization agency controlled by American bishops. Aware of the growing problems burdening Catholic higher education, Francis Howard, bishop of Covington, Kentucky and a major figure in the National Catholic Educational Association, sought to obtain aid from the hierarchy in 1932.[93] But just as bishops had responded to a similar plea in 1907, many of Howard's fellow prelates wanted assurances about the educational quality and religious orthodoxy of Catholic institutions. Consequently, Howard proposed that the hierarchy and Catholic colleges and universities jointly agree on standards, thus satisfying episcopal concerns and also encouraging improvements in Catholic postsecondary schools. In return, the bishops would assist Catholic higher education. The members of the American episcopacy seemed favorably disposed to Howard's plan and directed him to consult with college and university leaders on additional steps.[94]

Jesuits reacted ambivalently to the bishops' overtures, partly because they judged that some prelates wanted exclusive control of Catholic colleges and universities. Also, Jesuit educators feared subjecting their institutions to the scrutiny of the hierarchy, many of whom were not university men and possessed little awareness of the problems troubling contemporary Catholic higher education. Macelwane wrote Ledochowski that the bishops could make decisions "which would be disastrous to the best interests of the Church and which they themselves would regret later on." Yet, as Ledochowski reminded the provincials in late 1932, for years American Jesuits had complained about the indifference and opposition of bishops. With episcopal support now a possibility, they should not dismiss the plan as "an impossibility or an open encroachment on our rights." Rather, every attempt should be made to cooperate, and the provincials should seek counsel with experts, especially members of the former Commission on Higher Studies. For the next eighteen months, Jesuit officials and representatives of the hierarchy periodically discussed the concept of a Catholic standardization agency.[95]

Initiatives of Ledochowski, the Jesuit Commission on Higher Studies, Catholic University officials, and certain bishops in the early 1930s broadened intellectual perspectives within Jesuit higher education. As a result, more Jesuits became aware of contemporary educational trends and the academic needs of American Catholics, and they supported calls for revamping Jesuit schools. But the differing educational visions of reformers and traditionalists within the Jesuit order prevented basic agreement on how Jesuit colleges and universities should respond to current conditions. In 1933 and 1934, as Jesuits debated questions about future academic policy and sent reactions to their superiors, reform seemed stalled, reminiscent of the 1920s when proposals of the Inter-Province Committee on Studies generated interest but produced minor improvements. After returning from Rome where he had discussed recommendations of the Commission on Higher Studies with Ledochowski, a discouraged Edward Tivnan, one of the commission members, wrote Macelwane in June 1933 that "I have not the least hope that anything will come of all our work even if the General [Ledochowski] does take the modified action I expect."[96]

But on August 15, 1934, Ledochowski acted decisively, issuing an "Instruction" concerning Jesuit education in the United States that incorporated many of the ideas suggested by the Commission on Higher Studies.[97] The document called for establishment of a national association of Jesuit schools headed by a "National Secretary of Education" as a means of fostering union and cooperation among American Jesuits and their institutions. This innovation reflected criticisms that existing Jesuit organizational forms perpetuated isolation and mediocrity. It also manifested Ledochowski's agreement with reformers that present structures could not quickly eliminate defects in Jesuit schools nor enable Jesuit colleges and universities to compete effectively in American higher education.

Though not repudiating previous emphases on protecting the faith of Catholics, Ledochowski's plan emphasized the necessity of academic professionalism. It specified that Jesuit schools should modernize administrative practices and become members of regional accrediting associations. The entire third section of the "Instruction" dealt solely with the training of Jesuits. One paragraph in it directed superiors to select men for doctoral studies and send them to preeminent universities, preferably Catholic institutions but non-Catholic schools if necessary.[98]

Ledochowski informed the provincials separately that Daniel O'Connell, S.J., a member of the Chicago Province, would be the national secretary and that he would have the power of a "commissarius" or commissioner, possessing all the authority needed to implement the prescriptions of the "Instruction."[99] Furthermore, Ledochowski advised that he had directed O'Connell to give special attention to Jesuit graduate schools, "which have hitherto received so little public recognition" and which must be "brought to the level of the best in the country."[100]

Ledochowski's promulgation of the "Instruction" and appointment of an "educational czar" represented the turning point of Jesuit educational reform during the interwar period. His actions mandated sweeping revisions in policy and perspective, breaking the grip of conservatism and inertia; and they also created the organizational structure necessary to achieve needed improvements in Jesuit institutions. By World War II, the Jesuit Educational Association (JEA), the national organization prescribed by the "Instruction," and its executive committee of province directors of education had become an effective, functioning mechanism for strengthening Jesuit postsecondary education, especially through presentations and discussions at its annual meetings. As commissarius, O'Connell tirelessly promoted academic excellence, pointing out defects and calling for higher standards. The JEA Committee on Graduate Studies drafted norms in 1936 and 1937 for faculty hiring, institutional organization, library holdings, research facilities, and degree requirements, the first general statements of graduate school standards in American Catholic higher education.[101] Largely because of the "Instruction" and advocacy by JEA leaders, Jesuit provinces took greater interest in research and committed themselves to the graduate training of their men in an unprecedented way; seventy Jesuits were engaged in doctoral studies in 1941, more than the total number with doctorates two decades earlier.[102]

Still, various problems prevented Jesuit colleges and universities from making rapid progress toward the "Instruction's" twin goals of academic excellence and national cooperation. Because of the Depression, Jesuit higher education in the 1930s could not afford costly improvements in facilities and faculty. Samuel Horine, S.J., provincial of the Missouri Province, wrote to Francis McMenamy, S.J., a former provincial, in 1934 that the new expenses resulting from the "Instruction" "can hardly be solved satisfactorily in view of the heavy debts we are carrying everywhere." Zacheus Maher, S.J., provincial of the California Province, explained to O'Connell in 1935 that he was not sending more men to graduate studies because the schools under his jurisdiction could not afford to hire replacements for Jesuits. Moreover, the province was essentially bankrupt, forced to borrow from one of its schools to pay for the ordinary training of Jesuits.[103]

Clashes between O'Connell and Jesuit superiors in the United States led to a reduction in his power and eventually to his replacement, crippling the drive for a unified approach and slowing advancement toward educational quality. Responding to steady complaints, Ledochowski in 1936 suspended the broad powers given to O'Connell two years earlier and in 1937 removed him as national secretary. Moreover, he drastically curtailed the authority of the next head of the JEA, making him subordinate to the provincials.[104]

In addition, regional and institutional rivalries continued to retard the development of Jesuit higher education. Though the JEA Executive Committee and Ledochowski urged a pooling of resources to enable at least one Jesuit university to become a member of the Association of American Universities and thus enhance the image of all Jesuit colleges and universities, the provinces and schools would not subordinate their local interests for a greater good. If O'Connell had been in office with his full powers, he might have been able to demand cooperation and to implement his plan of concentrating Jesuit graduate education at Fordham and St. Louis Universities.[105]

The changes in Catholic postsecondary institutions during the interwar period pointed to five significant developments occurring in Catholic higher education and the larger Catholic community during these years. First, the Catholic Church in the United States committed itself to a comprehensive system of higher education. In 1920, the network of Catholic colleges and universities consisted of 130 schools enrolling 34,000 students, mainly in undergraduate and professional programs. Twenty years later, Catholic higher education had grown to 193 colleges and universities, and attendance had risen to 162,000. By 1940, Catholic postsecondary institutions offered graduate instruction in eighty-two fields, including twenty-eight on the doctoral level.[106]

Second, pressured by accrediting associations and their Catholic clientele, Catholic educators began conforming in attitudes and policies to the dominant secular academic culture. They modified the long-standing humanistic, structured approach of Catholic higher education, with its stress on classical languages and Scholastic philosophy, to accommodate desires for electivism, a broader curriculum, and graduate and professional programs. Besides previous emphases on religious formation and transmission of Catholic beliefs, leading Catholic schools added the goal of discovering knowledge.[107] Religious orders like the Jesuits sent more personnel to doctoral studies, frequently in non-Catholic institutions. Administrators in Catholic colleges and universities commonly accepted the necessity of accreditation by secular accrediting organizations to have standing in American higher education. Recognizing that a separate standardization agency for Catholic schools was futile and superfluous, the National Catholic Educational Association discontinued its accreditation program in 1938.[108]

Third, while the changes in Catholic higher education during the 1920s and 1930s produced widespread improvements, they also undermined traditional Catholic educational theory and practice. Robert Hutchins criticized Catholic schools for failing to uphold the Catholic intellectual heritage. He told a meeting of midwestern Catholic educators in 1937 that "Catholic education is not Catholic enough," and he added that Catholic educators have "imitated the worst features of secular education and ignored most of the good ones." William McGucken, S.J., director of education for the Missouri Province of the Jesuit order, acknowledged that Catholic educational personnel "have been so busy meeting problems of organization, administration, and the like that we haven't really had time to study the extremely important problem of imparting a Catholic culture to our students."[109]

Fourth, though members of a church known for its vertical authority structure and priority on doctrinal unity, the vast majority of Catholic educators opposed plans to centralize control of academic policies and institutional growth in Catholic higher education.[110] Even at the height of the Depression when personnel, financial, and morale problems seemed overwhelming, Catholic colleges and universities continued to duplicate programs and to compete for scarce manpower and money, especially on the graduate level. In doing so, they sacrificed the last chance for a coordinated, national system of Catholic higher education and continued a pattern of debilitating competition.

Fifth, by 1940, Catholics had become more confident and more involved in American society than ever before. The percentage of Catholics in the 17-25 age group enrolled in college during the Depression decade moved ahead of that of Lutherans and almost matched that of Baptists; and by World War II, Catholics had advanced to within 1% of the national average for college attendance.[111] An estimated 200,000 members of the Catholic Church attended non-Catholic colleges and universities by the end of the 1930s. Attacks on the Newman Movement, common in the Catholic press in the mid-1920s, diminished as Catholic fears about loss of faith in a Protestant culture lessened.[112] After the 1932 presidential elections, Catholics received unprecedented recognition in national affairs, signalling a new era for them. Franklin Roosevelt skillfully cultivated Catholic voters by appointing Catholics to his cabinet, the Supreme Court, and the federal judiciary.[113]

Tensions between Catholicism and non-Catholic society remained on the eve of World War II, and opposition to educational reform persisted in Catholic higher education. But during the interwar period, Catholics began to end their isolation from American culture, and Catholic educators moved to adapt their institutions to the increasing social and educational expectations of their Catholic clientele, higher academic standards, and a more secular intellectual environment. Doing so laid the foundations for Catholic advances after 1945.

Notes

1. Garland G. Parker, "50 Years of Collegiate Enrollments: 1919-20 to 1969-70," *School and Society* 98 (January 1970): 150; and Harris, *A Statistical Portrait of Higher Education*, 926.

2. Greeley, *The American Catholic*, 41.

3. The term "custodial" is from Michael J. Buckley, S.J., "The Catholic University as Pluralistic Forum," *Thought* 46 (June 1971): 203. To gain a sense of the concerns and atmosphere on a Catholic university campus during the interwar years, see "Survey of Fifteen Religious Surveys, 1921-1936," *Bulletin of the University of Notre Dame* 34 (March 1939).

4. Everard Beukers, S.J., "Memorial of the Visitation of the Missouri Province, August 31, 1920-September 13, 1921," 7, AMPSJ.

5. For an analysis of the reaction of Catholics to World War I and their attitudes between 1920 and 1940, see William M. Halsey, *The Survival of American Innocence: Catholicism in an Era of Disillusionment, 1920-1940* (Notre Dame, Ind.: University of Notre Dame Press, 1980). See also Hennesey, *American Catholics*, 234-36; and Robert T. Handy, *A History of the Churches in the United States and Canada* (New York: Oxford University Press, 1976; paperback, 1979), 399-400.

6. See "Program of Social Reconstruction," in *Pastoral Letters of the United States Catholic Bishops*, ed. Hugh J. Nolan (Washington, D.C.: United States Catholic Conference, 1984), vol. 1, 1792-1940, 255-71; and "The Pastoral Letter of 1919," ibid., 272-333. For an account of the origins, contents, and reception of the bishops' social program, see Joseph M. McShane, S.J., *'Sufficiently Radical': Catholicism, Progressivism, and the Bishops' Program of 1919* (Washington, D.C.: Catholic University of America Press, 1986), 136-238.

7. For a list of Catholic organizations started between 1918 and 1940, see Halsey, *The Survival of American Innocence*, 57.

8. Carleton J. H. Hayes, "A Call for Intellectual Leaders," *Catholic Mind* 20 (22 July 1922): 261-75; George N. Shuster, "Have We Any Scholars?" *America*, 15 August 1925, 418-19; R. R. MacGregor, "The Catholic Lay Professor," *America*, 12 September 1925, 513-14; and James Burns, C.S.C., "Failures of Our Higher Schools," *Commonweal*, 3 November 1926, 634-36. See also Albert Fox, S.J., "Our Scorn of Higher Schooling," n.p., n.d., Archives, Marquette University (hereafter cited as AMU).

9. *Woodstock Letters* 49 (1920), Appendix I; ibid., 59 (1930): 190-91; and Evans, *The Newman Movement*, 55, 99, 210, fn. 1. Approximately 25% of the freshman class at Columbia University in 1932 belonged to the Catholic Church; see Synott, *The Half-Opened Door*, 18.

10. Francis J. Crowley, "Catholic Education in the United States," in *The Official Catholic Yearbook, 1928* (New York: P. J. Kennedy & Sons, 1928), 418-19; and Bernard J. Weiss, "Duquesne University and the Urban Ethnic," in *American Education and the European Immigrant*, ed. Bernard J. Weiss (Urbana: University of Illinois Press, 1982), 185. In 1928, 49% of the students at Duquesne University were registered in the business school.

11. C. Molanphy, "Catholic Colleges," *Commonweal*, 23 September 1925, 481-82.

12. ? to Joseph Piet, S.J., 29 July 1929, "Old Corr.—IPCS and Fr. Charles Carroll," ACPSJ. Judging from the name of the file, the letter writer was Charles Carroll, S.J., director of education for the California Province.

13. For criticisms of Jesuit higher education, see reports of the Inter-Province Committee on Studies, 1921-1925, 1928, and 1929, Drawer 73, ACPSJ; and minutes of the Jesuit Commission on Higher Studies, 26-28 June 1931, 2; 12-20 February 1932, 79-80; and 3-23 July 1932, 16, ACPSJ.

14. "Topics to be discussed at the meeting of the Presidents of the Jesuit Colleges of the Missouri Province, April 2, 1917," 3, AJCSLU; Plough, "Catholic Colleges and the Catholic Educational Association," 435-39; and Davis, *A History of the North Central Association*, 46.

15. For a description of professionalism in education and its relationship to the emergence of a middle class, see Burton J. Bledstein, *The Culture of Professionalism: The Middle Class and the Development of Higher Education in America* (New York: W. W. Norton and Company, Inc., 1976).

16. *The Province News-Letter* 1 (15 May 1920): 29-30, AMPSJ; and "Accredited Higher Institutions," *Educational Record* 1 (October 1920): 71-80.

17. F. P. Donnelly, S.J., "Is the American College Doomed?" *American Ecclesiastical Review* 60 (April 1919): 359-65; reports of the Inter-Province Committee on Studies, 1924, 1928, and 1929, Drawer 73, ACPSJ; and E.W.K., letter to the editor, *America*, 13 February 1932, 464.

18. Evans, *The Newman Movement*, 60-61; Hennesey, *American Catholics*, 243-53; and report of the Inter-Province Committee on Studies, 1923, 2-3, Drawer 73, ACPSJ. For a recent examination of the conflict in Oregon, see Thomas J. Shelley, "The Oregon School Case and the National Catholic Welfare Conference," *Catholic Historical Review* 75 (July 1989): 439-57.

19. Donald P. Gavin, *John Carroll University: A Century of Service* (Bowling Green, Ohio: Kent State University Press, 1985), 142-45 and 492, fn. 28; and minutes of provincials' meeting, St. Louis University, 22-23 May 1923, ACPSJ.

20. In the fall of 1918, hearings started in Congress on the Smith Bill, which called for a federal department of education and provided federal aid to public education but not to private schools; see Plough, "Catholic Colleges and the Catholic Educational Association," 455.

21. Minutes of provincials' meeting, Georgetown University, 16 October 1918, ACPSJ; and ibid., Campion House, New York City, 21-22 April 1920, AMPSJ.

22. Contemporaries credited Fox with proposing the interprovince meeting; see *The Province News-Letter*, Missouri Province, 2 (May 1921): 60, AMPSJ; and Labaj, "The Development of the Department of Education at Saint Louis University, 1900-1942," 62-63. For a study of Fox as an educational leader, see Kenneth J. Gawrysiak, "The Administration of Albert C. Fox, A Portrait of Educational Leadership at Marquette University, 1922-1928" (Ph.D. dissertation, Marquette University, 1973).

23. For the origins of the IPCS, see minutes of the Jesuit Commission on Higher Studies, 15-18 November 1931, 21, and 3-23 July 1932, 200-1, ACPSJ; Edward B. Rooney, S.J., address to Jesuit philosophy students, St. Louis University, 3 May 1948, Folder 14, Box 19, Edward B. Rooney, S.J. Papers, ABC; and Ledochowski to American provincials, 20 October 1921, "Fr. General to American Provincials (1918-1932)," ACPSJ.

24. Elizabeth McKeown, "The National Bishops' Conference: An Analysis of Its Origins," *Catholic Historical Review* 66 (October 1980): 565-83; and *Directory of Catholic Colleges and Schools*, 1921, 972-73.

25. See reports of the Inter-Province Committee on Studies, 1921-1931, Drawer 73, ACPSJ; and Paul FitzGerald, S.J., *The Governance of Jesuit Colleges in the United States, 1920-1970* (Notre Dame, Ind.: University of Notre Dame, 1984), 1-20.

26. "Report of the Committee on the Course of Studies," St. Louis, 21 June 1920, ACPSJ; and "Revised Program of Studies for the Colleges and High Schools of the Maryland-New York Province, 1923," AMPSJ. For studies of curriculum changes in Jesuit schools between 1880 and 1923, see Miguel Bernad, S.J., "The Faculty of Arts in the Jesuit Colleges in the Eastern Part of the United States: Theory and Practice, 1782-1923" (Ph.D. dissertation, Yale University, 1951); and Roman Bernert, S.J., "A Study of the Responses of Jesuit Educators in Theory and Practice to the Transformation of Curricular Patterns

in Popular Secondary Education Between 1880 and 1920" (Ph.D. dissertation, University of Wisconsin, 1963).

27. *Woodstock Letters* 64 (1935): 280-81; and *The Province News-Letter* 13 (1936): 345, AMPSJ. In 1939, Percy Roy, S.J., president of Loyola University in New Orleans, became head of the Southern Association of Colleges and Universities, the first Catholic priest to hold the office; see *Jesuit Educational Quarterly* 2 (June 1939): 63.

28. Gannon, *Up to the Present,* 161; John F. Bannon, S.J., "The Department of History, Saint Louis University, 1925-1973," St. Louis University, 1980, 2 (mimeographed).

29. David R. Dunigan, S.J., *A History of Boston College* (Milwaukee: Bruce Publishing Company, 1947), 229-30; McKevitt, *The University of Santa Clara,* 195-201; William B. Faherty, S.J., *Better the Dream: Saint Louis: University & Community* (St. Louis, n.p., 1968), 285-86; and Gannon, *Up to the Present,* 165-66.

30. Minutes of provincials' meeting, Fordham University, 19-20 August 1924, 4, ACPSJ; and reply of provincials to the 1927 report of the Inter-Province Committee on Studies, Drawer 73, ACPSJ.

31. For intimations of Jesuit attitudes toward degrees, see minutes of provincials' meeting, St. Ignatius Residence, New York City, 23-24 April 1914, AMPSJ; "Topics to be discussed at the meeting of the Presidents of the Jesuit Colleges of the Missouri Province, April 2, 1917," Box VI, "C," AMPSJ; and Leo S. Simpson, S.J. to Joseph Piet, S.J., provincial of the California Province, 6 April 1931, Drawer 74, "Various Reports, 1912-1932," ACPSJ.

32. Minutes of provincials' meeting, St. Ignatius Residence, New York City, 23-24 April 1913, 6, and 23-24 April 1914, 3-4, AMPSJ. Concerning teacher legislation passed in 1913 and 1914, see James E. Delzell, *Twenty-Third Biennial Report of the State Superintendent of Public Instruction to the Governor of the State of Nebraska* (Lincoln: Woodruff Press, 1914), 176; Clay J. Daggett, *Education in Wisconsin* (Whitewater, Wis.: Whitewater Press, 1936), 243; and Lee J. Bennish, S.J., *Continuity and Change: Xavier University, 1831-1981* (Chicago: Loyola University Press, 1981), 122.

33. Alexander J. Burrowes, S.J. to Jesuit presidents, 1 March 1917, AJCSLU. Distribution of diplomas took place without ceremony; one contemporary related that he found his degree on his bed when he returned to his room. See Labaj, "The Development of the Department of Education at Saint Louis University, 1900-1942," 76.

34. Data on Jesuits with doctorates were obtained from personnel records of the Missouri Province with the generous assistance of John F. Bannon, S.J., professor emeritus of history at St. Louis University, and Paul Distler, S.J., assistant to the provincial of the Missouri Province.

35. McAvoy, "Notre Dame, 1919-1922," 431-50; and David L. Salvaterra, "The Apostolate of the Intellect: Development and Diffusion of an Academic Ethos among American Catholics in the Early Twentieth Century" (Ph.D. dissertation, University of Notre Dame, 1983), 157-64 and 174-80.

36. Evans, *The Newman Movement,* 55.

37. Evans, *The Newman Movement,* 74-75; see also two brochures prepared by the education section of the National Catholic Welfare Conference: *Opportunities for Foreign Students at Catholic Colleges and Universities in the United States,* 1921; and Crowley, compiler, *Why a Catholic College Education?,* 1926.

38. Charles N. Lischka, "The Attendance of Catholic Students at Non-Catholic Colleges and Universities," *Catholic Educational Association Bulletin* 22 (November 1925): 103; J. Elliot Ross, C.S.P., "Catholics in Non-Catholic Colleges," *Religious Education* 21 (August 1926): 399-405; and *Catholic Educational Association Bulletin* 23 (November 1926): 86.

39. For a discussion of *America* articles on the Newman question, see Evans, *The Newman Movement,* 78-83.

40. Minutes of provincials' meeting, Jesuit High School, New Orleans, 3-4 April 1928, ACPSJ.

41. See Herbert Noonan, S.J., "The Need of Jesuit Universities," *Woodstock Letters* 54 (1925): 238-48; Thomas J. Livingstone, S.J., "Attendance at Secular Universities," *The Province News-Letter* 7 (October 1925): 10, AMPSJ; and Mario Barbera, S.J., "Catholic Foundations in Secular Universities," *Woodstock Letters* 57 (1928): 14-32.

42. "Accredited Higher Institutions," *Educational Record* 1 (October 1920): 71-80, and 11 (April 1930): 129-47; *Directory of Catholic Colleges and Schools*, 1932-1933, 10; and Association of American Universities, *Journal of Proceedings and Addresses, Forty-Ninth Annual Conference*, 28-30 October 1948, 133-39.

43. "Report of the Committee on Graduate Instruction," *Educational Record* 15 (April 1934): 192-234. For Catholic reactions to the report, see Deferrari, *Memoirs*, 115-22; Matthew J. Fitzsimons, S.J., "The *Instructio*, 1934-1949," *Jesuit Educational Quarterly* 12 (October 1949): 69; and William J. McGucken, S.J., letter to the editor, *Commonweal*, 31 May 1935, 35.

44. Association of American Universities, *Proceedings*, 1948, 133-39; and minutes of the Jesuit Commission on Higher Studies, 3-23 July 1934, 172.

45. Compilers of these data apparently counted only personnel with Ph.D.s; they made no reference to Jesuits holdings ecclesiastical doctorates in theology or philosophy. See Charles F. Carroll, S.J. to James B. Macelwane, S.J., 27 May 1932, "Charles Carroll," Box 15, JEA Collection, ABC; "Jesuits of the New Orleans Province with the Doctorate," 28 April 1932, ibid.; Edward P. Tivnan, S.J. to Macelwane, 30 April 1932, "Tivnan," Box 16, JEA Collection, ABC; and Charles J. Deane, S.J. to Macelwane, 30 April 1932, "Deane, Rev. Charles J., S.J.," Box 15, ibid. The JEA Collection does not include data on the number of midwestern Jesuits with doctorates in 1932. But according to Missouri Province personnel records, fifty-four members had earned doctoral degrees by 1932 (41 Ph.D.s, 11 S.T.D.s, 1 J.C.D., and 1 S.S.D.).

46. Minutes of the Jesuit Commission on Higher Studies, 15-18 November 1931, 17, and 5-7 January 1932, 27, ACPSJ. Macelwane reiterated the negative assessments in his letter to Ledochowski, 9 May 1932, "Ledochowski," Box 15, JEA Collection, ABC.

47. Gleason, "Immigration and American Catholic Intellectual Life," 154-56; Steinberg, *The Academic Melting Pot*, 65; and Ellis, *American Catholicism*, 53.

48. Ryan to friends of Catholic University, 28 September 1932, "Commission on Higher Studies," Box 15, JEA Collection, ABC.

49. David J. O'Brien, *American Catholics and Social Reform* (New York: Oxford University Press, 1968), 215-17; and Evans, *The Newman Movement*, 77 and 83.

50. Ledochowski told the provincials that Cardinal Merry del Val had asked to talk with him about an American Jesuit "whose action in an educational matter had been denounced to the Roman Tribunal. His Eminence afterwards took occasion to lay before me in friendly and courteous terms certain information which had been presented to the same Holy office about Our Universities in the United States." See Ledochowski to the American provincials, 12 March 1927, ACPSJ.

51. The sources of the accusations were not named; but Ledochowski acknowledged in 1934 that certain bishops had objected on a few occasions that "in some of our Universities the Catholic atmosphere was not sufficiently in evidence." In a 1942 speech, Zacheus Maher, S.J., Ledochowski's assistant for the United States, described the critics as "men in high places." See Ledochowski to American provincials, 15 August 1934, ACPSJ; and Zacheus Maher, S.J., "Address to the Delegates, Jesuit Educational Association," *Jesuit Educational Quarterly* 5 (June 1942): 11-12.

52. Ledochowski also sought information about policies concerning the admission of women students. For a copy of the questions, see FitzGerald, *The Governance of Jesuit Colleges in the United States*, Appendix A.

53. Ledochowski to American Jesuits, 7 June 1928, AMPSJ.

54. John Tracy Ellis, *Catholic Bishops: A Memoir* (Wilmington, Del.: Michael Glazier, Inc., 1983), 25-27. For additional information on resistance to Ryan's plans, see Deferrari, *Memoirs*, 80-106, 141-46, and 403-12.

55. William K. Selden, *Accreditation: A Struggle Over Standards in Higher Education* (New York: Harper & Brothers, 1960), 37-38.

56. For reactions to North Central Association policies, see Daniel O'Connell, S.J., academic dean of Xavier College in Cincinnati, to Samuel Horine, S.J., assistant to the provincial of the Missouri Province, 23 March 1927, "North Central Association," Box VI, AMPSJ; and Albert Fox, S.J. to Horine, 6 April 1927, ibid. See also the tougher endowment regulations for Catholic institutions announced by North Central in 1930: "Report of the Committee on Financial Standards for Catholic Institutions," *North Central Association Quarterly* 5 (September 1930): 191-92.

57. Report of the Inter-Province Committee on Studies, 1927, 2, Drawer 73, ACPSJ; Gannon, *Up to the Present*, 196-97; Germing to Ledochowski, 27 December 1930, "Letters to Fr. General, 1926-1941," AMPSJ; Walter Fitzgerald, S.J., "Some notes on 'Report of the Inter-Province Committee on Studies,' Detroit, 1929," "Inter-Province Committee on Studies," Drawer 73, ACPSJ.

58. Faherty, *Better the Dream*, 286; Dunigan, *A History of Boston College*, 230; McKevitt, *The University of Santa Clara*, 195-201; and Gannon, *Up to the Present*, 166. Interestingly, between 1921 and 1925 Notre Dame raised one million dollars for endowment and a similar amount for buildings, thanks in part to gifts from the General Education Board and the Carnegie Foundation of $200,000 and $75,000, respectively. See Thomas T. McAvoy, *A History of the Catholic Church in the United States* (Notre Dame, Ind.: University of Notre Dame Press, 1969), 398; and McAvoy, "Notre Dame, 1919-1922," 443 and 446.

59. Paul L. Blakely, S.J., "The Educational Year," *America*, 31 December 1927, 296. Notre Dame and Columbia College (now Loras College) each possessed one million dollars in endowment. In 1936, eighty-six Catholic colleges and universities reported $40.3 million in endowment; see Francis M. Crowley, "American Catholic Universities," *Historical Records and Studies* 29 (1938): 104-5.

60. David Allan Robertson, ed., *American Universities and Colleges* (New York: Charles Scribner's Sons, 1928), 16.

61. Matthew Germing, S.J. to Ledochowski, 3 January 1930, AMPSJ. See also James B. Macelwane, S.J. to Charles Cloud, S.J., president of St. Louis University, 21 July 1928, AJCSLU; and Cloud to Germing, 4 December 1929, AJCSLU.

62. Magee to Matthew Germing, S.J., 28 December 1929, "Letters to Fr. Gen.," AMPSJ. See also Alphonse Schwitalla, S.J. to Charles Cloud, S.J., 29 November 1929, AJCSLU.

63. For an assessment of Catholic seminary education, see essays by John Tracy Ellis, "The Formation of the American Priest: An Historical Perspective" and Michael V. Gannon, "Before and After Modernism: The Intellectual Isolation of the American Priest," in *The Catholic Priest in the United States: Historical Investigations*, ed. John Tracy Ellis (Collegeville, Minn.: Saint John's University Press, 1971), 3-110 and 293-383, respectively.

64. The 1930 and 1931 reports of the Inter-Province Committee on Studies recommended major changes in Jesuit training. For representative objections from scholasticate faculty, see the comments of William J. Young, S.J. in "Summary of Criticisms of the Los Angeles Schedule by Professors in the Juniorate at Milford," and M. J. Ahern, S.J. in "Suggestions for Scholasticate Schedule from Weston College," File "Inter-Province Committee, 1931," Box VI, AMPSJ; and statements by Jesuits Charles Walsh, Leo Martin, and William Donnelly, "Various Reports, 1912-1932," Drawer 74, ACPSJ.

65. Carroll to Joseph Piet, S.J., 23 August 1932, "Various Reports, 1912-1932," Drawer 74, ACPSJ.

66. For sketches of various American bishops in the twentieth century, see Ellis, *Catholic Bishops*; and Gerald P. Fogarty, S.J., ed., *Patterns of Episcopal Leadership* (New York: Macmillan Publishing Company, 1989), chaps. 10-14.

67. See Kelly to Tierney, 25 January 1925; Tierney to Kelly, 27 January 1925; Kelly to Tierney, 31 January 1925; Kelly to Ledochowski (excerpt), 19 February 1925; and Ledochowski to Kelly (excerpt) 20 March 1925. This correspondence is filed with minutes of the provincials' meeting, Provincial's Residence, New York City, 22 April 1925, ACPSJ.

68. Minutes of the Jesuit Commission on Higher Studies, 5-7 January 1932, 28, ACPSJ. For additional comments on Jesuit leaders, see idem, 5-7 January 1932, 19 and 12-20 February 1932, 52-53 and 69, ACPSJ.

69. Minutes of provincials' meetings, St. Louis University, 22-23 May 1923, 3, and College of St. Francis Xavier, New York, 11 January 1924, 3, ACPSJ; and minutes of the Jesuit Commission on Higher Studies, 3-23 July 1932, 42-43, ACPSJ.

70. See digests of IPCS recommendations and provincials' responses, 1925 and 1930, Drawer 73, "Inter-Province Committee on Studies," ACPSJ.

71. For data on accredited Catholic institutions, see "Accredited Higher Institutions," *Educational Record* 11 (April 1930): 129-47; *Directory of Catholic Colleges and Schools, 1932-1933*, 10; and *Catholic Colleges and Schools in the United States*, 1940, 33.

72. Deferrari, *Memoirs*, 317-26; and Faherty, *Better the Dream*, 311.

73. For reports concerning Schwitalla's conferences with Ledochowski, see James King, S.J. to Richard Gleeson, S.J., 2 December 1930, "O'Connell," Drawer 74, ACPSJ; and "Topics which V.R. Father General discussed with Father Schwitalla," n.d., "Commission on Higher Education," Box 15, JEA Collection, ABC.

74. Deferrari, *Memoirs*, 26-35 and 89-114; David J. Arthur, "The University of Notre Dame, 1919-1933: An Administrative History" (Ph.D. dissertation, University of Michigan, 1973), 225-27. For a review of developments in Catholic graduate education between 1926 and 1931, see Alphonse Schwitalla, S.J., "Graduate Study in Catholic Colleges and Universities," *National Catholic Educational Association Bulletin* 28 (November 1931): 83-110.

75. Ledochowski to American provincials, 8 December 1930, in *Report of the Commission on Higher Studies of the American Assistancy of the Society of Jesus, 1931-1932*, Appendix I, ACPSJ.

76. The introduction to the commission's report stated that Ledochowski wrote his 1930 letter because of "his profound interest" in American Jesuit education and his "grave concern lest our failure to raise our universities, colleges and high schools to the highest possible standard, should result in eliminating us from the educational field, thus destroying an instrument so rich in possibilities for the glory of God and the salvation of souls"; see *Report of the Commission on Higher Studies*, 4, ACPSJ.

77. The idea for the special commission originated in a recommendation made by the New Orleans Province for consideration in 1930 by the Congregation of Procurators, a worldwide convocation of Jesuits periodically held in Rome to review the state of the Society of Jesus. John Hynes, S.J., president of Loyola University in New Orleans and his province's representative to the procurators' meeting, discussed the proposal for an evaluation team with Ledochowski. For references to the role of the New Orleans Province and John Hynes, see minutes of the Jesuit Commission on Higher Studies, 26-28 June 1931, 3, and 3-23 July 1932, 261, ACPSJ; James Macelwane, S.J. to Ledochowski, 21 May 1932, "Ledochowski," Box 15, JEA Collection, ABC; and "John W. Hynes, S.J.," *Jesuit Educational Quarterly* 14 (June 1951): back cover.

78. Besides Macelwane, the members included Charles F. Carroll, S.J., director of education for the California Province; Charles J. Deane, S.J., dean of liberal arts at Fordham; Albert C. Fox, S.J., dean at John Carroll University in Cleveland and former president of Campion College in Prairie du Chien, Wisconsin (1918-1922) and Marquette

University (1922-1928); John W. Hynes, S.J., president of Loyola University, New Orleans; and Edward P. Tivnan, S.J., treasurer of the New England Province and formerly president of Fordham (1919-1924) and rector of Weston College, a Jesuit seminary.

79. See the following correspondence: Ledochowski to Macelwane, 5 March and 16 April 1932, "Ledochowski," Box 15, JEA Collection, ABC; and Macelwane to Ledochowski, 9 May 1932, ibid. See also Hynes to Ledochowski, 6 May 1932 and Hynes to Macelwane, May 6, 1932, "Hynes," ibid.

80. Minutes of the Jesuit Commission on Higher Studies, Loyola University, New Orleans, 5-7 January 1932, 36, ACPSJ.

81. *Report of the Commission on Higher Studies*, 20-28, and 187-89. Albert Fox made the comment about the advantages of doctorates; see minutes of the Commission on Higher Studies, 5-7 January 1932, 34, ACPSJ.

82. For a sampling of reactions to the *Report*, see Edward Whelan, S.J., a consultor of the California Province, to Zacheus Maher, S.J., provincial, 17 September 1932, "Various Reports 1912-1932," Drawer 74, ACPSJ; Maher to Ledochowski, 8 November 1932, "Interprovince Committee on Studies," Drawer 73, ACPSJ; Tivnan to Macelwane, 26 June 1933, "Commission on Higher Studies," Box 15, JEA Collection, ABC; and FitzGerald, *The Governance of Jesuit Colleges*, 32-33.

83. For instance, see William S. Ament, "Religion, Education, and Distinction," *School and Society* 26 (24 September 1927): 399-406; Karl F. Herzfeld, "Scientific Research and Religion," *Commonweal*, 20 March 1929, 560-62; and Harvey C. Lehman and Paul A. Witty, "Scientific Eminence and Church Membership," *Scientific Monthly* 33 (December 1931): 544-49.

84. See James H. Ryan, "Foundations of Culture," *Commonweal*, 30 April 1930, 729-31; idem, "The Catholic University of America: Focus of National Catholic Influence," *American Ecclesiastical Review* 85 (July 1931): 25-39; Roy J. Deferrari, "Catholics and Graduate Study," *Commonweal*, 24 June 1931, 203-5; and idem, "Are the Popes in Error?" *Commonweal*, 16 December 1931, 181-82.

85. James H. Ryan to friends of Catholic University, 28 September 1932, "Commission on Higher Studies," Box 15, JEA Collection, ABC; and Eugenio Cardinal Pacelli to Michael J. Curley, Archbishop of Baltimore, 12 October 1932, and "A National Plan for Higher Catholic Education" [editorial from *Catholic University Bulletin* (January 1933)] in "Rooney Correspondence with Fr. Maher, 1937-1942," Box 20, JEA Collection, ABC.

86. Sheehy to Wilfred Parsons, S.J., editor of *America*, 18 June 1932, "Catholic University," Box 15, JEA Collection, ABC; and Deferrari, *Memoirs*, 63-65.

87. Minutes of the Jesuit Commission on Higher Studies, 3-23 July 1932, 55; and Parsons to Edward C. Phillips, S.J., provincial of the Maryland-New York Province, 20 April 1933, in "Minutes of the 1933 provincials' meeting," ACPSJ. Phillips told the American provincials at their annual session in 1934 that the drive for money by Catholic University "looks like war to the death against our own Graduate Schools"; Charles Cloud, S.J., provincial of the Chicago Province, commented he thought there was a well-planned campaign in operation to discredit all Catholic graduate schools except Catholic University. See minutes of the provincials' meeting, Mt. St. Michael's, Spokane, 2-3 May 1933, ACPSJ.

88. Certain Jesuits had opposed the founding of CU, fearing competition with Georgetown; and tensions increased in 1894 when Archbishop Francis Satolli, the Apostolic Delegate from the Vatican to the United States, tried to transfer the law and medical schools of Georgetown to Catholic University. See John Tracy Ellis, *The Formative Years of the Catholic University of America* (Washington, D.C.: American Catholic Historical Association, 1946), 103-9; Power, *Catholic Higher Education in America*, 217-18; and "Historical Notes: Father Joseph Havens Richards' Notes on Georgetown and the Catholic University," *Woodstock Letters* 83 (February 1954): 77-101.

89. See statistics reported by Wilfred Parsons, S.J. at a meeting of Jesuits attending the National Catholic Educational Association convention in St. Paul, 26-29 June 1933, "Interprovince Committee on Studies," Drawer 73, ACPSJ.

90. Macelwane informed the Commission on Higher Studies on 12 April 1932 that Crowley "is writing a series of three articles for the *Commonweal* in reply to the attack on Catholic graduate schools made by Fr. De Ferrari [sic] of the Catholic University"; see minutes of the Commission's meeting, 12-17 April 1932, 6-7, ACPSJ. Sheehy reported that *Commonweal* had refused to publish the responses; see his letter to Robert S. Johnston, S.J., president of St. Louis University, 18 July 1932, "Catholic University," Box 15, JEA Collection, ABC.

91. See Crowley's articles in *America*: "Catholic Graduate Schools," 21 May 1932, 163-64; "Only One Graduate School?" 11 June 1932, 234-35; and "Institutionalism in Higher Education," 18 June 1932, 257-58. Sheehy protested to Wilfred Parsons, S.J. on 18 June 1932 and to Robert S. Johnston, S.J., president of St. Louis University, on 18 July 1932 that Crowley did not understand the intentions of Catholic University; see the letters in "Catholic University," Box 15, JEA Collection, ABC.

92. Minutes of the Jesuit Commission on Higher Studies, 3-23 July 1932, 54; and the Commission's *Report*, 21, ACPSJ.

93. The Catholic Educational Association added the word "National" to its title in 1927.

94. Howard sent a draft of his proposal to John Hynes, S.J., president of Loyola University, New Orleans, asking for a reaction. See Howard to Hynes, 8 October 1932 and 4 November 1932, "Education #200," Drawer 75, ACPSJ.

95. Hynes to Macelwane, 10 November 1932, "Hynes," Box 15, JEA Collection, ABC; Macelwane to Ledochowski, 15 November 1932, "Education #200," Drawer 75, ACPSJ; and Ledochowski to American provincials, 12 December 1932, "Letters of Fr. General," AMPSJ.

96. Tivnan to Macelwane, 26 June 1933, "Commission on Higher Studies," Box 15, JEA Collection, ABC.

97. Ledochowski explained in an introductory letter that recent papal legislation on ecclesiastical studies had delayed his "long promised Instruction on Studies and Teaching."

98. "Instructio Pro Assistentia Americae De Ordinandis Universitatibus, Collegiis Ac Scholis Altis Et De Praeparandis Eorundem Magistris" [Instruction for the American Assistancy Concerning the Administration of Universities, Colleges, and High Schools and the Preparation of Their Teachers], 15 August 1934, ACPSJ. John Hynes, S.J. had been called to Rome to assist Ledochowski in preparing the "Instructio"; see minutes of JEA Executive Committee, 1-3 April 1953, Drawer 73, ACPSJ.

99. Macelwane was the logical choice for national secretary, given his experience as chairman of the Commission on Higher Studies, academic achievements, and administrative abilities; but Ledochowski did not appoint him, perhaps because some Jesuits considered Macelwane too identified with secular educational ideas. Also, Jesuit superiors may have felt that Macelwane, one of the few American Jesuits in the 1930s with a national reputation in science, should remain in research and teaching.

100. Ledochowski to American provincials, 15 August 1934, ACPSJ. To the intense embarrassment of Jesuits, no doctoral program in a Jesuit university had been judged satisfactory in an evaluation released by the American Council on Education and publicized by the *New York Times* in April 1934. See "63 Are Designated Graduate Schools," *New York Times*, 2 April 1934, 18; and Fitzsimons, "The *Instructio*," 69.

101. Gannon, *Up to the Present*, 197-200; and FitzGerald, *The Governance of Jesuit Colleges*, 39-53. For the norms and comments on their significance, see Power, *A History of Catholic Higher Education*, 237 and Appendix E.

102. "Graduate Studies in the Assistancy," *Jesuit Educational Quarterly* 5 (September 1942): 129-31.

103. Horine to McMenamy, 22 October 1934, McMenamy Papers, AMPSJ; Maher to O'Connell, 5 July 1935 and 1 August 1935, "O'Connell," Drawer 74, ACPSJ.

104. See comments by William J. McGucken, S.J., director of education in the Missouri Province, on revision of the "Instruction," [1937] and a one-page evaluation of O'Connell (undated and unsigned but probably by Samuel Horine, provincial of the Missouri Province) in "Instructio," File Section III, Education, AMPSJ. See also minutes of provincials' meeting, Loyola High School, Los Angeles, 5-6 May 1936, ACPSJ; and FitzGerald, *The Governance of Jesuit Colleges*, 54-58.

105. Minutes of JEA Executive Committee meeting, 2-5 November 1938, "JEA Ex. Comm., 1935-1939," Drawer 74, ACPSJ; and McGucken to Peter Brooks, S.J., provincial of the Missouri Province, 15 March 1941, "Assoc. of Am. Univs.," AMPSJ.

106. See data concerning Catholic higher education during the 1920-1940 period in *Catholic Colleges and Schools in the United States*, 1942, 6-13; and "Report of the Committee on Graduate Study," *National Catholic Educational Association Bulletin* 38 (August 1941): 120.

107. For objections to the trend toward research in Catholic higher education, see George Bull, S.J., "The Function of the Catholic Graduate School," *Thought* 13 (September 1938): 364-80; for rebuttals, see Thurber M. Smith, S.J., "At Variance with Fr. Bull," *Thought* 13 (December 1938): 638-43; and Martin R.P. McGuire, "Catholic Education and the Graduate School," in *Vital Problems of Catholic Education in the United States*, ed. Roy J. Deferrari (Washington, D.C.: Catholic University of America Press, 1939), 112.

108. See *National Catholic Educational Association Bulletin* 35 (August 1938): 122, 135, and 141-46.

109. Robert Hutchins and William J. McGucken, S.J., "The Integrating Principle of Catholic Higher Education," *College Newsletter, Midwest Regional Unit, N.C.E.A.*, May 1937, 1 and 4. See also Roy J. Deferrari, "Catholic Education and the Approving Agencies," in *Vital Problems*, 44-45.

110. In addition to the plans of Ryan, Deferrari, the hierarchy, and Daniel O'Connell, Daniel Lord, a midwestern Jesuit, informed his provincial in August 1932 that Maurice Sheehy, assistant to the rector of Catholic University, wanted Catholic officials to unite in support of "a great Catholic University of America," governed by a committee of bishops, Catholic University personnel, and Jesuits; Sheehy also called for elimination of certain graduate and professional programs to strengthen Catholic higher education. For a statement of Sheehy's ideas, see Daniel Lord, S.J. to Samuel Horine, S.J., 4 August 1932, "Catholic U. and Jesuits," AMPSJ. Edward Tivnan, S.J. thought the idea of a national Jesuit University had merit; see Tivnan to Macelwane, 6 October 1932, "Deane, Rev. Charles," Box 15, JEA Collection, ABC.

111. Greeley, *The American Catholic*, 40-47. Irish Catholics exceeded the national norm for enrolling in college by 1920; except for a decline during the 1920s, Catholics of German extraction remained close to the national average, but Polish, Slavic, and Italian Catholics, more recent immigrants, lagged behind until the 1950s.

112. Evans, *The Newman Movement*, 82 and 210, fn. 1; and Zacheus Maher, S.J. to Edward Rooney, S.J., head of the Jesuit Educational Association, 14 February 1938, "Rooney Corr. with Maher, 1937-1942," Box 20, JEA Collection, ABC. Ledochowski told American Jesuits in 1932 and 1933 to end their criticism of the Newman apostolate; see his letters to American provincials: 21 November 1932, *Acta Romana* 7 (1932-1934): 194-97; and 4 April 1933, "Inter-Province Committee on Studies," JEA Collection, ABC.

113. For an analysis of the relationship between the Roosevelt administration and American Catholics, see George Q. Flynn, *American Catholics & the Roosevelt Presidency* (Lexington, Ky.: University of Kentucky Press, 1968).

3

Catholics and Coeducation

Numerous Catholic colleges and universities founded to educate men began admitting women before World War II. But the movement toward coeducational instruction conflicted with the long-standing Catholic policy of maintaining separate higher educational facilities for male and female students, and it met stiff opposition from many leading educational and religious figures in the Catholic Church, particularly during the 1920s and 1930s. An examination of the origins and development of coeducation in Catholic postsecondary institutions before 1940 provides a further perspective on currents within American Catholicism during the early twentieth century. In particular, it highlights the increasing status and aspirations of women as well as changing attitudes toward authority, tradition, and sexual morality in the Catholic Church.

Most Americans in the nineteenth century exalted women, regarding them as naturally religious and pure, and they relied on females to uphold virtue, rear children, and nurture family life. Magazines and religious literature during these years described the true woman as one who subordinated herself to her husband and who confined her interests to domestic affairs. This prevailing view also held that intellectual activity by women threatened feminine identity. Consequently, few colleges and universities admitted female students.[1]

But after the Civil War, such factors as industrialization, westward migration, and growth of the public school system introduced new perspectives and opportunities for American females. Motivated by concerns about protecting family life, an increasing number of women moved outside the traditional female sphere, campaigning for temperance, suffrage, and labor unions. More women also sought higher education, especially as teaching emerged as a respectable female profession and demand grew for competent instructors. Though men filled most classroom positions in the antebellum period, women composed an estimated 59% of elementary and secondary teachers in 1870, 70% in 1900, and 86% in 1920.[2]

The growing intellectual desires among women and the shortage of trained teachers precipitated two major developments in American higher education. First, new women's colleges were founded, designed to offer a curriculum comparable to men's institutions. Schools like Vassar (1865), Smith and Wellesley (1875), and Bryn Mawr (1885) helped set the dominant pattern for the collegiate training of women in the East and dispelled stereotypes that females were intellectually inferior to males. By 1901, 119 colleges for women existed in the United States.[3]

Second, numerous colleges and universities in the United States gradually introduced coeducation. By 1870, state universities in Wisconsin, Iowa, Kansas, Washington, Indiana, Minnesota, Missouri, Michigan, and California admitted both men and women; and in 1903, Wabash was the only non-Catholic college in the Midwest which did not accept female applicants. When Boston University opened in 1869, it enrolled both men and women; and women students entered Cornell in 1872. By the 1890s, MIT, Brown, Tufts, and the Yale Graduate School allowed women to register for classes; and Harvard and Columbia had established institutional links with Radcliffe and Barnard, respectively.[4]

Coeducational instruction spread for various financial, social, and intellectual reasons. It saved money, eliminating duplication of facilities and teachers. Its advocates further argued that educating men and women on the same campus fitted more naturally with American life, where both sexes associated freely. They also insisted that coeducation had a refining effect on male and female students and that it improved academic performance.[5]

The advent of coeducation provoked strong resistance in some parts of the nation, especially in the East. Many feared that coeducational classes would lead to moral lapses or that they would introduce distractions to serious study. Between 1900 and 1910, journals like the *Educational Review* and *The Independent* printed articles debating whether men and women should be educated together since colleges currently possessed the wealth and size to provide separate and equal facilities. Critics suggested that coeducation was destroying the traditional ideal of collegiate education.[6]

Prominent figures raised intellectual, psychological, and physiological objections to coeducational environments. In defending Harvard's policy of denying entrance to women, Charles Eliot suggested in 1873 that females were intellectually inferior to men and thus unsuited for the academic demands of Harvard. Dr. Edward Clarke of Boston attracted wide publicity in the mid-1870s after he published a book reporting his clinical observations that the stress of a "male" education endangered the health of women and consequently threatened the future of the human race. Writing in *Munsey's Magazine* in 1906, G. Stanley Hall warned of two impending dangers resulting from coeducational classes: (1) the feminization of education and (2) reduced desire for marriage caused by frequent association of the sexes in school.[7]

Growing doubts about the wisdom of coeducation led to reactionary measures in some schools. After the percentage of women at Stanford had reached 40% of total attendance in 1899, Mrs. Leland Stanford imposed a limit of 500 on female enrollment, a restriction which continued until 1933. In 1902, the University of Chicago, which had opened in 1891 as a coeducational institution, established a junior college for women only, despite strong dissent about the move from some faculty and alumni. Tufts decided to place women in a separate college in 1907; and following protests by male undergraduates, the governing board of Wesleyan voted in 1909 to exclude female students entirely.[8]

Yet despite persistent objections, coeducation grew in popularity. Between 1892 and 1902, the percentage of women registered at Grinnell, Knox, Beloit, and Carleton in the Midwest climbed from 33% to 59%, and females outnumbered males in the undergraduate population at the University of Michigan by the end of the nineteenth century. By 1900, 71% of American colleges and universities had become coeducational, and women amounted to 40% of those seeking postsecondary training in the United States.[9]

The changing social roles of women, rising female academic aspirations, and higher teacher qualifications also affected Catholic culture. By the 1880s, some Catholic parents were expressing interest in securing higher education for their daughters. In 1892, a woman entered the newly opened medical program at Creighton, the first female student ever to enroll in an American Jesuit university. Catholic liberals like Bishop John Lancaster Spalding of Peoria and Father Issac Hecker, founder of the Paulist religious order, called for development of women's intellectual capacities.[10]

But Catholic ideology and educational practice prevailing before World War I did not encourage collegiate instruction for female

Catholics. Like numerous Americans, many Catholics in the late nineteenth and early twentieth centuries believed that women should subordinate themselves to their husbands and prepare for careers as wives and mothers. Reflective of contemporary Catholic views concerning the proper role of females in society, Eleanor Donnelly declared in 1893 that "Woman's true sphere is the domestic one. God made her to be the queen of the home." She recommended that women model their lives after Mary, the Mother of God, who largely confined her activities to caring for her husband and family.[11]

Such restrictive views of women's function led some Catholic conservatives to deprecate the importance of higher learning for females. Bishop William Stang of Fall River, Massachusetts maintained in a book published in 1905 that "A grammar course in a parochial school or, if parents can afford it, a convent school (academy) education will equip woman for her sphere in life." He labeled higher education for women "an article of luxury." Father Thomas Shields, a well-known professor of psychology and education at Catholic University, wrote in 1917 that while female academic training should prepare for employment, it "should aim for the development of the future mother and homemaker."[12]

Until the mid-1890s, Catholic schooling for women consisted mainly of elementary and secondary schools whose curricula emphasized personal virtue and domestic arts, despite the call for teacher training issued by the American hierarchy at the Third Council of Baltimore in 1884. Only a small percentage of Catholic academies for girls offered any college-level courses to their students. Most Catholic men's institutions before 1914 displayed little interest in training nuns and Catholic laywomen to become teachers.[13]

Furthermore, the vast majority of Catholic educators before World War I strongly opposed coeducation. Primarily, they feared that educating men and women in the same institution would foster sexual immorality, a concern they shared with adherents of numerous other religious denominations. Speaking to the Catholic Educational Association convention in 1916, Albert Muntsch, a Jesuit from St. Louis, argued that common classrooms for male and female students would feminize the males, citing research of G. Stanley Hall to support his position. Other Catholic educational officials maintained that preparation to fulfill the different roles of men and women adults required separate schooling. In addition, partially reflecting their own training in sex-segregated seminaries and convents, most members of the male and female religious orders conducting Catholic higher education early in the twentieth century preferred to continue their traditions of operating different institutions for men and women students.[14]

Given the ideological and moral climate prevailing within Catholicism and American higher education at the turn of the century, the only viable option for Catholics wanting to provide a Catholic liberal arts education for women, especially school teachers, was to found colleges specifically for female students. Despite lack of money and faculty, various religious orders of women took up the challenge. The School Sisters of Notre Dame opened the first Catholic college for women (the College of Notre Dame of Maryland) in 1895, and another thirteen institutions were in operation by 1910. Increasing rapidly in succeeding decades, Catholic women's colleges numbered seventy-four in 1930 and enrolled 24,000 students; and by 1967, they had expanded to 120 institutions and 96,000 students.[15]

The growth of Catholic colleges for women and the activities of their graduates in the Catholic community fostered interest in higher education for female Catholics. Many alumnae of these institutions became Catholic school teachers, functioning as effective role models and breaking down stereotypes of educated women. A reported 70% of the 1921 graduating class of the College of St. Catherine entered the teaching profession. According to a 1923 survey of 655 alumnae of nine Catholic women's colleges, 46% were teachers, and another 14% had become members of religious orders and thus were also likely involved in education.[16]

But the key factors in changing Catholic ideas regarding female higher education and coeducation were the increasing personnel needs of Catholic schools and concerns about the faith of Catholics attending non-Catholic colleges and universities. As the Catholic parochial educational system expanded from 400,000 students in 1880 to over two million pupils by World War II, it required more staff, a problem exacerbated by rising state standards for teachers.[17] Anxious to safeguard the Catholic character of their institutions and to communicate Catholic values, Catholic school leaders sought teachers and administrators educated in a Catholic environment and thus presumably more familiar with Catholic educational goals and less influenced by secularism. Father Ralph Hayes told delegates attending the 1922 convention of the Catholic Educational Association that "we [Catholic educators] cannot afford to lessen by one jot or tittle the Catholic atmosphere of our schools, much less can we afford to place the professional training of religious teachers in an ambient that might mar their character as Catholic teachers in Catholic schools." Some Catholic officials urged bishops to enforce regulations requiring nuns to obtain episcopal permission before enrolling in non-Catholic colleges and universities.[18]

After 1900, a steadily rising number of Catholic women registered in secular academic institutions, doing so for such reasons as lower cost, geographic proximity, special programs, and social advantage. According to a 1907 survey, 1,557 Catholic women attended 220 non-Catholic colleges and universities, with Radcliffe, Cornell, Iowa, Wisconsin, and California each enrolling at least forty Catholic females.[19] Alexander Burrowes, S.J., a former president of Jesuit schools in Milwaukee, Chicago, and St. Louis, judged in 1919 that Catholic women attended non-Catholic colleges and universities "by the hundreds."[20]

Convinced that secular schools threatened the faith of Catholics, Catholic lay and clerical leaders frequently urged Catholic students to choose Catholic schools. But Catholic women's colleges could not satisfy the educational desires of their potential student clientele nor meet the needs of the Catholic school system. The approximately forty institutions for Catholic women founded by 1920 enrolled only 4,400 students (attendance at twenty-three schools was fewer than 100), and they lacked the facilities and trained faculty to accommodate large numbers. Many of these schools were located in isolated areas, often at the headquarters of the founding religious order. As late as 1920, no Catholic institution for women existed in such major centers of Catholic population as Detroit, Milwaukee, Pittsburgh, or Philadelphia; and Chicago and Boston had one each.[21]

Besides limited capacity and remote locations, many of these institutions, especially those started after World War I, suffered from serious academic problems which further restricted their appeal and effectiveness. Victims of overexpansion and competition for scarce resources, only 38% of the seventy-four Catholic women's colleges operating in 1930 qualified for membership in regional accrediting associations.[22]

Without accreditation, these schools could not provide the classes needed by Catholic teachers to fulfill state certification requirements; nor could the institutions enable students to complete prerequisites for graduate and professional programs. In addition, since none of the Catholic colleges for women offered doctoral and professional programs, they could not prepare faculty needed to strengthen Catholic higher education for women; and they could not satisfy preferences for training in business, law, and social service.[23]

The need for trained teachers in Catholic schools and concerns about maintaining the faith of Catholics in secular institutions prompted some Catholic academic and religious leaders to consider ways of providing postsecondary training for women in a Catholic setting. In 1906, Thomas Sherman, a Jesuit priest and a son of Civil War general William Sherman, raised the subject of women's education for the first time at a Catholic Educational Association convention. He urged the church to ensure that female Catholics received intellectual preparation equivalent to their non-Catholic counterparts. While ostensibly rejecting coeducational instruction as a threat to femininity and morality, Sherman proposed that Catholic colleges and universities adopt the Oxford University policy of admitting female students to all classes and registering them in women's colleges. Or if they preferred, schools could establish coordinate institutions in the pattern of Harvard and Radcliffe.[24]

Officials at St. John's College in Brooklyn, operated by the Vincentian order, introduced extension classes in "general pedagogy" for men and women in 1908.[25] The shift in Catholic attitudes toward women and coeducation manifested itself even more the next year, when Marquette University announced plans to hold a summer school (unprecedented in Catholic higher education) and to allow nuns to enroll. The fragmentary data available suggest that several factors contributed to the Marquette decision. During its 1908-1909 session, the Wisconsin legislature had passed a law requiring that all candidates for minimum teacher certification attend a professional school for teachers for six weeks and fulfill standards in pedagogy and school management. Marquette was the only Catholic institution of higher education in Milwaukee, and it had been expanding since its advance to university status in 1907, adding law and engineering schools in 1908. Probably influenced by the new teacher certification requirements and Marquette's addition of new programs, certain Catholics asked Marquette officials to admit women students, a request supported by Archbishop Sebastian Messmer.[26]

But the teachers at Marquette opposed coeducation and recommended the foundation of a Catholic women's college in the city, a position consistent with the Jesuit tradition of educating only males. Various religious orders of women expressed willingness to start such schools if Marquette would provide necessary training for their members. To obtain women's colleges and thus reduce pressure to admit female students, Marquette would have to admit religious women for a time.

To placate his faculty and yet provide instruction to nuns, James McCabe, S.J., the president of Marquette, endorsed the idea of a summer school. But when Rudolph Meyer, S.J., provincial of midwestern Jesuits, learned that a few laywomen had also registered for the classes, he objected and suggested that all courses be cancelled. McCabe resisted and exercised his right to appeal to the superior general of the Jesuit order. The summer school convened as scheduled, pending a reply from Rome. For unknown reasons, three years passed before a decision was reached; in the spring of 1912, Jesuit authorities granted Marquette permission to allow "'ladies and even nuns'" to attend its summer courses.

While waiting for the answer, McCabe negotiated an affiliation in 1910 between his institution and a local music conservatory enrolling many women. He also reached agreement the following year with the Sisters of Charity, headquartered in Dubuque, to conduct a women's college at Marquette.[27] McCabe's firm advocacy of courses for nuns and his efforts to increase female enrollment suggest that he always favored at least some form of permanent coeducation for Marquette. By 1916, Marquette's student body included 375 women.[28]

The entrance of female students to Marquette represented a turning point in the development of Catholic higher education for women. Though not signifying general permission for coeducation in Jesuit schools or other Catholic colleges and universities, Marquette's new policy set an influential precedent for the admission of women and undermined the existing Catholic rationale for single-sex institutions. In starting a summer school open to nuns and laywomen, Marquette focused attention on the educational needs and aspirations of female Catholics; and it indicated its approval of them. Also, by pressing for coeducation against their provincial superior and institutional heritage, officials at Marquette emphasized the urgency of providing academic training for women. Finally, the introduction of coeducation at Marquette signalled a softening in resistance among Catholic leaders to educating men and women in the same classroom. When forced to choose between coeducation or no Catholic schooling for American Catholic women, Jesuit superiors in Rome and eventually other educational and religious figures in the Church chose to meet contemporary needs rather than to maintain a long-standing tradition.

Swayed by these new viewpoints and anxious to assist Catholic education, Catholic colleges and universities for men began admitting women on a limited basis between 1910 and 1920. They concentrated on teacher education but also accepted female students into business and professional programs. In 1911, both Catholic University and DePaul established summer schools; and a year later, CU opened a college solely for members of female religious orders, though forbidding the sisters to come on campus, use the library, or attend classes with other students.[29]

But in contrast to Catholic University, other Catholic colleges and universities for men proceeded much more cautiously, restrained by tradition as well as by various psychological and pedagogical objections to coeducation common within the Catholic Church. At first, they offered summer and part-time courses for women, mainly for the convenience of teachers in parochial and public schools needing to satisfy state certification requirements.[30] Such classes also had the advantage of introducing coeducation with a minimum of controversy since they did not meet during the regular school day.

Creighton established a summer school in 1913, and both Loyola University of Chicago and Fordham did so in 1918. American Jesuit provincials agreed at their annual meeting in 1918 that their colleges and universities could confer degrees on nuns.[31] By 1920, members of female religious orders could study during the summer at twenty-four Catholic institutions, including ten Jesuit schools. That year summer programs at Notre Dame, Creighton, Villanova, Loyola (New Orleans), and St. Louis University each attracted 350 or more female students, most of them religious women. For instance, in 1920, Creighton enrolled 475 nuns and 100 other people in summer classes, and Loyola University of Chicago attracted 740 sisters to its summer session.[32]

In 1914, Chicago's Loyola University began offering late afternoon and early evening courses for credit "towards degrees and for promotion in the public schools"; and by 1920, its programs, including summer school, registered 1,730 women. Fordham admitted teaching personnel to classes in 1916; and a decade later, 720 women attended its Teachers College (80% of the enrollment) and the Fordham Graduate School reported 300 women among its 450 students. By the early 1920s, teachers could attend part-time classes at such schools as Canisius, Loyola University in New Orleans, Villanova, St. Louis University, and Creighton.[33]

Besides preparation for careers in teaching, some Catholic laywomen in the early decades of the twentieth century sought and obtained admission to business and professional programs, benefiting from two factors. First, Catholic universities like Marquette, DePaul, and St. Louis had either purchased or signed affiliation agreements with law and medical schools already enrolling female students; and they maintained existing enrollment policies both from obligation and from need to attract a sufficient number of applicants. Second, the greater age of those registering for professional education mitigated fears about moral offenses stemming from immaturity.[34]

In 1910, Marquette granted a law degree to a woman; and the next year, St. Louis University graduated five women from its law school, the first females to receive diplomas from the institution. Because of requests from women, Duquesne began admitting females to its law and business schools in 1915; Detroit adopted a similar policy the next year. Xavier (Cincinnati) announced in 1918 that it would admit female students to its School of Commerce, perhaps influenced by local needs for trained women to fill vacancies caused by wartime draft calls. During the 1925-1926 academic year, ninety-five coeds (7% of the total enrollment) attended the Fordham Law School, and women constituted 34% of business school students at DePaul (112 of 330 students).[35]

In the decade before 1920, Catholic higher education also expanded to provide training in the academic discipline of sociology and to prepare Catholic social workers. Pope Leo XIII's encyclical *Rerum Novarum*, issued in 1891, and the appalling social and industrial conditions publicized during the Progressive period, strengthened desires of Catholic leaders to inject the church's teachings into the American society. They especially urged Catholic educational institutions to communicate the church's social doctrine.[36]

Without better academic preparation, Catholic candidates, most of them women, could not fulfill job requirements in the increasingly professionalized field of social work. Attempting to meet the needs of the church and its female members involved in social service activities, Loyola University of Chicago admitted both men and women to its School of Sociology, founded in 1914. Fordham started a similar program in 1916; and during the 1925-1926 school year, it enrolled nineteen men and 148 women. A third institution, the National Catholic School of Social Service, opened in Washington, D.C. in 1921.[37]

Coeducation spread among Catholic colleges and universities for men during the interwar period as prominent institutions expanded their efforts to educate women. St. Louis University opened a school of education in 1925; female students enrolling in it could cross-register into regular classes in arts and sciences, in effect giving them access to the same courses and degrees as men. Creighton adopted a similar plan in 1931, when it organized its University College.[38] Catholic University allowed nuns to register for graduate programs in 1928 and extended the same privileges to laywomen a year later. In 1929, Duquesne dropped its ban on coeds attending classes in its daytime humanities division. During the 1930s, Seattle University, Quincy College (Quincy, Ilinois), and the University of Dayton began admitting female students on the undergraduate level. By 1940, forty-six of the seventy-four Catholic colleges and universities for men accepted women applicants, though fewer than ten of these schools were fully coeducational.[39]

As emotional and institutional barriers to coeducation fell within Catholicism, female enrollment increased in Catholic colleges and universities for men, further evidence of the rising aspirations of Catholic women and their improving status. In 1924, female students represented 44.5% of the total attendance in all Catholic institutions of higher learning; by 1940, their share had grown to 52.7%. Women totaled 37,000 (33%) of the 113,000 students registered in Catholic men's institutions in 1940 compared to approximately 13,000 females (28%) among the 46,000 enrolled in Catholic postsecondary schools for males in 1924. Between 1928 and 1940, the number of women attending Catholic University jumped from 40 to 2,100; it rose from 3,200 to 5,700 at DePaul and tripled at St. John's in Brooklyn, rising from 524 to 1,605. Available data do not allow for an exact comparison, but apparently the increase of female students in Catholic higher education during the interwar period differed from the national pattern. After an 11% rise between 1900 and 1920, the proportion of women among students in colleges and universities in the United States fell from 47.3% in 1920 to 40.2% in 1940.[40]

Detailed statistics on female attendance in Catholic higher education before World War II have yet to be compiled. But registration totals for Jesuit colleges and universities in 1938-1939 provide information concerning the academic interests of Catholic women and the extent of their access to various programs. During that year, Jesuit postsecondary schools included 10,500 females among their 41,800 students, about one-third of the women in Catholic men's institutions. Approximately 72% of the females in Jesuit colleges and universities sought preparation in the liberal arts and in teaching, most of them enrolled in late afternoon, evening, and extension classes. Nursing attracted 17.3% of all women students in Jesuit higher education, and another 6.9% chose business. Women constituted 1.6% of students in Jesuit schools of law, medicine, dentistry, and pharmacy; and they were present in three of five medical divisions, four of six dental programs, seven of twelve law schools, and all three pharmacy colleges operated by Jesuit universities.[41]

Compared to the distribution of female students in American higher education one year earlier, Jesuit schools in 1938-1939 registered 14% fewer women in undergraduate and graduate classes. But they enrolled a higher percentage of females for training in business (6.9% to 3.2%), nursing (17.3% to 1.6%), and the professions of law, medicine, dentistry, and pharmacy (1.6% to .85%). These different enrollment patterns reflected the concentration of Catholic business and professional programs in Jesuit institutions. They also indicated greater willingness among Jesuit officials to accept women applicants who were older (and therefore regarded as more mature and capable of maintaining their moral integrity in a coeducational environment than undergraduates) and who were registering for courses outside the traditionally all-male Jesuit colleges of arts and sciences.[42]

Certain social and economic factors supported the development of coeducation in Catholic colleges and universities during the interwar years. The suffrage movement, culminating in the passage of the

Nineteenth Amendment, encouraged wider ambitions among women and also made it harder to deny them equal educational opportunities. More liberal social attitudes emerging in the aftermath of World War I also allowed American females to expand their educational and occupational goals.[43] As the American Catholic hierarchy observed in its 1919 pastoral letter, "The present tendency in all civilized countries is to give woman [sic] a larger share in pursuits and occupations that formerly were reserved to men. The sphere of her activity is no longer confined to the home or to her social environment; it includes the learned professions, the field of industry and the forum of political life."[44] The rising status of women in Catholic society in the 1920s and 1930s coincided with higher female enrollment in Catholic colleges and universities. Conceivably, a reciprocal relationship existed between these two changes. Increased prestige and leisure may have led female Catholics to become interested in academic training; and recognition that educational achievements enhanced social standing possibly motivated some Catholic women to seek college degrees.

Furthermore, women had achieved greater prominence in Catholic higher education by the 1920s, helping to break down resistance to coeducation based on female stereotypes. Though more conservative members opposed, the Catholic Educational Association began admitting females to its annual meetings in 1910. In 1916, a woman delivered a paper at a CEA convention; and the following year, representatives of Catholic women's colleges received permission to organize a special group within the Association to discuss common problems.[45]

Economic pressures further eroded opposition to coeducation within the Catholic Church. In 1928, 1,125 (53%) of 2,129 Catholic high schools admitted both male and female students, a policy often dictated by shortage of money to construct and operate separate educational facilities.[46] The success of coeducational classes in Catholic elementary and secondary schools allayed fears about educating both sexes in the same school, and it also fostered support for coeducation among American Catholics. In addition, like other institutions of higher education in the United States, some Catholic colleges and universities accepted women students to offset falling male enrollment and declining revenues. Responding to an inquiry concerning the presence of women at Marquette, the provincial of the Missouri Province informed his superior general in 1931 that the university, which was near bankruptcy, could not afford to stop enrolling female students. Seattle University began allowing women to attend classes in 1933, mainly because it needed the added tuition money to survive financially.[47]

Even though Catholic schools on all levels in the United States admitted both male and female students by the 1920s, the Catholic Church still had not accepted the principle of coeducation. Pope Pius XI reiterated the official Catholic position in his encyclical *Christian Education of Youth*, issued on December 29, 1929. Clearly concerned about growing secularism and attempts in various nations to reduce the role of the family and church in educating children, the Pope described the "so called method 'coeducation'" as false and harmful to Christian education. He asserted that its foundations lay in the acceptance of naturalism, the denial of original sin, and "a deplorable confusion of ideas that mistakes a leveling promiscuity and equality for the legitimate association of the sexes." Nothing in God's plan of creation or the nature of men and women indicated that their training should be equal. Instead, the obvious differences in temperament and abilities between the sexes should be "maintained and encouraged during their years of formation" to complement one another in the family and society.[48]

Wlodimir Ledochowski, S.J. was another powerful foe of coeducation. While superior general of the Jesuit order from 1915 to 1942, he consistently objected to the presence of female students in Jesuit institutions, regarding it as against Jesuit educational traditions and the mind of the church. Only with great reluctance did he permit Jesuit universities to operate summer programs for nuns, and he insisted that Jesuit high schools and colleges deny admission to women students. In a major policy statement sent to American Jesuits in 1928, Ledochowski announced his intention to revoke permission for the attendance of women at Jesuit universities as soon as the present "special urgent necessity no longer exists." Until then, the enrollment of women "must be discouraged rather than invited, nor must they be admitted to any department where they are not already at the present time." In succeeding years, he remained adamant on the extension of coeducation, denying requests for it made by officials of the University of San Francisco, Spring Hill College, and Gonzaga University. When officials at Spring Hill pleaded in 1938 that the college must admit women students to survive, Ledochowski told them to close.[49]

Pius XI and Ledochowski represented a mind-set in Catholicism that stressed the value of tradition as a protection against secular trends threatening the faith. Like many of their contemporaries in the Catholic Church, both relied heavily on theory, not personal experience, as a basis for forming or justifying decisions. While not against women seeking higher education, they objected to coeducational classes, convinced that such instruction endangered the moral integrity of students and conflicted with Catholic educational traditions. The pope and Ledochowski also maintained that coeducation was based on an unsound pedagogy.

A similar ideology prevailed among various Catholic educators and religious superiors in the United States. For example, officials of the Holy Cross order banned laywomen from Notre Dame's summer school in 1927, perhaps because they considered these women a temptation to seminarians who also attended the summer program. After protests from the university administration, a compromise was reached. Laywomen could be accepted to the summer school but only to classes taught by lay faculty members or religious approved by the provincial. In another incident, William McCabe, S.J., president of Creighton and a consultor of his provincial superior, agonized in 1946 over his vote concerning a proposal to construct a new residence-classroom facility for Jesuit philosophy students at St. Louis University. Though agreeing that solid reasons had been advanced in the project's favor, he felt "that quite apart from obedience to the General and the Pope, the University should be willing to pay the price of eliminating coeducation (as a danger to religious spirit both of scholastic students and Jesuit faculty), in order to have the scholasticate attached."[50]

Representatives of American Catholic colleges and universities for men also argued against the admission of women on the grounds of tradition and pedagogy.[51] Edward Phillips, S.J., a former provincial of the Maryland-New York Province of the Society of Jesus, insisted in 1939 that coeducation conflicted with the traditional policies and ideals of the church and the Jesuit order, and "this tradition is based not on variable social customs but on the divinely established differences and relationships of the two sexes." Zacheus Maher, S.J., a zealous opponent of coeducation as a university president, provincial, and assistant to Ledochowski, held that the different natures and roles of men and women made it "pedagogically unsound" to educate them in the same classroom. Unexpressed in these theoretical defenses of single-sex schools but quite likely influencing some of the defenders was an emotional attachment to a strictly masculine educational experience. Adversaries of coeducation in the 1920s and 1930s probably shared the motivation of Hugh Duce, S.J., director of education for the California Province of the Jesuit order, who acknowledged in 1950 that his opposition to admitting women students stemmed "first from sentiment and secondly from a conviction that the American practice of co-education . . . is psychologically unsound."[52]

Opposition to coeducation within American Catholicism caused major problems because of the limited educational opportunities available for female Catholics. Catholic colleges for women alone could not accommodate the desires of female Catholics for liberal arts, business, and professional training under Catholic auspices. Nor could these institutions supply the Catholic parochial school system with enough certified teachers. Unless Catholic institutions founded to educate men admitted women, large numbers of Catholic females would have to sacrifice certain educational and career goals or else enroll in secular schools, regarded by many Catholics as threats to their faith.

Consequently, various supporters of coeducational classes in Catholic higher education argued that in the present circumstances, authority and tradition should yield to pastoral need and allow women to enter Catholic colleges and universities for men. In contrast to their opponents within the church, Catholics advocating coeducation did not fear that admitting female students would threaten the moral lives of male faculty and students or require the sacrifice of essential traditions. Nor did they believe that women had to be sheltered from contemporary society. Perhaps their more positive view of women and coeducation resulted from personal experience. Especially between 1910 and 1920, many of those urging Catholic schools to admit women lived in the Midwest, where male and female students commonly attended the same classrooms without major problems. But such staunch Jesuit foes of coeducation as Zacheus Maher and Edward Phillips had no direct contact with it, either as students or later as faculty and administrators.[53]

Two groups of leaders in the Catholic Church worked to remove obstacles to women's education in Catholic colleges and universities. First, various bishops pressed Catholic institutions for men to accept female students, undeterred by the generally conservative climate within Catholicism and the male educational traditions of these schools. Patrick Hayes, Cardinal-Archbishop of New York, asked Fordham in 1916 to open a coeducational school of social work. In subsequent years, members of the hierarchy in Buffalo, Boston, New Orleans, Mobile, Seattle, Los Angeles, and Kansas City called on Jesuit colleges and universities to sponsor programs for women. Even after the strong papal criticism of coeducation in 1929, American bishops apparently made no attempt to stop Catholic colleges and universities for men from accepting female students because the coeducational movement in Catholic higher education accelerated in the 1930s.[54]

Certain Catholic educators and officials within the religious orders conducting Catholic colleges and universities for men also endorsed the academic goals of women. But unlike bishops, who possessed nearly autonomous authority in their jurisdictions, they could not immediately translate their opinions into concrete programs. They functioned within an organizational structure characterized by centralized control and uniformity. A major policy change like the admission of women required approval from higher superiors, but many high-ranking ecclesiastics were wedded to tradition and also lacked awareness of changes in contemporary culture, especially the growing aspirations of women. Consequently, they often regarded coeducation as an undesirable deviation from the educational heritage of the Church and their institutions.

To overcome such opposition, Catholic proponents of coeducation employed three main strategies. First, they pleaded "necessity," stressing the emergency situation of Catholic teachers and schools caused by accrediting demands. They also emphasized that unless Catholic institutions for men offered courses in teacher training and other fields, Catholic women would be forced to enter "godless" secular institutions. Jesuit provincials agreed in 1918 that Jesuit colleges and universities could confer degrees on nuns; otherwise, diplomas will "be procured from secular universities, where doctrines contrary to the Faith and teaching of the Church are disseminated." William McGucken, a Jesuit widely known in Catholic educational circles, warned in 1938 that "If the Catholic universities refuse to admit women, they will go, as they are going in increasing numbers, to secular institutions where they will be indoctrinated with a purely naturalistic philosophy, which in turn they will pass on to those who come under their influence."[55] The force of these arguments gradually convinced those in power to authorize summer and extension courses for women.[56]

Second, Catholics advocating coeducation on the college and university level resorted to varying degrees of subterfuge, fully aware that traditionalists would protest any quick or controversial increase in female presence on Catholic campuses. Officials at institutions like Marquette, the University of Detroit, and St. John's College in Brooklyn slowly allowed women to enroll in late afternoon and evening courses in undergraduate, graduate, and professional schools, sometimes presuming permission to do so. After female students had become less of a novelty, they could enroll in larger numbers and without restrictions.

Enabling women to attend classes in colleges of arts and sciences, particularly to fulfill graduate and professional requirements, called for more elaborate deceptions in some schools. Catholic colleges and universities commonly faced strong resistance from those who wanted to maintain the daytime division of liberal arts as a traditional bastion for males. Probably to avoid objections and yet meet requests from women, Marquette allowed female students to attend classes in arts and sciences by World War I but registered them in its journalism school until 1926.[57]

In 1925, officials at St. Louis University obtained approval from their superiors in Rome for a professional school of education and then used it for the next two decades as an "umbrella" to register coeds into regular classes in the liberal arts. Since these students were not officially enrolled in the college of arts and sciences, reports to Rome affirmed that "'There were no women in the College.'"[58] Need for additional revenue during the Depression made Seattle College even more daring. In 1933, it began an extension division offering afternoon and evening classes for both men and women. But James McGoldrick, S.J., the dean, effectively made the school coeducational by starting "afternoon" classes at ten o'clock in the morning. Supported quietly by the bishop of Seattle and his provincial, he prevailed against Ledochowski and all other critics.[59] The expansion of coeducation by presumption or subterfuge chipped away at existing concepts of authority and tradition. Often receiving at least the tacit support of local authorities, it encouraged other Catholic colleges and universities to start or enlarge programs for women.

In the late 1930s and early 1940s, prominent educational leaders among American Jesuits followed a third strategy in support of coeducation. They directly challenged the prohibition against female students in their colleges and universities, and they also adamantly defended coeducation against attempts by Ledochowski, their superior general, and Maher, his assistant for the United States appointed in 1935, to eliminate it.

The struggle over coeducation within the Society of Jesus entered a critical phase in 1937, one affecting the subsequent place of women in American Catholic higher education. Leaders of the Jesuit Educational Association feared that Ledochowski would influence the General Congregation of the Jesuit order scheduled for the next year to enact more stringent legislation against the admission of women in Jesuit institutions. Consequently, at their December 1937 meeting, they drafted a strong defense of coeducation for use if necessary by American delegates to the congregation. Their document repeated familiar assertions about the inadequacy of existing graduate and professional training in Catholic institutions available to women. It also warned about the dangers to faith and morals of female Catholics forced to attend secular schools in search of necessary education.[60]

But the JEA Executive Committee also introduced two new arguments, based on changing perceptions of women and the place of American Catholicism within the larger Roman Catholic Church. Because women "are taking their place alongside of men in important positions of responsibility" in American society and because the Jesuit order has traditionally sought to prepare leaders, Jesuit higher education in the United States should admit women. Moreover, the committee suggested that the criticism of coeducation made by Pope Pius XI in 1929 did not extend to the United States, noting that the papal statement included the qualification "'due regard being had for time and place.'"[61]

A year later William McGucken, S.J., a member of the JEA Executive Committee, argued for coeducation in an especially significant journal article.[62] His essay marked the first public advocacy of coeducational instruction in Catholic colleges and universities by a major Catholic educator. Furthermore, instead of simply accepting papal statements like many of his contemporaries, McGucken interpreted the 1929 encyclical in its European context and from a distinctively American Catholic perspective. He pointed out that Pius XI was criticizing coeducation based on naturalism and insisted that the Pope hardly intended to condemn coeducational Catholic universities in Milan, Louvain, and Lille, each conducted by the hierarchy and with the express approval of the Holy See. Finally, McGucken concluded that if American bishops and pastors could justify coeducation in elementary and secondary schools, the same reasoning applied to higher education.

To resolve differences among Jesuits about coeducation, Maher authorized JEA leaders in November 1938 to formulate general norms concerning the admission of women. In March 1939, Ledochowski told the American provincials to appoint a special commission to study the whole issue, reminding that its members should bear in mind decisions of the Vatican and founding documents of the Society. Four months later, he reaffirmed his long-standing view that coeducation was against the mind of the church and the fundamental law of the Jesuit order, and he prohibited any expansion in the number of female students in Jesuit schools without his explicit permission.[63]

But the final report of the Commission on Coeducation, submitted on February 12, 1940, generated further controversy, maintaining that present conditions required Jesuit colleges and universities to admit women and in some cases made it desirable. The commission mistakenly thought from conversations with Maher in late 1939 that its purpose was to regularize present practice and plan for the future, not root out the presence of female students. Consequently, its members drafted guidelines to help their superiors determine whether to approve the admission of female students, and they also specified personnel and facilities needed by institutions adopting coeducation.[64]

Predictably, Maher rejected the commission's analysis and most of its recommendations, though agreeing that graduate, professional, and part-time programs could enroll women, a major concession. Furthermore, he proposed "Tentative Norms" to end increases in female enrollment and gradually to eliminate coeds on the undergraduate level.[65] For the next two years, he and the commission members debated policy concerning coeducation, but the basic differences in their views left them largely at an impasse. After considering the various opinions, Ledochowski announced in May 1942 that undergraduate schools currently admitting coeds could continue to do so as a temporary measure, but they were to reduce the number of women "as soon as can possibly be done without serious harm" to the institutions. In addition, graduate and professional programs could accept women applicants, though preferably these sessions would be held off campus. But with male students in scarce supply during World War II, Jesuit schools could not afford to reduce the enrollment of women, and thus coeducation remained.[66]

Authority and tradition in the Catholic Church continued to yield to pressures for coeducation after World War II. Delegates to the 1946 Jesuit General Congregation affirmed arguments that coeducation did not conflict with the constitutions of their order. By 1949, Creighton, St. Louis, and Gonzaga had obtained formal permission to admit coeds to their colleges of arts and sciences.[67] Once the influx of veterans slowed in the late 1940s, more Catholic institutions for men began accepting female students, disturbing some Catholic colleges for women and encouraging them to become coeducational.[68]

An instruction on coeducation issued by the Vatican in 1957 specifically excluded higher education from its provisions. When changing social and economic conditions in the 1960s and 1970s touched off further criticism of single-sex education, numerous Catholic schools adopted a policy of complete coeducation. Along with Harvard, Princeton, and Dartmouth, such Catholic institutions as Holy Cross, Georgetown, and Notre Dame ended limitations on female enrollment. In 1988, Boston College, Fordham, Loyola University of Chicago, the University of San Francisco, and fifteen other Jesuit institutions enrolled more women than men, especially ironic considering the opposition to coeducation within the Jesuit order before 1945.[69]

By 1984, every Catholic college or university founded to educate men admitted female students without restriction, except for St. John's University in Collegeville, Minnesota, which maintained an extensive coordinate relationship with a nearby Catholic college for women. Moreover, approximately seventy-five Catholic women's colleges either adopted coeducation or merged with men's schools between 1950 and 1980.[70]

Efforts to introduce female students into Catholic colleges and universities for men in the early twentieth century mirrored important developments among Catholics in the United States during these years and left a rich legacy. Such advocacy of coeducation resulted in large part from the growing desires of Catholic women for academic training, the needs of the Catholic school and social welfare systems, and concerns about protecting the faith of female Catholics. In addition, support for coeducational instruction reflected awareness of the changing roles of women in American society and desires to assist the upward mobility of Catholics. Moreover, the gradual emergence of coeducational classes in Catholic institutions of higher learning manifested the willingness of some Catholics to adapt to the American social and educational environment. In the process, they developed new attitudes toward authority and tradition, and they also displayed a surprising degree of flexibility and tenacity.

Finally, the struggles to admit female students into Catholic colleges and universities before World War II prepared the way for the triumph of coeducation in subsequent decades. They also contributed to later advances in the status of Catholic women. When James McCabe, S.J. decided in 1909 to inaugurate a summer school at Marquette for female Catholics, he could not have imagined the consequences for Catholic higher education and the Catholic Church in the United States.

Notes

1. Barbara Welter, "The Cult of True Womanhood: 1820-1860," *American Quarterly* 18 (Summer 1966): 151-74; idem, "Anti-Intellectualism and the American Woman, 1800-1860," *Mid-America* 48 (1966): 258-70; and Carl Degler, *At Odds: Women and the Family in America from the Revolution to the Present* (New York: Oxford University Press, 1980), 309-11.

2. Degler, *At Odds*, 312-27; David B. Tyack, *The One Best System: A History of American Urban Education* (Cambridge: Harvard University Press, 1974), 59-65; and Barbara Solomon, *In the Company of Educated Women* (New Haven: Yale University Press, 1985), 43-61.

3. Brubacher and Rudy, *Higher Education in Transition*, 66-67; and Roberta Wein, "Women's Colleges and Domesticity, 1875-1918," *History of Education Quarterly* 14 (Spring 1974): 31-47. For a partial listing of women's colleges in operation before 1860, see Burke, *American Collegiate Populations*, 341.

4. Saul D. Feldman, *Escape from the Doll's House: Women in Graduate and Professional School Education* (New York: McGraw-Hill Book Company, 1974), 28; Brubacher and Rudy, *Higher Education in Transition*, 67-68; and Rudolph, *The American College and University*, 314 and 319-23.

5. Feldman, *Escape from the Doll's House*, 28-29; Brubacher and Rudy, *Higher Education in Transition*, 67-68; and David Starr Jordan, "The Question of Coeducation," *Munsey's Magazine* 34 (March 1906): 683-88.

6. For these arguments against coeducation, see John C. Maxwell, "Should the Educations of Boys and Girls Differ? A Half Century of Debate—1870-1920," (Ph.D. dissertation, University of Wisconsin, 1966), chap. 6.

7. Maxwell, "Should the Educations of Boys and Girls Differ?" 25-27 and 172-77; and G. Stanley Hall, "The Question of Coeducation," *Munsey's Magazine* 34 (February 1906): 588-92.

8. Thomas Woody, *A History of Women's Education in the United States*, vol. 2 (New York: Science Press, 1929), 280-89; Maxwell, "Should the Educations of Boys and Girls Differ?" 137-38 and 148-50; and Orrin L. Elliot, *Stanford University: the First Twenty-Five Years* (Stanford: Stanford University Press, 1937), 132-34.

9. Rudolph, *The American College and University*, 322 and 324; Joan Grace Zimmerman, "College Culture in the Midwest, 1890-1930" (Ph.D. dissertation, University of Virginia, 1978), 123; and Burke, *American Collegiate Populations*, 215-17.

10. Mary Mariella Bowler, "A History of Catholic Colleges for Women in the United States of America" (Ph.D. dissertation, Catholic University of America, 1933), 18-22; "4 Histories: Medicine, Dentistry, Pharmacy, and Law," *Alumnews*, Creighton University (August 1978): 5; and Cross, *The Emergence of Liberal Catholicism*, 132.

11. Eleanor C. Donnelly, "The Home Is Woman's Sphere," *Catholic World* 57 (August 1893): 677-81. See also Katherine E. Conway, "Woman Has No Vocation to Public Life," ibid., 681-84; Cross, *The Emergence of Liberal Catholicism*, 133; and James J. Kenneally, "Eve, Mary and the Historians: American Catholicism and Women," *Horizons* 3 (Fall 1976): 191. For a recent study of how women's roles evolved in American Catholic culture since the Civil War, see Colleen McDannell, "Catholic Domesticity, 1860-1960," in *American Catholic Women: A Historical Exploration*, ed. Karen Kennelly, C.S.J. (New York: Macmillan Publishing Company, 1989), 48-80.

12. William Stang, *Socialism and Christianity* (New York: Benziger Brothers, 1905), 178-80; and Thomas Shields, *Philosophy of Education* (Washington: Catholic Education Press, 1921), 289-91.

13. Power, *Catholic Higher Education in America*, 273-75 and 303-4; and Bowler, "A History of Catholic Colleges for Women," 18-19.

14. *Catholic Encyclopedia*, 1913, s.v. "Co-education," by Thomas Shields; Albert Muntsch, S.J., "Coeducation from a Catholic Standpoint," *Catholic Educational Association Bulletin* 13 (November 1916): 352-66; and Jencks and Riesman, *The Academic Revolution*, 377-78.

15. Mary J. Oates, C.S.J., "The Development of Catholic Colleges for Women, 1895-1960," *U.S. Catholic Historian* 7 (Fall 1988): 413; Bowler, "A History of Catholic Colleges for Women," 89-90; and Andrew M. Greeley, *From Backwater to Mainstream: A Profile of Catholic Higher Education* (New York: McGraw Hill Book Company, 1969), 30.

16. Bowler, "A History of Catholic Colleges for Women," 94; Crowley, compiler, *Why a Catholic College Education?*, 17.

17. Power, *Catholic Higher Education in America*, 303-4; Buetow, *Of Singular Benefit*, 179; M. Jane Coogan, B.V.M., *The Price of Our Heritage*, vol. 2 (Dubuque: Mount Carmel Press, 1978), 344; and *Catholic Colleges and Schools*, 1942, part 3, 21.

18. Ralph L. Hayes, "The Problem of Teacher Certification," *Catholic Educational Association Bulletin* 19 (November 1922): 368-69; Alphonse Schwitalla, S.J. to Charles Cloud, S.J., 13 July 1929, Schwitalla personal file, AMPSJ. See also Mary J. Oates, "Learning to Teach: The Professional Preparation of Massachusetts Parochial School Faculty, 1870-1940," 3-4, Working Paper Series 10, no. 2 (Fall 1981), Cushwa Center for the Study of American Catholicism, University of Notre Dame.

19. Farrell "The Catholic Chaplain at the Secular University," 151-58. Such schools as Adelphi, Boston University, Smith, Syracuse, Michigan, and Valparaiso also reported a minimum of forty Catholic women in 1907.

20. Burrowes, "Attitude of Catholics towards Higher Education," 160.

21. Sister M. Catherine, "The Higher Education of Women under Catholic Auspices," *Catholic Educational Association Bulletin* 18 (November 1921): 429-40; Bowler, "A History of Catholic Colleges for Women," 124; and *Directory of Catholic Colleges and Schools, 1921.*

22. Bowler, "A History of Catholic Colleges for Women," 123 and 94; and *Educational Record* 11 (April 1930): 129-42. Until they could gain individual accreditation, certain Catholic women's colleges in the St. Louis area became "corporate colleges" of St. Louis University in 1925, retaining financial independence and much academic autonomy while gaining the advantage of the university's recognition by the North Central Association. See John F. Bannon, S.J. and Elvis Patea, "Notes for an Academic History of Saint Louis University—Suggested by the Record of Degrees Awarded during Its 163 Years of Service," Office of University Registrar, St. Louis University, 1982, 43-44; and Faherty, *Better the Dream,* 282.

23. For a summary of the problems faced by Catholic colleges for women before 1940, see Sr. Thomas Aquinas, O.S.U., "Some Problems of the Catholic Women's College," *Catholic Educational Association Bulletin* 21 (November 1924): 271-77; and Grace Dammann, R.S.C.J., "The American Catholic College for Women," in *Essays on Catholic Education in the United States,* ed. Roy J. Deferrari (Washington, D.C.: Catholic University of America Press, 1942; reprint ed., Freeport, N.Y.: Books for Libraries Press, 1969), 173 and 184-94.

24. Thomas Ewing Sherman, S.J., "Higher Education of Catholic Women," Catholic Educational Association, *Report of the Proceedings and Addresses of the Third Annual Meeting,* Cleveland, Ohio, 9-12 July 1906, 90-98; Joseph T. Durkin, S.J., *General Sherman's Son* (New York: Farrar, Straus and Company, 1959), 173. For other statements arguing for women's education under Catholic auspices, see *Higher Education for Catholic Women: An Historical Anthology,* ed. Mary J. Oates (New York: Garland Publishing, Inc., 1987).

25. *Bulletin of St. John's College,* 1948-1949, 12.

26. Daggett, ed., *Education in Wisconsin,* 243. For details on the introduction of coeducation to Marquette, see Raphael Hamilton, S.J., *The Story of Marquette University* (Milwaukee: Marquette University Press, 1953), 124-27; and Coogan, *The Price of Our Heritage,* vol. 2, 345-49. William McGucken, S.J., a student at Marquette in 1909, wrote Edward B. Rooney, S.J. in 1941 that "It was only after persistent urging of the Ordinary, Archbishop Messmer, that Marquette undertook the education of women." See McGucken to Rooney, 21 April 1941, File 134.02, Box 32, JEA Collection, ABC.

27. The institution never opened because James Keane, who became Archbishop of Dubuque in 1911, believed that the sisters' college in Dubuque needed the faculty trained for the proposed Milwaukee venture. See Coogan, *The Price Of Our Heritage,* vol. 2, 346-49.

28. Hamilton, *The Story of Marquette University,* 127. In 1917, McCabe became president of Xavier University in Cincinnati; within a year, Xavier began admitting women students to summer, evening, and extension courses. See Bennish, *Continuity and Change,* 126-27.

29. Deferrari, *Memoirs,* 230-31; and John F. Schenk, S.J., "The History of Coeducation in Catholic Colleges and Universities in the United States" (M.A. thesis, St. Louis University, 1943), 90. On page 227 of his book *Catholic Higher Education in America,* Edward Power states that in 1914 DePaul became the first Catholic college or university to become fully coeducational, but for conflicting evidence, see Kantowicz, *Corporation Sole,* 90.

30. Delegates to the 1914 Catholic Educational Association convention passed a resolution which first noted that secular schools did not seem to be "fitting places" of study for nuns and then praised Catholic colleges and universities for "providing courses in education and for opening summer schools where women and especially those of religious communities may be taught." See "General Resolutions," *Catholic Educational Association Bulletin* 11 (November 1914): 34.

31. Schenk, "History of Coeducation in Catholic Colleges and Universities," 67-68; *Creighton University Information Bulletin* 32 (1940-1942), 21; and minutes of provincials' meeting, New York, April 10-11, 1918, 4, AMPSJ.

32. For enrollment data, see *Directory of Catholic Colleges and Schools*, 1921; and Labaj, "The Development of the Department of Education at St. Louis University, 1900-1942," 105-6.

33. *Bulletin of Loyola University*, February 1917, 52; David Allan Robertson, ed., *American Universities and Colleges* (New York: Charles Scribner's Sons, 1928), 418-19; *Datelines: Canisius College, 1870-1980* (Buffalo: Canisius College, 1981), 3; Schenk, "The History of Coeducation in Catholic Colleges and Universities," 68 and 110; Faherty, *Better the Dream*, 277-78; and *Creighton University Bulletin* 24 (15 April 1932), 41.

34. Jesuit Educational Association, "Report of the Commission on Coeducation," 12 February 1940, 6, "Education #7, 1939," Drawer 74, ACPSJ. During their formative years, graduate schools may have accepted women more readily because "they needed all the qualified students they could find." See Feldman, *Escape from the Doll's House*, 32. For information about involvement of Catholic laywomen in the professions, see Mary J. Oates, "Catholic Laywomen in the Labor Force," in *American Catholic Women*, 97-124.

35. Hamilton, *The Story of Marquette University*, 124; Bannon and Patea, "Notes for an Academic History of Saint Louis University," 70; *Duquesne University Bulletin* 25 (October 1938), 31; Herman J. Muller, S.J., *The University of Detroit, 1877-1977, A Centennial History* (Detroit: n.p., 1976), 117; Bennish, *Continuity and Change*, 126; Robertson, ed., *American Universities and Colleges*, 401-2 and 418-19.

36. J.W. Maguire, "Why Sociology Should Be Taught in Our Catholic Colleges," *Catholic Educational Association Bulletin* 13 (November 1916): 108-13; Thomas E. Mitchell and Lucian L. Lauerman, "The Catholic Schools of Social Work in the United States," in *Essays on Catholic Education in the United States*, 299-301; and Gannon, *Up to the Present*, 145-47.

37. Burrowes, "Attitude of Catholics Towards Higher Education," 168-69; Helen E. Kean, "History of Women in Jesuit Colleges," *Proceedings of the Jesuit Educational Association Workshop for Jesuit Student Personnel Programs and Services*, Regis College, Denver, 18-30 July 1965, 90-93; and Mitchell and Lauerman, "Catholic Schools of Social Work," 301.

38. Bannon and Patea, "Notes for an Academic History of Saint Louis University," 69-70; Faherty, *Better the Dream*, 279-80; and *Creighton University Bulletin* 24 (15 April 1932), 41 and 44.

39. Deferrari, *Memoirs*, 235-36; *Duquesne University Bulletin* 18 (July 1929), 47; and Schenk, "The History of Coeducation in Catholic Colleges and Universities," 96-104 and 163-66.

40. For enrollment data, see *Catholic Colleges and Schools*, 1930, 1936, and 1942; and U.S. Department of Health, Education, and Welfare, *Digest of Educational Statistics, 1983-1984* (Washington: Government Printing Office, 1984), 101.

41. See "Report of the Commission on Coeducation," 12 February 1940, ACPSJ. In contrast to women, most male students in Jesuit schools in 1938-1939 attended class full-time, 56% were enrolled in liberal arts and education classes, 20% of them sought degrees in the law, medicine, dentistry, and pharmacy, and 17% were registered in business.

42. For data on female enrollment in American higher education for 1937-1938, see U.S. Office of Education, *Statistics of Higher Education, 1937-1938* (Washington, D.C.: Government Printing Office, 1940).

43. Lois W. Banner, *Women in Modern America: A Brief History* (New York: Harcourt Brace Jovanovich, Inc., 1974), 125-26; Frederick Lewis Allen, *Only Yesterday: An Informal History of the 1920s* (New York: Harper & Row, Publishers, 1931, reprint ed., 1964), 79-81; and "Report of the Commission on Coeducation," 12 February 1940, 13, ACPSJ.

44. "The Pastoral Letter of 1919," in *Pastoral Letters of the United States Catholic Bishops*, vol. 1, 314.

45. For comments on the status of women in the early years of the Catholic Educational Association, see Plough, "Catholic Colleges and the Catholic Educational Association," 287-88; and Julius W. Haun, "The Contribution of the College and University Department of the National Catholic Educational Association to the Growth and Development of Catholic Higher Education in the Past Fifty Years," *National Catholic Educational Association Bulletin* 50 (August 1953): 172-73.

46. James E. Cummings, "Pertinent Facts on Catholic Secondary Education," *Catholic Educational Review* 28 (October 1930): 450; and Buetow, *Of Singular Benefit*, 261.

47. Buetow, *Of Singular Benefit*, 261; Mabel Newcomer, *A Century of Higher Education for American Women* (New York: Harper and Brothers Publishers, 1959), 38; Matthew Germing, S.J., provincial of the Missouri Province, to Ledochowski, 25 August 1931, "Letters to Fr. General, 1926-1941," AMPSJ; and Wilfred P. Schoenberg, S.J., *Paths to the Northwest: A Jesuit History of the Oregon Province* (Chicago: Loyola University Press, 1982), 392.

48. Claudia Carlen, compiler, *The Papal Encyclicals 1903-1939* (Wilmington, N. C.: McGrath Publishing Company, 1981), 363. For an analysis of the educational views expressed in the document, see Edward A. Fitzpatrick, "Theology of Education in the Encyclical on Xian Education," *National Catholic Educational Association Bulletin* 44 (February 1948): 6-26.

49. For a sampling of Ledochowski's views on coeducation, see Joseph Rockwell, S.J., provincial of the Maryland-New York Province, to American provincials, 27 November 1919, "Fr. General to American Provincials," ACPSJ; Ledochowski to American Jesuits, 7 June 1928, "Letters of Fr. Ledochowski," Box 15, JEA Collection, ABC; Ledochowski to American provincials, 15 July 1939, "Education-Coeducation," Drawer 77, ACPSJ; Zacheus Maher, S.J., provincial of the California Province, to Daniel M. O'Connell, S.J., 22 May 1935 and 4 July 1935, "O'Connell file," Drawer 74, ACPSJ; Maher to Edward Rooney, S.J., 12 April 1940, "Education-Coeducation," Drawer 77, ACPSJ; and Maher to Raphael McCarthy, S.J., president of Marquette University, 2 January 1943 and 18 January 1943, "American Assistant Correspondence, 1943," AMPSJ.

50. Arthur, "The University of Notre Dame, 1919-1933," 191-92; and McCabe to Francis X. McMenamy, S.J., 4 March 1946, McMenamy Papers, AMPSJ. For another statement of opposition to coeducation, see I.J. Semper, "The Church and Higher Education for Girls," *Catholic Educational Review* 29 (April 1931): 215-25.

51. Resistance to coeducation or even outright refusal to enroll female students in the 1930s and 1940s was not unique to Catholic educators. In 1940, Amherst, Dartmouth, Princeton, and Williams accepted only male students. Harvard did not allow coeds from Radcliffe into its classrooms until 1943, when faculty shortages during World War II forced a more efficient use of personnel, and the Harvard Medical School first admitted women applicants in 1945. See Clarence S. Marsh, ed., *American Universities and Colleges* (Washington, D.C.: American Council on Education, 1940), 1066-67; and Synnott, *The Half-Opened Door*, 204.

52. Phillips to Edward Rooney, S.J., 15 August 1939, File 134.02, Box 32, JEA Collection, ABC; Maher to Edward Rooney, S.J., 12 April 1940, "Education-Coeducation," Drawer 77, ACPSJ; and Duce to [Joseph O'Brien, S.J.], provincial of the California Province, 2 September 1950, ibid.

53. Phillips acknowledged in 1939 that "I have never had direct contact with the problem of coeducation—never having taught any mixed classes, nor ever having been stationed in any of our schools where coeducation exists." See Phillips to Edward Rooney, S.J., 15 August 1939, File 134.02, Box 32, JEA Collection, ABC. All of Maher's educational training after grade school was in male institutions, and his assignments in

the Jesuit order never gave him direct contact with coeducation. See his autobiographical sketch, November, 1951, ACPSJ.

54. Gannon, *Up to the Present*, 145-47; "Report of the Commission on Coeducation," 12 February 1940, 6, "Education #7, 1939," ACPSJ; and Power, *Catholic Higher Education in America*, 274.

55. Minutes of provincials' meeting, New York, 10-11 April 1918, 4, AMPSJ; and William J. McGucken, S.J., "Should We Have Coeducation in Catholic Colleges and Universities?" *Thought* 13 (December 1938): 539.

56. For the responses of various institutions, see Schenk, "The History of Coeducation in Catholic Colleges and Universities," chaps. 2 and 3.

57. A.C. Penny, Director of the Department of Statistics, Marquette University to John Schenk, S.J., 12 October 1942, quoted in Schenk, "The History of Coeducation in Catholic Colleges and Universities," 94.

58. Bannon and Patea, "Notes for an Academic History of Saint Louis University," 69-70.

59. Schoenberg, *Paths to the Northwest*, 390-92 and 411; and Neill R. Meany, S.J., "Seattle University Founder Fr. McGoldrick Dies," *National Jesuit News*, June 1983, 27. Ledochowski's first reaction to the introduction of coeducation at Seattle "was a vigorous order to do away with it. Earnest pleading, because of the 'fait accompli,' made him change the order for immediate cancellation to an honest and serious endeavor to do away with it as soon as possible." See Zacheus Maher, S.J. to Edward Rooney, S.J., 12 April 1940, 5, "Education-Coeducation," Drawer 77, ACPSJ.

60. See "Concerning the Admission of Women to Our Colleges and Universities," supplement to the minutes of the JEA Executive Committee meeting, 12-13 December 1937, Loyola University, Chicago, "Education #6," Drawer 74, ACPSJ.

61. Ibid.

62. McGucken, "Should We Have Coeducation in Catholic Colleges and Universities?" 537-40.

63. Minutes of the JEA Executive Committee, 2-5 November 1938, 16, "JEA Ex. Comm., 1935-39," Drawer 74, ACPSJ; William McGucken, S.J. to Peter Brooks, S.J., provincial of the Missouri Province, n.d., McGucken personal file, AMPSJ; Ledochowski to American provincials, 24 March 1939, 1939 provincials' meeting, ACPSJ; and idem, 15 July 1939, "Education-Coeducation," Drawer 77, ACPSJ.

64. "Report of the Commission on Coeducation," 12 February 1940, "Education #7, 1939," ACPSJ. For the beliefs of its members and their understanding of their assignment, see William McGucken, S.J. to Edward Rooney, S.J., 13 September 1939, File 134.02, Box 32, JEA Collection, ABC; Edward C. Phillips, S.J., to Rooney, 23 May 1940, File 134.06, ibid.; McGucken to Rooney, 21 April 1941, File 134.02, ibid.; and Samuel Knox Wilson, S.J., president of Loyola University, Chicago, to Rooney, n.d., ibid.

65. Zacheus Maher, S.J. to Edward Rooney, S.J., 12 April 1940, "Education-Coeducation," Drawer 77, ACPSJ; and [Maher], "Tentative Norms on Coeducation," May 1941, File 134.02, Box 32, JEA Collection, ABC.

66. Minutes of the Commission on Coeducation, New York, 4-5 October 1941, File 134.02, Box 32, JEA Collection, ABC; Maher to the American provincials, 2 November 1941, ibid.; and Ledochowski to Maher, 2 May 1942, "Education-Coeducation," Drawer 77, ACPSJ.

67. John B. Janssens, S.J., superior general of the Society of Jesus, to Leo Robinson, S.J., provincial of the Oregon Province, 23 April 1947, 1947 provincials meeting, ACPSJ; Vincent McCormick, S.J., assistant to Janssens for the United States, to Joseph Zuercher, S.J., provincial of the Missouri Province, 18 April 1948, Letters of Fr. General, AMPSJ; Schoenberg, *Paths to the Northwest*, 442; and Janssens to Zuercher, 7 February 1949, Letters of Fr. General, AMPSJ.

68. Power, *Catholic Higher Education in America*, 321 and 445-46; and "Panel on Coeducation and Education of Women," *National Catholic Educational Association Bulletin* 51 (August 1954): 284-304.

69. Aidan M. Carr, "The Church on Coeducation," *Homiletic and Pastoral Review* 58 (September 1958): 1147-51; Power, *Catholic Higher Education in America*, 445-46; and *Directory Association of Jesuit Colleges and Universities*, 1989-90, 7.

70. John R. Crocker, S.J., *The Student Guide to Catholic Colleges and Universities* (San Francisco: Harper and Row, Publishers, 1982); and Susan G. Broyles and Rosa M. Fernandez, compilers, *Educational Directory Colleges and Universities, 1983-1984* (Washington, D.C.: National Center for Education Statistics, 1984).

4

The Rise of the Laity in
American Catholic Higher Education

The number, religious affiliation, and status of laity involved in American Catholic higher education changed greatly during the twentieth century. In the early 1900s, lay academic personnel in Catholic postsecondary schools represented a small minority, usually belonged to the Catholic Church, and exercised little influence in their institutions. But by the 1970s, lay people, many of them non-Catholics, constituted the vast majority of faculty, administrators, and trustees in Catholic colleges and universities. In addition, they commonly helped shape and execute academic policies. An analysis of the rise of Catholic and non-Catholic laity on Catholic campuses reveals the growing aspirations, responsibilities, and prestige of nonclerics in Catholic culture since 1900. It also illuminates the evolution of lay-clerical relations in Catholicism and the development of more ecumenical attitudes in American society in recent decades.

Lay Catholics played a minor role in Catholic higher education at the start of the twentieth century. Between 1891 and 1906, Marquette College functioned with only one full-time lay professor and a limited number of M.A. students teaching for brief periods while completing their degrees. In 1900, the collegiate department at St. Ignatius College in Chicago consisted of nine Jesuits teaching liberal arts courses and three laymen providing instruction in commercial subjects. That same year the faculty of St. Vincent's College in Los Angeles, operated by the Vincentian order, included ten priests and three nonclerics; and all eight professors teaching college-level courses at St. Ignatius College in San Francisco were members of the Society of Jesus. In 1903, St. Benedict's College in Atchison, Kansas did not employ a single lay teacher.[1]

Even fewer lay people served as administrators in Catholic colleges and universities in the early 1900s, except in professional programs. Clergy and religious also maintained tight control of governing boards. According to data on 216 trustees serving in thirty-five Catholic postsecondary schools in 1900, only two were laymen. When Thomas McCluskey, S.J., president of Fordham, proposed in 1912 that the university invite non-Jesuits, including certain lay Catholics, to be trustees, the superior general of the Jesuit order denied permission for the move.[2]

The minor roles of laity in Catholic postsecondary schools before World War I reflected the subordinate position, attitudes, and expectations of nonclerics in the Catholic Church. Lay activism had shown signs of developing among American Catholics in the 1880s and early 1890s. During these years, Catholic laymen in St. Paul formed a Catholic Truth Society to respond to attacks on the church and to spread information about Catholicism. Numerous diocesan newspapers employed lay editors, and the *Catholic World* printed a series of articles discussing the place of lay Catholics in the church. Supported by liberals among the American bishops, prominent Catholic laity organized national congresses in 1889 and 1893 to consider Catholic social teachings and to discuss contemporary cultural, political, and economic issues.[3]

But the promise of these initiatives was never fulfilled. Many Catholic priests and bishops in the United States feared that activities by lay Catholics would encroach on clerical control of the church and harm Catholic unity. Increased involvement of laity in Catholic affairs became suspect as the liberal wing of the American hierarchy, advocates of an expanded role for lay Catholics, came under increasing attack from conservative clerics in America and Rome. Pope Leo XIII sent a letter to Cardinal Gibbons in 1899 criticizing any American Catholics who maintained that the church should introduce greater liberty so that "each one of the faithful may act more freely in pursuance of his own natural bent and capacity." The condemnation of theological liberalism by Pope Pius X in 1907 further discouraged innovation, particularly any attempt to broaden the role of laity in the Catholic Church.[4]

Most lay Catholics in the United States willingly deferred to the clergy in the early decades of the twentieth century, partly out of respect and a sense of tradition but also because of self-consciousness about their own lack of skills, education, and priestly ordination. In particular, the large majority of lay Catholics in the early 1900s regarded higher education as the responsibility of clergy and religious. Reporting to his fellow Jesuits about the 1907 convention of the Catholic Educational Association, John Conway, S.J. noted that except for book agents and newspaper reporters, "it is rare, indeed, to find a Catholic layman in the audience." He added that he could recall only one instance in the past four years when a layman had delivered a paper at a CEA meeting.[5]

During the twentieth century, certain Catholics, both lay and religious, launched efforts to increase the number, religious diversity, and standing of laity in Catholic colleges and universities; but they struggled against various obstacles. First, lay Catholics often lacked the academic qualifications to be hired as administrators and teachers in Catholic higher education, especially in the 1920s and 1930s. In 1929, the president of Creighton observed to his provincial that "if circumstances should create several vacancies calling for new Deans, it would be fairly impossible at the present time to fill the positions with properly qualified lay Catholics." James Macelwane, S.J., dean of the graduate school at St. Louis University, wrote that same year that "The great difficulty that we [Catholic academic leaders] all face is that of obtaining Catholics with the training that is needed for positions on our faculties. Our American Catholic laymen have not been entering the teaching profession."[6] In 1939, members of the Executive Committee of the Jesuit Educational Association drew attention to the continued scarcity of "good Catholic lay teachers," and they stressed the importance of encouraging students in Jesuit institutions "to prepare for those fields of teaching where there is need and opportunity, viz., education, economics, sociology, etc."[7]

While more Catholics obtained doctorates after 1945, recruiting Catholic faculty still remained difficult. Edward Rooney, S.J., president of the Jesuit Educational Association, informed Harold Small, S.J., assistant to the Jesuit superior general for the United States, in 1963 that "Try as we may it is frequently difficult, sometimes impossible, to find Catholic laymen to fill positions that are open in Catholic institutions of higher learning."[8] Postwar expansion in Catholic schools and other institutions of higher education heightened competition for the comparatively limited number of trained Catholic teachers and administrators. In addition, unlike many of their counterparts in the 1920s and 1930s, fewer Catholics earning graduate degrees after World War II restricted their career choices to Catholic institutions, especially those completing programs at the best American colleges and universities. As one Jesuit remarked in 1977 about applicants for faculty openings at his school, "'The young Catholic scholar of real quality waiting in line for a position at Marquette is a mythical figure.'"[9]

Despite the shortage of qualified Catholic faculty and administrators, the religious climate prevailing in Catholic higher education, particularly before 1940, discouraged employment of non-Catholic academic personnel to fill vacancies. Responding to criticism that Jesuit colleges and universities in the United States needed to strengthen their Catholic character, Wlodimir Ledochowski, S.J., head of the Jesuit order, urged American Jesuit superiors in 1928 to "take steps at once to secure teachers for our college departments who are Catholic both in name and in practice." Furthermore, he prohibited hiring of non-Catholic deans in the future and called for the replacement of any presently in office "wherever it can be prudently done." Data from eighty-seven Catholic colleges and universities compiled by the National Catholic Educational Association in 1937 revealed that fifty-four of these institutions excluded non-Catholics from being department chairmen.[10]

Because of widespread concerns about maintaining a pervasively Catholic institutional atmosphere, administrators of Catholic colleges and universities in the 1920s and 1930s hired few non-Catholic teachers. Of 3,784 faculty in ninety-three Catholic postsecondary schools surveyed in 1937, 3,550 (94%) identified themselves as Roman Catholics. In 1940, only 7% (80) of 1,156 liberal arts faculty members in twenty-two Jesuit institutions did not belong to the Catholic Church.[11]

Chronic financial problems further retarded the rise of laity in Catholic higher education. Lacking endowment and often in debt, Catholic colleges and universities depended largely on tuition revenue and the contributed services of clergy and religious to finance operations. They commonly economized by paying low salaries to laity on their faculties. Consequently, they found it difficult to attract and retain lay teachers and administrators, particularly those with superior abilities.[12] The highest faculty salary at Notre Dame during the 1919-1920 academic year amounted to $2,000, and the median was about $1,500; in comparison, the national average totaled about $2,100. A 1947 study of ninety-nine Catholic and non-Catholic postsecondary institutions in the eastern United States reported that assistant, associate, and full professors in Catholic colleges and universities received considerably less money than their peers in other schools. The greatest pay variations occurred among the highest-ranked teachers. The average *maximum* salary ($3,838) for a full professor in a Catholic institution fell $400 short of the average *minimum* ($4,225) earned by his counterpart on a non-Catholic campus.[13]

Budget pressures also hindered the professional advancement of laity in Catholic higher education. Few Catholic colleges and universities could afford to hire the extra faculty required to reduce teaching loads. Nor could many of them fund research activities or establish sabbatical programs, measures which would have created a better environment for scholarly achievement and thus raised the status of individual professors. Hugh Duce, S.J., director of education for the California Province of the Jesuit order, observed in 1939 that because of inadequate finances, most Jesuit postsecondary schools "put nothing by for research, or to allow a good man to take a year's leave of absence on some worthwhile project." Interviewed in 1965 and 1966 about problems in their institutions, officials in ninety-eight Catholic postsecondary schools frequently complained that lack of money resulted in inadequate assistance for research and advanced study, heavy reliance on part-time faculty, and above average teaching responsibilities.[14]

Besides educational, religious, and financial problems, supporters of a wider role for laity in Catholic colleges and universities contended against ideological opposition, particularly concerning three issues. First, a bias against lay academic personnel existed in Catholic higher education. For instance, nonclerics constituted just slightly more than 20% of the speakers at conventions of the National Catholic Educational Association between 1904 and 1953, even though lay people made up over 50% of the total faculty in Catholic postsecondary institutions after 1920.[15] The superior general of the Jesuit order refused in 1939 to permit non-Jesuits to become associate members of the Jesuit Educational Association. In 1948, Jesuit educational leaders organized a national meeting to discuss the curriculum in Jesuit colleges of liberal arts and business; but they excluded lay faculty and deans, even though lay professors outnumbered Jesuits in the Jesuit higher educational network and lay deans directed nine of the fourteen business schools in Jesuit institutions.[16]

Such treatment of laity stemmed largely from doubts that lay people could communicate the religious traditions, academic values, and institutional goals of Catholic higher education as effectively as priests and religious.[17] When Seattle College hired lay professors in the early 1930s, the local bishop complained about the "irreligious staff" in the institution. While acknowledging that circumstances might justify the use of non-Jesuit faculty, John Janssens, S.J., the Jesuit superior general, declared in 1947 that a Jesuit school "loses much of the character that the Society [the Jesuit order] wishes to give it, when the number of lay teachers is very large."[18]

Second, Catholic ecclesiastical and educational leaders before 1960 generally rejected concepts of academic freedom and faculty rights prevailing in non-Catholic American higher education. In 1939, Henry Crimmins, S.J., president of St. Louis University, dismissed a lay faculty member of twenty-three years for joining other St. Louisans in sponsoring a former Irish priest's lecture on the Spanish Civil War. Perhaps under pressure from the local archbishop, Crimmins judged that the professor had compromised the university's reputation as a Catholic school. During a lengthy mid-1960s dispute over salaries and the proper role of faculty in institutional governance, administrators at St. John's University in New York discharged approximately twenty faculty members whom they regarded as troublemakers. The trustees of Catholic University attempted to discipline certain professors in 1968 for publicly dissenting from *Humanae Vitae*, the papal encyclical concerning birth control.[19]

Catholic educators prior to the 1960s commonly insisted that their responsibilities to ensure religious orthodoxy and to maintain the Catholic character of their institutions required the right to intervene against faculty in certain instances. Many shared the position of Wilfred Mallon, S.J., dean of the college of liberal arts at St. Louis University. In an address at the 1942 National Catholic Educational Association convention, he declared that violations of Catholic doctrine, moral principles, or "of the essential proprieties of Catholic life, on the campus or off the campus, render a man unfit for service in a Catholic college."[20]

Consequently, faculty contracts in Catholic colleges and universities often specified that professors could be dismissed for violating Catholic doctrine and morality. For instance, faculty members beginning at Notre Dame in 1953 signed an agreement which stated that "If the said appointee in his teaching or professional activities shall have been guilty of an offense against Catholic doctrine or morality, or if he shall have been involved in a crime or scandal, or shall have been knowingly engaged in or lent his name to any subversive activity, then the University may dismiss him summarily without notice." Marquette University statutes in the early 1950s declared that all faculty were expected to teach "nothing contrary to Catholic doctrine nor to American principles as these are embodied in the Declaration of Independence and the Constitution of the United States." Professors at Marquette were also required to "show a respectful and sympathetic attitude toward Catholic doctrine and American principles of government. Obviously, any grave offense against these canons must be considered just cause for dismissal from the Marquette University faculty."[21]

The emphasis in the Marquette statutes on loyalty to American political principles and form of government fitted with widespread contemporary concerns about the advance of communism in China and Europe as well as accusations of communist infiltration in the federal government made by Senator Joseph McCarthy. But manifestations of patriotism and commitment to democracy in Catholic education predated the Cold War and McCarthyism. Noting current interest about Americanization and education for citizenship, a national committee of Jesuit educators recommended in 1921 that "it should be made clear that the training given in our colleges illustrates the fundamental principles of real patriotism and is the best preparation for successful citizenry." After the outbreak of World War II, Zacheus Maher, S.J., head of the American branch of the Jesuit order, wrote President Roosevelt pledging the loyalty of Jesuits and offering Jesuit institutions "for the defence [*sic*] of the country or the promotion of the common good."[22]

Third, some Catholic educators and laity feared that appointment of lay people to key positions in Catholic higher education would deprive clergy and religious of institutional control and eventually result in secularization. Priests, brothers, and nuns traditionally dominated American Catholic higher education. In large part, their initiative, resourcefulness, and sacrifices had accounted for the founding and development of most Catholic postsecondary institutions in the United States. Clergy and religious functioned as fund raisers, policy makers, and guardians of orthodoxy. They filled the major administrative offices in Catholic higher learning before the 1960s, and most governing boards excluded lay members. Data collected in 1977 concerning 108 Catholic colleges and universities revealed that in 1960 lay men and women served as trustees in only nine of these institutions.[23]

Attached to their institutions and accustomed to power and influence, many clerics and religious objected to lay participation in the formation and execution of Catholic higher educational policy. For instance, when Marquette University started a lay board of governors in 1927, Ledochowski, the Jesuit superior general, questioned the move, warning that it could inhibit the freedom of Jesuit administrators. While he did not disapprove of seeking the advice of lay people about institutional affairs, Ledochowski subsequently expressed his judgment that formally organized advisory groups violated the fundamental law of the Jesuit order because "they seem to cede to externs some of the authority and independence of action of our Superiors."[24]

Concerns among some clergy and religious about their declining importance in Catholic postsecondary institutions deepened after World War II as schools expanded in size, programs, and lay faculty.

Starting in the early 1950s, Jesuit educational and religious officials debated how to maintain an effective presence in their professional schools, divisions staffed almost entirely by nonclerics.[25] Certain anonymous Jesuits complained to their superiors in Rome between 1957 and 1960 that laymen exercised excessive influence in American Jesuit higher education; in particular, they objected to the appointment of lay vice-presidents. Because of unfavorable reports about American Jesuit higher education, John Janssens, S.J., the Jesuit superior general, appointed four Jesuits in November 1958 to evaluate religious and academic conditions in Jesuit universities. In particular, he charged his "inspectors" to determine whether laymen had too much authority in setting academic policy and filling administrative positions.[26]

Most of all, some Catholic leaders worried that the increasing delegation of power to laity and the declining role of clergy and religious would result in the secularization of Catholic colleges and universities, as had happened to many Protestant schools in the late nineteenth and early twentieth centuries. In a 1958 editorial, *America* praised efforts to grant more responsibility to lay faculty and administrators in Catholic colleges and universities, but it also warned that "there is a point beyond which delegation obviously cannot go—when this means loss of basic control."[27] Plans in the late 1960s to reorganize governing boards and to grant majority control to laity provoked particularly vigorous opposition.[28] Despite strong endorsements from leading Jesuits, the majority of Jesuit presidents and chief academic officers voted in June 1966 against a resolution encouraging one or more Jesuit institutions to add lay people to their boards of trustees. In a 1967 journal article, Dennis Bonnette, a lay faculty member at St. John's University in New York, insisted that separating Catholic educational institutions from ecclesiastical authority and eliminating religious orders as the owners and operators of Catholic postsecondary schools was "a blueprint for the complete secularization of Catholic higher education."[29] Also that year, John Ford, S.J., a well-known theologian, argued that proposals to transfer institutional control to lay people violated canon law and provided no legal guarantee that the schools would remain Catholic institutions.[30]

Yet in spite of unfavorable conditions, Catholic and non-Catholic laity advanced in number and influence in Catholic higher education during the twentieth century. The percentage of lay teachers in Catholic colleges and universities increased from perhaps 10% to 15% in 1900, to over 50% in 1920, and to 85-90% in 1980. This growth began in the early 1900s when certain Catholic institutions, mainly those located in urban areas with large Catholic populations, added business, law, medicine, dentistry, and other professional schools to their existing small colleges of arts and sciences. For example, reflecting trends in American higher education and the desires of its Catholic supporters, Fordham opened law and medical programs in 1905 and pharmacy in 1911. Marquette started law and engineering divisions in 1908, added business in 1910, and incorporated medicine and dentistry in 1913.[31]

Catholic institutional leaders relied almost solely on lay people to conduct business and professional divisions in their schools. Few clergy and religious possessed the necessary training, and Catholic educators commonly believed that the religious and academic goals of Catholic education could be achieved best if priests, brothers, and nuns taught undergraduate classes in the arts and sciences.[32] Data on 106 Catholic colleges and universities collected in 1920 revealed that the 1,300 laity teaching in business and professional schools represented 88% of the faculty in these divisions, and they also constituted 68% of lay professors and 38% of all teachers in Catholic colleges and universities. In 1926, two-thirds of the lay professors on the faculties of Catholic postsecondary institutions still were concentrated outside the liberal arts.[33]

Unlike in Catholic business and professional programs, the number of lay teachers in Catholic liberal arts colleges did not increase significantly before World War I. During the 1908-1909 academic year, laity represented 17% (two of twelve) of liberal arts teachers at St. Ignatius College in Chicago, 23% (five of twenty-two) at Fordham, 27% (three of eleven) at St. Ignatius in San Francisco, and 28% (five of eighteen) at both St. Vincent's College in Los Angeles and Georgetown.[34] Laity averaged 21% of professors in the liberal arts divisions of six Jesuit colleges and universities in the Midwest (Creighton; Loyola University of Chicago; Marquette; St. Mary's, St. Mary's, Kansas; Regis, Denver; and Xavier, Cincinnati) in 1914, the same percentage as in 1909. In 1920, nonclerics accounted for about 25% of arts and sciences faculty in Jesuit schools and about 30% of all liberal arts teachers in Catholic higher education. Statistics compiled on 106 Catholic colleges and universities in 1920 indicated that nonclerics teaching in liberal arts constituted about 17% of their total faculties.[35]

But the proportion of lay professors in Catholic higher education outside business and professional programs rose steadily after 1918 as Catholic colleges and universities expanded to meet the growing educational aspirations of American Catholics. Between 1919 and 1924, the percentage of lay faculty in six Midwestern liberal arts colleges operated by the Jesuit order rose from 30% to 55%.[36] By 1940, nonclerics amounted to 49% of teachers in twenty-four Jesuit liberal arts programs, almost double the percentage in 1920; and they totaled

50.4% (6,600) of all instructors in Catholic higher education. William McGucken, director of education for the Missouri Province of the Society of Jesus, remarked in 1939 that "increased enrolment and a more diversified curriculum" ended the earlier domination of college and university faculties by clergy and members of religious orders.[37]

The laicization of Catholic colleges and universities accelerated during the educational expansion following World War II. For example, between 1940 and 1981, the percentage of lay teachers at the College of St. Catherine rose from 30% to 75%, from 27% to 82% at Trinity College in Washington, D.C., from 35% to 95% at Villanova, and from 52% to 91% at the University of Santa Clara.[38] Within the Jesuit network of higher education, the proportion of Jesuits among full-time faculty fell from 31.1% in 1948, to 27.5% in 1958, to 16.3% in 1968, and to 13.3% in 1972.[39]

In addition to numerical growth, shifts occurred in the religious composition of lay faculty in Catholic higher education. The vast majority of professors in Catholic postsecondary institutions before the 1950s belonged to the Catholic Church. For instance, 93% of those teaching in the liberal arts divisions of twenty-two Jesuit colleges and universities in 1940 identified themselves as Catholics, including 480 of 563 nonclerics. A 1952 survey of 9,166 arts and sciences teachers in 216 Catholic institutions reported that 93% (8,540) were Catholics. Non-Catholics amounted to only 15% (560 of 3,768) of undergraduate, graduate, and professional faculty in twenty-six colleges and universities operated by the Jesuit order in 1953.[40]

But in more recent decades, the number of Catholics teaching in Catholic postsecondary institutions has decreased. For example, the percentage of Catholic faculty at Seattle University dropped from 89% in 1953 to less than 50% by the late 1970s.[41] Non-Catholics represented 35% of the full-time faculty at Marquette in 1970 and 42% in 1977. Of 775 teachers at Notre Dame in 1984, almost 40% did not belong to the Catholic Church.[42] The declining number of Catholic faculty in Catholic higher education reflected the growing pluralism in American church-related postsecondary schools. A 1980 study of faculty in Lutheran colleges reported that only 33% were members of Lutheran churches.[43]

The status of nonclerics teaching in Catholic higher education also changed greatly after 1945. Many Catholic schools established retirement programs and raised salaries for lay faculty, a boost to the laity's morale and an aid to recruiting better academic personnel. Like many other American colleges and universities in 1945, only seven of seventy-five Catholic postsecondary institutions responding to a survey conducted by the National Catholic Educational Association offered benefits to retired professors, but by 1951 seventy-five schools had instituted retirement plans.[44] Furthermore, by the 1960s, the income gap between academic personnel in Catholic and secular higher education had narrowed, particularly for those in lower faculty ranks.[45] Between 1958 and 1968, faculty pay at the University of Santa Clara climbed from the $4,500-$8,000 range to $7,200-$16,000. By 1966, compensation at Boston College, Fordham, Georgetown, Notre Dame, and other leading Catholic schools ranked B+ on the salary scale maintained by the Association of American University Professors. Of seventy-two Catholic colleges and universities submitting data on faculty compensation to the AAUP in 1968, 60% rated the rank of "C" or better, while 64% of all higher educational institutions included in the survey ranked in the "C" or above categories.[46]

In addition, the image and job security of lay faculty in Catholic higher education also improved as Catholic schools recognized the legitimacy of tenure and academic freedom. A 1942 investigation of academic regulations in a representative sample of Catholic and non-Catholic postsecondary institutions revealed that 35% of the forty-eight Catholic colleges and universities surveyed granted tenure, while 92% of the 161 non-Catholic schools examined did so. During the late 1940s and early 1950s, only four of twenty-seven Jesuit colleges and universities offered tenure. But by the 1960s, Catholic post-secondary institutions commonly followed the tenure procedures prevailing in American higher education.[47]

Similarly, Catholic educators gradually accepted a broader definition of academic freedom. In 1966 and 1967, Catholic organizations of historians, philosophers, sociologists, and economists endorsed the "1940 Statement of Principles on Academic Freedom and Tenure" of the AAUP. In 1967, twenty-six prominent Catholic educational and religious officials issued a position paper which affirmed that "To perform its teaching and research functions effectively, the Catholic university must have a true autonomy and academic freedom in the face of authority of whatever kind, lay or clerical, external to the academic community itself." By the 1970s, faculty in most Catholic colleges and universities had the same protection from outside interference in research and teaching as their peers in non-Catholic institutions.[48]

Furthermore, lay faculty gained a voice in the governance of Catholic postsecondary education after 1945. Acknowledging the growing importance of laity in their schools, Jesuit leaders gave permission in 1958 for lay academic personnel to attend regular meetings of the Jesuit Educational Association, sessions previously restricted to members of the Jesuit order.[49] Also, institutions increasingly appointed nonclerics as department chairmen, positions once held mainly by clergy and religious. For instance, lay men and women in 1958 directed twenty-three of thirty-two departments at the University of Detroit, eleven of eighteen at Creighton, and thirteen of seventeen at St. John's in New York.[50] The lay-dominated faculties in Catholic colleges and universities gained further prominence in the 1960s and 1970s. Institutional leaders at schools like Fordham, Boston College, and St. Louis approved proposals for academic senates and wider consultation about decisions concerning curriculum, tenure, and professional standards. By 1969, faculty senates or councils functioned at twenty-five of twenty-eight Jesuit colleges and universities, with eighteen of the groups having been started after 1964. In its first official decision, the reorganized board of trustees of Notre Dame in 1967 approved a new faculty handbook which placed all academic decisions in the hands of professors and their elected representatives. Other Catholic postsecondary institutions subsequently conferred similar responsibilities on their faculties.[51]

The role of lay administrators in Catholic postsecondary institutions also developed after 1900. Their advance began in the early decades of the twentieth century as Catholic higher education expanded to include numerous business and professional programs. For instance, nonclerics in 1920 headed the divisions of law, commerce and finance, and engineering at the University of Detroit; and they served as deans of law, medicine, and pharmacy at Fordham. In 1945, lay deans administered forty of fifty-three Jesuit business and professional schools.[52]

Laity obtained other administrative positions in Catholic colleges and universities after World War I. Marquette selected a layman to be dean of its graduate school in 1924, and Catholic University made a similar appointment in 1930. John Carroll University in Cleveland chose a noncleric as vice-president of development in 1955, the first lay person to reach that rank in the Jesuit higher educational system. By 1960, almost 50% of the registrars, business managers, library directors, and assistant deans in Jesuit schools were lay men and women.[53]

Yet before the early 1960s, clergy and religious held almost all top-level positions in Catholic higher education outside business and professional divisions. In 1960, no lay person functioned as dean of liberal arts in the twenty-eight Jesuit colleges and universities. In addition, nonclerics numbered only two of twelve graduate school deans and four of thirty-four vice presidents in Jesuit institutions. A similar administrative pattern prevailed at such Catholic schools as Notre Dame, Providence, Trinity (Washington, D.C.), Duquesne, College of St. Catherine, and Manhattan.[54]

But during the 1960s and 1970s, many Catholic colleges and universities promoted laity to high-level posts. In 1965, Marquette appointed a layman to be academic vice-president, an innovation in Jesuit higher education. Two years later, Loyola College in Baltimore became the first Jesuit institution to choose a non-Jesuit as dean of liberal arts. In 1988, fifteen of twenty-six academic vice-presidents and nineteen of twenty-eight liberal arts deans in Jesuit schools were lay people. That year nonclerics filled 110 of approximately 135 positions of vice-presidential rank in Jesuit higher education.[55] Furthermore, lay presidents directed about 25% (fifty-five) of Catholic colleges and universities in 1981, mainly smaller schools founded by local dioceses and religious orders of women.[56]

Little information has been collected on the church membership of laity appointed to prominent positions in Catholic higher education since the early 1960s, but fragmentary data indicates that some did not belong to the Catholic Church. In 1966, Fordham selected non-Catholic deans for its colleges of education and performing arts. Two of seven laymen in the central administration of Marquette in 1977 were not Catholics, and Wheeling College hired a Protestant to be academic vice-president in 1983. At least two of the lay presidents of Catholic institutions in 1977 were not Catholics.[57]

In addition to their rising status as faculty and administrators during the twentieth century, numerous Catholic and non-Catholic laity became increasingly involved in the governance of Catholic higher education. At first, they contributed mainly as members of lay advisory groups. Notre Dame established a "Board of Lay Trustees" in 1921 to manage money for endowment received from the General Education Board, the Carnegie Foundation, and a planned fund drive. In correspondence with the head of the General Education Board, James Burns, C.S.C., Notre Dame's president, indicated that no fewer than two of the trustees would be non-Catholics.[58] Well-known St. Louis businessmen, including some who were not Catholics, agreed in 1909 to join the board of advisors at St. Louis University. Leaders at Marquette and Loyola University of Chicago started similar organizations in 1924 and 1930, respectively.[59] By 1954, lay advisory groups functioned at twenty-one of twenty-seven Jesuit colleges and universities.[60]

Traditionally, priests, brothers, and nuns formed the governing boards in Catholic higher education. Statistics on 108 Catholic institutions in 1960 showed that ninety-nine of them had only clergy and religious as trustees. But starting in the early 1960s, leaders of Catholic colleges and universities began inviting lay men and women to become board members. By 1977, at least one lay person served as a trustee in 110 (92%) of 119 Catholic postsecondary institutions surveyed; and of the nearly 2,500 trustees in these 110 schools, 62% were lay people. In 1986 nonclerics represented 69.4% of 875 trustees in the twenty-eight American Jesuit colleges and universities.[61]

Many Catholic colleges and universities granted the majority of seats on their boards of trustees to nonclerics. St. Louis University and Notre Dame announced plans in 1967 to reconstitute their governing boards and transfer control from priests to lay men and women, decisions commanding wide influence. By 1977, lay people outnumbered clergy and members of religious orders on the boards of at least seventy-seven Catholic institutions of higher education.[62]

Numerous non-Catholics served on the reorganized governing boards in Catholic higher education, sometimes in key positions. Of eighteen laymen named to the new board at St. Louis in 1967, nine were not Catholics. In 1977, Catholics totaled less than half of the lay trustees at Marquette; and that year, 120 Catholic colleges and universities reported that of 1,579 lay men and women on their boards, 24% (385) did not belong to the Catholic Church.[63] In the late 1970s, non-Catholics acted as chairmen of the trustees in approximately 20% of Catholic colleges and universities having lay board members.[64]

Various factors accounted for the changing number, religious backgrounds, and status of laity in Catholic higher education after 1900. First, the sheer need for faculty and administrators compelled Catholic educational leaders to hire large numbers of lay personnel. The religious orders and dioceses operating Catholic postsecondary schools could not meet the demand for staff created by increasing enrollment. As early as 1924, a committee of Jesuit educators observed that "It is becoming increasingly evident that we shall not be able to man our high schools and colleges exclusively with Jesuit teachers."[65]

The lack of qualified priests, brothers, and nuns to fill teaching and administrative vacancies in Catholic higher education became acute during the educational boom following World War II. Institutional expansion far exceeded growth in the pool of religious men and women available for academic assignments. Statistics on Jesuits and their schools illustrate the problem. Jesuit priests and seminarians in the United States rose from 5,006 in 1945 to a peak of 7,677 in 1964, an increase of 53%; and the number of Jesuit doctoral students more than doubled between 1945 and 1965 (from 141 to 300). But starting in the mid-1960s, the total of men entering and remaining in the American branch of the Jesuit order began dropping sharply, including numerous individuals trained for scholarship and academic administration. Between 1964 and 1989, the number of Jesuit priests and students for the priesthood in the United States decreased by 40% to 4,481.[66]

In contrast, the number of students in Jesuit postsecondary institutions grew from approximately 40,000 in 1945, to 140,000 in 1965, and to 175,000 in 1988.[67] Furthermore, other parts of the Jesuit order sought additional Jesuits, exacerbating the manpower shortage in Jesuit higher education. The number of Jesuit high schools in the United States increased from thirty-eight in 1945 to fifty-four in 1970.[68] The Jesuit superior general pressured American Jesuit provincials in the 1950s and early 1960s to send men to foreign missions, particularly Japan and South America.[69]

Some Catholic officials, especially after 1945, warned that the increases in students, faculty, and degree programs threatened both the academic quality and distinctiveness of Catholic higher education. But advocates of growth argued that expansion would bring badly needed revenue, enhance the prestige of Catholic colleges and universities, and reduce the number of Catholics attending non-Catholic institutions. They recognized that higher enrollment would aggravate personnel shortages and strain institutional identity; yet they thought such problems could be resolved by hiring lay faculty and administrators with Catholic religious and educational backgrounds and also by placing clergy and religious in key positions. But often Catholics with necessary educational qualifications could not be hired to fill vacancies, forcing Catholic administrators to employ non-Catholics, particularly for openings in graduate, business, and professional schools.[70]

Changing aspirations in Catholic higher education after the mid-1960s also helped increase the number of non-Catholic faculty and administrators in Catholic schools. Seeking to improve their standing in American academic culture, many Catholic colleges and universities placed greater stress on strictly professional criteria in selecting personnel rather than on previous concerns about religious preference, value orientations, and familiarity with Catholic educational traditions. Thus, they frequently hired non-Catholic applicants with degrees from prestigious secular schools or work experience in them rather than Catholics holding doctorates from Catholic graduate programs or currently employed in Catholic institutions.[71]

Unprecedented militancy among lay faculty after World War II was another factor in the rise of laity in Catholic higher education. During the 1920s and 1930s, a few lay teachers had publicly criticized the inadequate pay, uncertain tenure, and low status of nonclerics in Catholic colleges and universities.[72] But such protests elicited little support. Many involved in Catholic higher education realized that Catholic postsecondary institutions simply could not afford to raise salaries. In addition, the climate within Catholicism did not encourage lay people to challenge the favored position of clergy and religious.

Theodore Maynard, a lay professor teaching at Catholic University, expressed the view of numerous Catholics when he wrote in 1935, "If it must be admitted that nowhere . . . are laymen admitted on equal terms with priests, I do not see that they have any right to object. After all, the Church must be controlled by priests, and laymen can be no more than consultants and auxiliaries."[73]

But after 1945, lay faculty increasingly complained about their meager compensation. For instance, writing in *America* in 1951, a professor with twelve years' experience in Catholic higher education described many teachers in Catholic institutions as vastly underpaid and forced to find ways to supplement their income, circumstances harming their scholarship and teaching. John Meng, a Catholic and president of Hunter College, told those attending the 1956 National Catholic Educational Association convention that numerous Catholic colleges and universities did not pay a living wage to their professors. In 1965, more than two hundred teachers at St. John's University in New York walked out of a general faculty meeting to protest stalled salary negotiations.[74]

Nonclerics also objected to their subordinate position in Catholic higher education. Willis Nutting, a much-respected faculty member at Notre Dame, observed in 1951 that most of the lay professors he knew in Catholic institutions felt administrators treated them as employees, leaving some teachers cynical and others deeply resentful.[75] Oscar Perlmutter of Saint Xavier College in Chicago provoked lively discussions in Catholic educational circles in 1958 when he described lay people teaching in Catholic higher education as "second-class citizens, like trusted colonials or like successful Negroes in the United States."[76] In his 1964 study of Catholic faculty, John Donovan discovered that lay professors regarded their lack of status as more troubling than inadequate pay.[77]

Unhappy with their standing, some lay faculty in Catholic higher education after the late 1940s sought to remedy problems by direct action. A sizable number joined the American Association of University Professors, hoping group efforts could obtain higher salaries and a share in institutional governance for professors. By 1967, fourteen Catholic colleges and universities each had 100 or more teachers active in the AAUP and a combined membership of 2,282. But a decade earlier, only 660 faculty in these schools belonged to the AAUP (65% of faculty from Catholic higher education in the organization), and three of the fourteen institutions did not have a local AAUP chapter.[78] Like professors in other postsecondary schools, teachers in Catholic higher education sought a larger role in policy formation. In particular, many of them supported efforts to organize faculty senates and to gain representation on college and university committees.[79]

In a few cases, laity took stronger steps to resolve grievances. Failure to settle disputes over pay increases and faculty rights at St. John's University resulted in a strike by 150 teachers in 1966, a radical move for college professors but especially so for teachers at a Catholic institution. Following a precedent set by certain public institutions in the late 1960s, faculty at St. John's voted in 1970 to organize the first teachers' union on a Catholic campus. In 1975, of seventy-one post-secondary schools with faculty unions, seven were Catholic institutions.[80]

New religious perspectives emerging in Catholicism and American society after the mid-1950s further encouraged a wider role for Catholic and non-Catholic laity in Catholic academic life. The election of John Kennedy as the first Catholic president of the United States in 1960 lessened Catholic defensiveness, and his presidency also helped dispel anti-Catholic prejudice in this country. The pontificate of Pope John XXIII achieved similar effects. While head of the Roman Catholic Church from 1958 to his death in 1963, he urged Catholics to move from isolation to involvement in contemporary culture. His personal popularity and interest in ecumenism fostered better relations between Protestants, Catholics, and Jews. In addition, the Second Vatican Council, which met in Rome between 1962 and 1965, produced theological statements stressing the importance of laity, ecumenical activities, and collegial forms of government in the Catholic Church.[81]

The changing religious climate within Catholicism affected the policy deliberations of Catholic educators. For instance, in a 1963 memorandum to his superiors in Rome, Edward Rooney, S.J., president of the Jesuit Educational Association, addressed the issue of whether Catholic postsecondary institutions should employ non-Catholic faculty and administrators. He maintained that the matter should be approached "in the spirit of much of the current literature on the Ecumenical Movement," and he advised that many Catholic administrators in the United States believed that numerous faithful Protestants and Jews made positive contributions to Catholic higher education.[82]

Decisions of Jesuit educational leaders also mirrored more ecumenical attitudes among Catholics. Twenty-three of twenty-eight Jesuit college and university presidents indicated in a 1961 survey that they thought non-Catholics should not be hired to teach theology in Catholic postsecondary schools. But in 1967, when a Vatican official questioned whether departments of theology in Catholic schools should employ non-Catholic theologians to teach undergraduate courses in the Old Testament, Jesuit presidents defended the practice. They argued in part that "A valuable contribution to the knowledge and acceptance of the word of God can also be made by those who do not share in the fullness of our Faith."[83]

Vatican II's emphasis on a greater role for laity in Catholic life specifically influenced Catholic colleges and universities to add nonclerics to their governing boards and in many cases to make them the majority of trustees. For example, in 1967, St. Louis University became one of the first major Catholic universities in the United States to transfer institutional control to a board of trustees dominated by lay men and women. Its leaders indicated that the change reflected in part a desire to give lay people "a clear-cut opportunity to participate in university life at the policy-making level, in line with the general movement within the Catholic Church, as expressed by Vatican II, to place laymen in highly responsible positions on all levels throughout the church."[84]

Financial pressures also promoted greater lay participation in Catholic higher education. In the early 1960s, many Catholic educational officials increasingly recognized that Catholic postsecondary institutions must strengthen academic programs, expand facilities, and boost meager endowments. They further realized that their schools could not rely solely on tuition income and gifts from existing benefactors for funds. In their estimation, Catholic colleges and universities could not make significant academic advances without building a broader base of community and financial support. In particular, Catholic schools needed to secure more assistance from prominent civic and business leaders, government agencies, and philanthropic organizations.[85]

But in the judgment of influential Catholic educators, lay people most able to help Catholic higher education would be unlikely to commit themselves personally and financially to a particular college or university unless they shared responsibility for the institution. Arguing for a reorganization of governing boards in Jesuit postsecondary schools, Paul Reinert, S.J., president of St. Louis University, maintained to his religious superiors in 1966 that few Catholic colleges and universities could obtain financial resources needed in the future "unless lay leaders with loyalty and a personal, proprietary interest in the institution can be placed in a position where they *share* with the Society [the Jesuit order] the obligation of guaranteeing the resources necessary for the support and stabilization of the institution; . . . only shared legal trusteeship will create that sense of responsibility which characterizes the members of the board of such institutions as Princeton, the University of Chicago, etc." Theodore Hesburgh, C.S.C., president of Notre Dame, insisted in 1967 that the only way his university could achieve its long-range fundraising and endowment goals was to create a lay-oriented power structure.[86]

Furthermore, a growing number of Catholic educational leaders after the mid-1960s feared that exclusive control of Catholic higher education by priests, brothers, and nuns jeopardized federal and state aid to Catholic postsecondary institutions. Such income had become essential for balanced budgets and new facilities in many Catholic colleges and universities. In 1966, the Maryland Court of Appeals reversed a lower court decision and ruled 4-3 that state construction grants to three church-related colleges, including two Catholic schools, violated Maryland's constitution. The majority of the judges held in part that the dominant role of clergy and religious in the administration and governance of the three institutions helped create a sectarian character in them. Consequently, state money could not be provided for projects on such campuses.[87]

When the United States Supreme Court declined in November 1966 to review the case, alarm spread among Catholic educators. Though the Maryland decision applied only in that state, many Catholic educational officials feared similar court tests and judicial opinions. Their apprehensions grew in 1968 when a suit was filed in Connecticut questioning whether the federal government could legally make construction grants to four Catholic colleges in the state.[88]

Concerned that the Maryland case might become the law of the land, attorneys for Catholic colleges and universities recommended that Catholic schools take certain steps to protect themselves against lawsuits challenging their eligibility for government money. For instance, Francis Gallagher, a lawyer who helped defend the four Maryland colleges in the suit filed by the Horace Mann League, advised Jesuit college and university presidents in 1967 to include more nonclerics as administrators and trustees in their institutions. In addition, he suggested that Catholic schools establish provisions for tenure, promotion, and sabbatical leaves for their lay faculty resembling those provided teachers in non-Catholic higher education. At a meeting of Jesuit educational leaders in 1968, Wilbur Katz, a professor at the University of Wisconsin Law School, stressed that acceptance of academic freedom in Catholic institutions strengthened arguments for federal and state funds.[89]

Finally, various clergy and religious played a decisive role in the advance of laity in Catholic colleges and universities, functioning as catalysts for change. First, priests holding major positions in Catholic higher education during the 1920s and 1930s defended employment of nonclerics as teachers in Catholic postsecondary schools, crucial support at a time when many Catholics doubted that lay people could be as effective in the classroom as priests, brothers, and nuns. James Burns, C.S.C., well known in Catholic circles as a historian of Catholic education and former president of Notre Dame, asserted in 1926 that excluding lay people from university faculties or restricting them to a small number would deprive institutions of badly needed talent as well as condemn the schools to relative academic inferiority. Edward Rooney, S.J. responded vigorously after Zacheus Maher, S.J., assistant to the Jesuit superior general for the United States, questioned whether non-Jesuits should be admitted to the JEA and described lay personnel as "here today and gone tomorrow." Writing to Maher in 1939, Rooney declared that lay professors "are a part of our system and . . . will be part of it for a long time to come. I do not see how we can ever get along without them in the graduate and professional schools."[90]

Furthermore, officials in leading Catholic colleges and universities took specific steps to obtain and keep qualified nonclerics as faculty members. To overcome the scarcity of Catholic lay professors, presidents of some Catholic schools helped finance graduate training for certain students and then offered them teaching positions once they had earned their degrees. The provincial of the Missouri Province of the Jesuit order reported to the Jesuit superior general in 1930 that "St. Louis University has paid for the higher education of several Catholic men who are now on its teaching staff. Marquette, I know, is doing the same." The president of Creighton followed a similar policy.[91]

In directives sent to the dean of liberal arts, Charles Cloud, S.J., president of St. Louis University, wrote in 1929 that lay professors "should all be made to feel that they are an intimate part of the University," having not only responsibilities but also opportunities to become involved in the institution's development. In 1937, one year after becoming president of Fordham, Robert Gannon, S.J. established policies on salary, rank, and tenure, the result of negotiations with faculty members.[92]

Certain priests and religious also campaigned after 1945 to improve the financial compensation paid to lay faculty in Catholic higher education.[93] In 1947, a special committee of the National Catholic Educational Association submitted a report recommending that Catholic schools establish retirement plans, increase salaries, and consider tenure for their lay professors. Also that year, John Janssens, S.J., the Jesuit superior general, stressed that all American Jesuit colleges and universities should provide retirement programs for nonclerics teaching on their faculties. In 1954, the Committee on Faculty Welfare of the NCEA publicized the necessity of increased pay for lay professors. By the early 1960s, major Catholic schools of higher learning offered retirement benefits, accepted the principle of tenure, and had begun to upgrade salaries for their lay academic personnel.[94]

In addition, certain Catholic educators after World War II focused attention on the need to raise the academic status of lay teachers in Catholic postsecondary institutions. Presidents and graduate deans from Jesuit colleges and universities in the Midwest emphasized at a 1952 meeting that "laymen need to be made more completely members of our academic family." Writing in his capacity as director of the Jesuit Educational Association, Edward Rooney, S.J. told his superior general in 1954 that to retain qualified lay teachers, Jesuit schools must "take them into the system, make them a part of it, never look on them as hired help."[95] In a 1960 report to his fellow Jesuit presidents, A. A. Lemieux, S.J. of Seattle University emphasized that nonclerics on the faculties of Jesuit colleges and universities must be given a voice in shaping policies and in institutional planning. Such views reflected growing opinion among Jesuit academic leaders; by 1964, lay men and women held the majority of seats on key committees overseeing graduate studies, undergraduate curriculum, and faculty appointments in Jesuit schools.[96]

Besides advocating the financial and academic advancement of lay faculty, certain clergy and religious effectively promoted the appointment of laity to be major administrators in Catholic higher education. In 1964, Paul Reinert, S.J. asserted in a speech delivered at the National Catholic Educational Association convention that "lay men and women must be placed in strategic administrative positions where they, together with the total faculty, can have an influential voice in determining academic policy." Also that year, the superior general of the Jesuit order informed American Jesuit leaders of his willingness to see lay people in all administrative positions in Jesuit schools except president and academic vice-president. John Tracy Ellis wrote in 1965 that while he did not think clergy should end their involvement in Catholic postsecondary institutions, "I do feel strongly that until the laity have been given really significant posts, i.e., policy-making posts, and have been made to feel that they are really a vital part of our colleges, we cannot look for the highest achievement."[97]

Furthermore, the movement in the late 1960s to reorganize the governing boards of Catholic colleges and universities originated among a small group of influential clergy and religious. Theodore Hesburgh and Paul Reinert, widely respected in both Catholic and non-Catholic educational circles, led efforts within Catholic higher education to add lay trustees and to give majority voice to nonclerics. They first convinced their fellow religious that relinquishing control to laity would strengthen their respective institutions, not secularize them; and both became public advocates of new governance structures. In January 1967, Hesburgh and Reinert announced that their universities planned to become the first major Catholic schools to revamp their boards of trustees. In the next five years, numerous Catholic postsecondary institutions made similar changes, following the pattern urged by Hesburgh, Reinert, and a few other leading Catholic educators.[98]

The rise of laity in Catholic higher education during the twentieth century mirrored the growing ambitions and prestige of lay Catholics in Catholic culture, increasing lay-clergy cooperation in Catholicism, and the development of more ecumenical attitudes in American society. Priests and religious dominated Catholic postsecondary institutions during the early decades of this century, mainly because of their better education and traditional status in the Catholic Church. Many lay Catholics lacked sufficient interest and training to pursue academic careers, and few of them could survive on the low salaries commonly paid by Catholic colleges and universities before World War II. Anxious to maintain the Catholic character of their schools, Catholic administrators hired non-Catholics with great reluctance before 1940. In addition, significant numbers of clergy and laity questioned whether lay teachers could fulfill the religious mission of Catholic higher education, and some feared that extensive lay involvement would result in secularization.

But conditions changed, especially after World War II. The dioceses and religious orders sponsoring Catholic postsecondary institutions could not provide sufficient personnel to meet the manpower needs resulting from educational expansion. Growing faculty militance influenced Catholic religious and academic officials to grant a larger role to lay professors. Moreover, continued domination of Catholic schools by clergy and religious threatened eligibility for federal and state aid, and the growing complexity and fiscal problems of Catholic institutions required a broader base of community and financial support. The warming religious climate in the United States encouraged Catholics to become involved in American culture and to include non-Catholics as faculty, administrators, and trustees in their colleges and universities. Finally, talented Catholic educators provided the leadership needed to incorporate lay people into all areas of the Catholic higher educational apostolate. Thus, Catholic and non-Catholic laity gradually moved from obscurity to prominence in Catholic higher education.

Notes

1. Hamilton, *The Story of Marquette University*, 268; *St. Ignatius College Catalogue*, Chicago, 1900-1901, 7-9; *St. Vincent's College Catalogue*, 1900-1901, 11-12; *St. Ignatius College Catalogue*, San Francisco, 1900-1901, 2; and *St. Benedict's College Catalogue*, Atchison, Kansas, 1903, 8-10.

2. Kernan, "The Catholic Layman in Higher Education," 381-85; Martin J. Stamm, "The Laicization of Corporate Governance of Twentieth Century American Catholic Higher Education," *Records of the American Catholic Historical Society of Philadelphia* 94 (March-December 1983): 88; and Gannon, *Up to the Present*, 139.

3. Daniel Callahan, *The Mind of the Catholic Layman* (New York: Charles Scribner's Sons, 1963), 62-71; and Cross, *The Emergence of Liberal Catholicism*, 168-69.

4. Cross, *The Emergence of Liberal Catholicism*, 168-69; Pope Leo XIII, "Testem Benevolentiae," in *Documents of American Catholic History*, ed. John Tracy Ellis (Milwaukee: Bruce Publishing Company, 1956), 556; and Callahan, *The Mind of the Catholic Layman*, 72-78.

5. O'Dea, *American Catholic Dilemma*, 109-27; Callahan, *The Mind of the Catholic Layman*, 52-78; and John A. Conway, S.J., "Conference of Catholic Colleges," *Woodstock Letters* 36 (1907): 258.

6. [William Agnew, S.J.] president of Creighton to [Matthew Germing, S.J.] provincial of the Missouri Province [late 1929], "Letters to Fr. Gen.," AMPSJ; Macelwane to Charles Cloud, S.J., president of St. Louis University, 23 November 1929, "Ledochowski and SLU reaction," AJCSLU.

7. Minutes of JEA Executive Committee meeting, Georgetown University, 10-12 April 1939, "Education: Coeducation," Drawer 77, ACPSJ.

8. Rooney to Small, 17 May 1963, "Memos on Special Subjects, 1961-1964," Box 20, JEA Collection, ABC.

9. Quoted in Gregory F. Lucey, S.J., "The Meaning and Maintenance of Catholicity as a Distinctive Characteristic of American Catholic Higher Education: A Case Study" (Ph.D. dissertation, University of Wisconsin-Madison, 1978), 195. For further perspectives on problems in hiring faculty in Catholic colleges and universities in recent decades, see Urban H. Fleege, "Our Resources: Actual and Potential in Catholic Higher Education," *National Catholic Educational Association Bulletin* 56 (August 1959): 113-15; Michael P. Walsh, S.J., "Catholic Universities--Problems and Prospects in the Changing Educational Scene," *National Catholic Educational Association Bulletin* 62 (August 1965): 163.

10. Ledochowski to American Jesuits, 7 June 1928, AMPSJ; National Catholic Educational Association, "Report on Faculty Competence according to Resolutions of the College and University Department, 1937 Louisville Convention," ACPSJ.

11. National Catholic Educational Association, "Report on Faculty Competence," 1937, ACPSJ; Jesuit Educational Association, "Report of the Commission on Liberal Arts Colleges," 10 April 1942, "Education #10," Drawer 74, ACPSJ.

12. Burns, "Failures of Our Higher Schools," 636; see also Andrew Corry, "Living Endowment," *Commonweal*, 19 October 1934, 580-81.

13. Arthur, "The University of Notre Dame, 1919-1933," 232-34; and "Report of the Committee on Insurance and Annuities," *National Catholic Educational Association Bulletin* 44 (August 1947): 217-18. See also John F. McCormick, S.J., "The Lay Instructor in the Catholic College," *National Catholic Educational Association Bulletin* 25 (August 1928): 148-50; Albert H. Poetker, S.J., "The Place of the Layman in Jesuit Schools," *Jesuit Educational Quarterly* 9 (June 1946): 13; and Power, *Catholic Higher Education in America*, 427.

14. Hugh Duce, S.J. to Edward B. Rooney, S.J., 18 August 1939, "1939-1940 JEA Ex. Comm.," Drawer 73, ACPSJ; and National Catholic Educational Association, "A Working

Paper: The Future Development of Catholic Institutions of Higher Education," 15 September 1966, "Educ-Phil.," Drawer 7, ACPSJ.

15. Salvaterra, "The Apostolate of the Intellect," 273; and *Directory of Catholic Colleges and Schools*, 1921.

16. Draft of JEA Constitution, 22 August 1938, "Rooney, #6," Drawer 74, ACPSJ; Ledochowski to American Jesuit provincials, 31 July 1939, ACPSJ; FitzGerald, *The Governance of Jesuit Colleges in the United States*, 85-88; and Jesuit Educational Association, *Directory, 1947-1948*, 3-18.

17. Oscar W. Perlmutter, "The Lay Professor," *Commonweal*, 11 April 1958, 31; Power, *Catholic Higher Education in America*, 386; and William Conley, "The Lay Teacher in Catholic Education," *National Catholic Educational Association Bulletin* 59 (August 1962): 26.

18. Schoenberg, *Paths to the Northwest*, 411; and John Janssens, S.J. to Leopold J. Robinson, S.J., provincial of the Oregon Province, 23 April 1947, "1947 provincials' meeting," ACPSJ.

19. Jesuit Educational Association, "Special Bulletin," 1 February 1939, ACPSJ; José Sanchez, "Cardinal Glennon and Academic Freedom at Saint Louis University: The Fleisher Case Revisited," *Gateway Heritage* 8 (Winter 1987-88): 2-11; John Leo, "Strike at St. John's," *Commonweal*, 28 January 1966, 504; and John F. Hunt and Terrence R. Connelly, *The Responsibility of Dissent: The Church and Academic Freedom* (New York: Sheed and Ward, 1969). For a recent study of the development and status of academic freedom on contemporary Catholic campuses, see James J. Annarelli, *Academic Freedom and Catholic Higher Education* (Westport, Conn.: Greenwood Press, 1987).

20. Wilfred M. Mallon, S.J., "Faculty Ranks, Tenure, and Academic Freedom," *National Catholic Educational Association Bulletin* 39 (August 1942): 194. See also Francis L. Meade, C.M., "Academic Freedom in Catholic Education," *National Catholic Educational Association Bulletin* 35 (August 1938): 109-14; Edward B. Rooney, S.J., "The Philosophy of Academic Freedom," in *A Philosophical Symposium on American Catholic Education*, ed. Hunter Guthrie, S.J. and Gerald G. Walsh, S.J. (New York: Fordham University Press, 1941), 116-28; and Philip Gleason, "Academic Freedom: Survey, Retrospect and Prospects," *National Catholic Educational Association Bulletin* 64 (November 1967): 67-73.

21. Robert Leader, "How the Landscape Has Changed," *Notre Dame Magazine* 13 (Spring 1984), 23; and "Marquette University Statutes (circa 1952)," in Lucey, "The Meaning and Maintenance of Catholicity," 305.

22. Report of the Inter-Province Committee on Studies, 1922, 6, Drawer 73, ACPSJ; and Maher to Roosevelt, 29 December 1941, "American Assistant," Box 20, JEA Collection, ABC. For perspectives on Catholic patriotism, see Dorothy Dohen, *Nationalism and American Catholicism* (New York: Sheed and Ward, 1967).

23. Power, *Catholic Higher Education in America*, 104-11 and 429-30; James J. Maguire, "A Family Affair," *Commonweal*, 10 November 1961, 71; and Stamm, "The Laicization of Corporate Governance of Twentieth Century American Catholic Higher Education," 88.

24. Ledochowski to Matthew Germing, S.J., provincial of the Missouri Province, 22 October 1927, "Letters of Fr. Gen.," AMPSJ; idem, 28 December 1927, ibid.; and minutes of the Jesuit provincials' meeting, Detroit, 23-24 April 1930, 10-11, ACPSJ. For similar reservations, see comments by William Fitzgerald, S.J., a member of the Oregon Province, concerning the 1929 report of the Inter-Province Committee on Studies, n.d., Drawer 73, ACPSJ.

25. For a summary of these deliberations, see Edward B. Rooney, S.J., "The Control of Jesuit Colleges and Universities," in "Proceedings of Conference of Presidents of Jesuit Colleges and Universities," Georgetown University, 3-4 January 1958, 20-27, ACPSJ; and FitzGerald, *The Governance of Jesuit Colleges*, 120-21.

26. Edward B. Rooney, S.J., personal memorandum of conference with Vincent McCormick, S.J., assistant to the Jesuit superior general for the United States, 18 August

1957, File 22.01, Box 35, JEA Collection, ABC; idem., 3-13 December 1959, "Confidential memoranda of Edward Rooney, S.J.," vol. 1, JEA Collection, ABC; minutes of JEA Executive Committee meeting, Loyola University, Chicago, 13-15 April 1960, 3, "1959-60 JEA Ex. Comm.," Drawer 73, ACPSJ; and Janssens to Leo D. Sullivan, S.J., 25 November 1958, "Confidential Memos of Edward Rooney, 1961-1965," Box 20, JEA Collection, ABC.

27. "Lay Professors in Catholic Colleges," *America*, 3 May 1958, 160.

28. For general reactions among Catholics, see Gerard J. Dalcourt, "Lay Control of Catholic Colleges," *America*, 14 October 1967, 412-14; and Andrew M. Greeley, "Myths and Fads in Catholic Higher Education," *America*, 11 November 1967, 422-25.

29. "Proceedings of the JEA Commission on Colleges and Universities," 22-27 June 1966, 44-46, ACPSJ; Dennis Bonnette, "The Doctrinal Crisis in Catholic Colleges and Universities and Its Effect upon Education," *Social Justice Review* 60 (November 1967): 222.

30. Pedro Arrupe, S.J., superior general of the Society of Jesus, to Linus Thro, S.J., provincial of the Missouri Province, 6 April 1967, "Letters of Fr. Gen.," AMPSJ; and John C. Ford, S.J., "Memorandum on Ownership and Government of St. Louis University in view of the contemplated enlargement of the Board of Trustees" [1967], "SLU Pres.," AMPSJ.

31. A.J. Brumbaugh, ed., *American Universities and Colleges* (Washington, D.C.: American Council on Education, 1948), 355 and 512.

32. For a discussion of the Catholic entry into professional education, see Power, *Catholic Higher Education in America*, 191-237.

33. Statistics on lay faculty in Catholic colleges and universities were compiled from institutional data published in *Directory of Catholic Colleges and Schools*, 1921; and idem, 1928, 38.

34. *St. Ignatius College Catalogue*, Chicago, 1908-1909, 26; *Fordham University Bulletin of Information*, 1908-1909, 16-17; *St. Ignatius College Catalogue*, San Francisco, 1908-1909, 2; *St. Vincent's College Catalogue*, Los Angeles, 1908-1909, 7; and *Georgetown University General Catalogue*, 1908-1909, 59-60.

35. Wilfred M. Mallon, S.J., "The Jesuit College: An Investigation into Factors Affecting the Efficiency of the Jesuit College in the Central States" (Ph.D. dissertation, St. Louis University, 1932), 381; and *Directory of Catholic Colleges and Schools*, 1921.

36. McCormick, "The Lay Instructor in the Catholic College," 143-44; Mallon, "The Jesuit College," 381. Similarly, of 281 liberal arts faculty in eleven Jesuit schools in the Midwest in 1927, 154 (55%) were laymen; see "Teaching Loads in 1927-28," *The Province News-Letter* 10 (February 1929): 38, AMPSJ.

37. Jesuit Educational Association, "Report of the Commission on Liberal Arts Colleges," 10 April 1942, "Education #10, Rooney, 1942," Drawer 74, ACPSJ; *Catholic Colleges and Schools in the United States*, 1942, 9; and William McGucken, S.J., "The White Steed and Education," *Thought* 14 (September 1939): 362-63.

38. See data on faculty in *Catholic Colleges and Schools*, 1942; and Crocker, *The Student Guide to Catholic Colleges and Universities*.

39. Paul J. Reiss, "Faculty and Administration: The Jesuit-Lay Character," *Jesuit Educational Quarterly* 32 (October 1969): 107; and *Project One: The Jesuit Apostolate of Education in the United States*, 6 vols. (Washington, D.C.: Jesuit Conference, 1974-1975), vol. 2: *An Overview*, 134.

40. "Report of the Commission on Liberal Arts Colleges," 10 April 1942, ACPSJ; James F. Whelan, S.J., compiler, *Catholic Colleges of the United States of America 1952-1953* (New Orleans: Loyola University, 1954), 131; and "Faculty: Jesuit Colleges and Universities 1953-1954," in "Lay Faculty in Jesuit Schools," Box 34, JEA Collection, ABC.

41. "Faculty: Jesuit Colleges and Universities, 1953-1954," in "Lay Faculty in Jesuit Schools," Box 34, JEA Collection, ABC; and Merrimon Cuninggim, "Examples of

Church-Related Colleges," in *Church Related Higher Education: Perceptions and Perspectives,* ed. Robert Rue Parsonage (Valley Forge: Judson Press, 1978), 62-63.

42. Lucey, "The Maintenance of Catholicity," 173; and Carol Weiss Rosenberg, "All in the Family," *Notre Dame Magazine* 13 (Spring 1984): 3. In 1987, approximately 50% of Marquette's faculty were not Catholics; see minutes, Committee on Faculty, Marquette University, 12 February 1987, 1.

43. Richard W. Solberg and Merton P. Strommen, *How Church-Related Are Church-Related Colleges?* (New York: Division for Mission in North America, Lutheran Church, 1980), 55.

44. Minutes of the JEA Executive Committee meeting, Loyola College, Baltimore, 29-30 September 1945, Drawer 73, "1945-46 JEA Ex. Comm.," ACPSJ; and "Report of the Committee on Faculty Welfare," *National Catholic Educational Association Bulletin* 54 (August 1957): 103-4.

45. W. Robert Bokelman and Louis A. D'Amico, "A Comparison of Salaries and Student Costs at Catholic Institutions with Salaries and Costs at Other Private Institutions, Including Regional Variations, 1960-61," *National Catholic Educational Association Bulletin* 58 (November 1961): 27-32.

46. McKevitt, *The University of Santa Clara,* 291; Robert Hassenger, "Catholic Colleges and Universities after the Second 100 Years," in *Catholics/U.S.A.,* ed. William T. Liu and Nathaniel J. Pallone (New York: John Wiley & Sons, Inc., 1970), 208; and Greeley, *From Backwater to Mainstream,* 52.

47. Mallon, "Faculty Ranks, Tenure, and Academic Freedom," 188-89; and Association of Jesuit Colleges and Universities, minutes of meeting, Cincinnati, 9-10 January 1971, AJCU file, Drawer 79, ACPSJ; and Power, *Catholic Higher Education in America,* 422-23.

48. American Association of University Professors, *AAUP Policy Documents and Reports* (Washington, D.C.: American Association of University Professors, 1977), 1; and "Land O'Lakes Statement: The Nature of the Contemporary Catholic University," in *The Catholic University: A Modern Appraisal,* ed. Neil McCluskey, S.J. (Notre Dame: University of Notre Dame Press, 1970), 336.

49. Responses of the JEA Board of Governors, 1958, Drawer 73, ACPSJ; and Fitz-Gerald, *The Governance of Jesuit Colleges,* 154.

50. "Lay Professors in Catholic Colleges," *America,* 3 May 1958, 160; Edward P.J. Corbett, "Letter on 'The Lay Professor,'" *Commonweal,* 9 May 1958, 154; and *St. John's University Bulletin,* 1958-59. See also Gerard Hinrichs, "Faculty Participation in the Government of Catholic Colleges and Universities," *American Association of University Professors Bulletin* 50 (December 1964): 336-42.

51. Power, *Catholic Higher Education in America,* 426-28; Paul C. Reinert, S.J., "The Imperatives Determining the Future of Jesuit Higher Education," *Jesuit Educational Quarterly* 32 (October 1969): 66; and Theodore Hesburgh, C.S.C., "The Changing Face of Catholic Higher Education," *National Catholic Educational Association Bulletin* 66 (August 1969): 56-57.

52. *Directory of Catholic Colleges and Schools,* 1921, 362 and 551; and *Directory, Jesuit Educational Association,* 1945.

53. Hamilton, *The Story of Marquette University,* 249; Deferrari, *Memoirs,* 89; *Directory, Jesuit Educational Association,* 1955-1956 and 1960-1961; and Edward B. Rooney, S.J., "1961 President's Report," Drawer 73, 73-74, ACPSJ.

54. *Directory, Jesuit Educational Association,* 1960-1961; *University of Notre Dame General Bulletin,* 1960-61, 6-8; *Bulletin of Providence College,* 1960-1961, 16; *Trinity College,* 1960-1961, 83; *Duquesne University: The Combined Catalog,* 1961-1962, 5; *Bulletin of the College of St. Catherine,* 1960-1962, 85; *Manhattan College Catalogue,* 1959-1960, 8-9.

55. Edward B. Rooney, S.J. to Pedro Arrupe, S.J., superior general of the Society of Jesus, 16 October 1965, "Corr. w. Fr. Gen./Vicar - 1965," Box 36, JEA Collection, ABC;

Directory, Jesuit Educational Association, 1967-1968; *Directory, Association of Jesuit Colleges and Universities*, 1988-89.

56. Statistics on the number of lay presidents were compiled from institutional descriptions in Crocker, *The Student Guide to Catholic Colleges.*

57. Jencks and Riesman, *The Academic Revolution*, 354, fn. 35; Lucey, "The Maintenance of Catholicity," 124; Gene I. Maeroff, "Jesuit Colleges Strive to Preserve Elite Tradition," *New York Times*, 27 March 1985, 10; and Martin J. Stamm, "Evaluating Presidential Leadership: A Case Study in Redefining Sponsorship," *Current Issues in Catholic Higher Education* 4 (Winter 1984): 29.

58. Arthur, "The University of Notre Dame, 1919-1933," 124-38.

59. Labaj, "The Development of the Department of Education at Saint Louis University, 1900-1942," 20, fn. 15; Albert Fox, S.J., president of Marquette University, to Francis McMenamy, S.J., provincial of the Missouri Province, 30 March 1924, Drawer 1, Barnett Papers, AMU; Eugene Weare, "Laymen on a College Council," *America*, 22 February 1930, 475.

60. "Summary of Answers, Questionnaire on a Lay Advisory Board" [1954 or 1955], in "Regents: Board of Regents," Drawer 9, ACPSJ; and Frederick E. Wefle, S.J., "Functions of the Advisory Board of Trustees," *Jesuit Educational Quarterly* 18 (October 1955): 87-94.

61. Goodchild, "The Mission of the Catholic University in the Midwest," 565-669 and 701-75; Stamm, "The Laicization of Corporate Governance," 88-89; and *Directory, Association of Jesuit Colleges and Universities*, 1986-1987, 19.

62. "An Innovation in Higher Education: The Board of Trustees of Saint Louis University," 1967, 1, AJCSLU; Thomas J. Schlereth, *The University of Notre Dame: A Portrait of Its History and Campus* (Notre Dame, Ind.: University of Notre Dame Press, 1976), 221; and Stamm, "The Laicization of Corporate Governance," 92.

63. Paul Reinert, S.J., "First Meeting of a Board," *Jesuit Educational Quarterly* 30 (October 1967): 116; Lucey, "The Maintenance of Catholicity," 124; Stamm, "The Laicization of Corporate Governance," 89.

64. Stamm, "The Laicization of Corporate Governance," 89; and idem, "The Emerging Guardianship of American Catholic Higher Education," *Occasional Papers on Catholic Higher Education* 5 (Summer 1979): 29, fn. 9.

65. Report of the Inter-Province Committee on Studies, 1924, 2, Drawer 73, ACPSJ.

66. *Project One*, vol. 1: *An Overview*, 55-59; and *Supplementum Catalogorum Societatis Iesu*, 1989, table 3.

67. *Jesuit Educational Quarterly* 8 (January 1946), after 180; idem., 23 (January 1965), table 2; and *Directory, Association of Jesuit Colleges and Universities*, 1989-90, 7.

68. *Directory of the Jesuit Educational Association*, 1945, 13-16, Drawer 3, Barnett Papers, AMU; and *Directory, Jesuit Secondary Education Association*, 1970-1971, 38-44.

69. John Janssens, S.J., superior general of the Jesuit order, to A. William Crandell, S.J., provincial of the New Orleans Province, 1 April 1953, "1953 Provincials' meeting," ACPSJ; Janssens to Henry Schultheis, S.J., provincial of the Oregon Province [29 July 1955?], "1955 Provincials' meeting," ACPSJ; and Janssens to Carroll O'Sullivan, S.J., provincial of the California Province, 3 March 1960, "1960 Provincials' meeting," ACPSJ.

70. Factors influencing the expansion of Catholic higher education after World War II will be analyzed in chapter 5 of this study.

71. For a discussion of revised hiring criteria in one Catholic university, changes typical of new approaches in Catholic higher education since 1965, see Lucey, "The Maintenance of Catholicity," 172-99. See also Jude P. Dougherty et al., "The Secularization of Western Culture and the Catholic College and University," *Current Issues in Catholic Higher Education* 2 (Summer 1981): 7-23.

72. See MacGregor, "The Catholic Lay Professor," 513-14; Corry, "Living Endowment," 580; Ward Stames, "The Lay Faculty," *Commonweal*, 12 April 1935, 667-68; and Jeremiah K.

Durick, "The Lay Faculty: A Reply," *Commonweal*, 19 April 1935, 699-700.

73. Theodore Maynard, "The Lay Faculty Again," *Commonweal*, 17 May 1935, 64.

74. Charles Rice [pseud.], "The Plight of the professor [sic]," *America*, 8 September 1951, 543-44 and 548; John J. Meng, "American Thought: Contributions of Catholic Thought and Thinkers," *National Catholic Educational Association Bulletin* 53 (August 1956): 117-18; and Francis Canavan, S.J., "Academic Revolution at St. John's," *America*, 7 August 1965, 136.

75. Willis D. Nutting, "Catholic Higher Education in America," *New Blackfriars* 32 (July 1951): 342-43.

76. Perlmutter, "The Lay Professor," 31-34. For responses, see *Commonweal*, 9 May 1958, 154-56 and 30 May 1958, 233-36; *America*, 3 May 1958, 160 and 5 July 1958, 394-95; and Stephen P. Ryan, "State of the Question," *America*, 4 October 1958, 17-19.

77. John Donovan, *The Academic Man in the Catholic College* (New York: Sheed and Ward, 1964), 173-74 and 183-84. See also John F. Brosnan, "Catholic Higher Education—A View from Outside the Institution," *National Catholic Educational Association Bulletin* 57 (August 1959): 118-19; and Robert O. Bowen, "The Lay Faculty on the Jesuit Campus," *Ramparts* 1 (March 1963): 16-20.

78. Donovan, *The Academic Man in the Catholic College*, 174; "Chapters with 100 or More Active Members," *AAUP Bulletin* 53 (March 1967): 84; and "Institutional Distribution and Chapter Officers," *AAUP Bulletin* 42 (Spring 1956): 212-30. See also Henry J. Browne, "Catholics and the AAUP," *Commonweal*, 5 October 1956, 10-12.

79. Leo Kennedy, "The Role of the Faculty in Academic Policy Formation," *National Catholic Educational Association Bulletin* 54 (August 1957): 157-60; and Francis E. Kearns, "Handkerchief Heads and Clerical Collars," *Ramparts* 2 (Winter 1964): 18.

80. Matthew W. Finkin, Robert A. Goldstein, and Woodley B. Osbourne, *A Primer on Collective Bargaining for College & University Faculty* (n.p., American Association of University Professors, 1975), i-ii. Concerning the formation of faculty unions in Catholic colleges and universities, see also Harold L. Stansell, S.J., *Regis: On the Crest of the West* (Denver: Regis Educational Corporation, 1977), 221-22; and Muller, *The University of Detroit*, 344-45. Faculty bargaining units existed at ten Catholic postsecondary institutions in 1988; see "Fact File: Colleges and Universities with Collective-Bargaining Agents in 1988," *The Chronicle of Higher Education*, 12 July 1989, 14 and 16.

81. Lerond Curry, *Protestant-Catholic Relations in America, World War I through Vatican II* (Lexington, Ky.: The University Press of Kentucky, 1972), 60-89; Eugene C. Bianchi, *John XXIII and American Protestants* (Washington, D.C.: Corpus Books, 1968); and Walter M. Abbott, S.J., general editor, *The Documents of Vatican II* (New York: America Press, 1966).

82. Rooney to Harold Small, S.J., assistant to the Jesuit superior general for the United States, 17 May 1963, "Memos on Special Subjects, 1961-1964," Box 20, JEA Collection, ABC.

83. "A Study of Some Problems in Administration of Jesuit Higher Educational Institutions," 26, in minutes of JEA Executive Committee meeting, San Francisco, 17-20 August 1962, Appendix B, Drawer 73, ACPSJ; "Background," May 1967 provincials' meeting, Drawer 85, ACPSJ; and minutes of JEA Commission on Colleges and Universities, Washington, D.C., 13-14 October 1967, Appendix A: "Non-Catholics as Teachers of Sacred Scripture in Jesuit Colleges, A Policy Statement," 18, in "Presidents' meetings, 1967," Drawer 9, ACPSJ.

84. St. Louis University, "An Innovation in Higher Learning," 2, AJCSLU; Schlereth, *The University of Notre Dame*, 221; and Earl J. McGrath and Gerald E. DuPont, S.S.E., *The Future Governance of Catholic Higher Education in the United States* (pamphlet), n.p., summer 1967, 5-6 and 20.

85. Paul Reinert, S.J., "The Responsibility of American Catholic Higher Education in Meeting National Needs," *National Catholic Educational Association Bulletin* 60 (August

1964): 140-41; Neil G. McCluskey, S.J., "Board of Trustees of a Jesuit College or University from an Academic and Administrative Standpoint," in "Proceedings of the Jesuit Educational Association Commission on Colleges and Universities," Spokane, 22-27 June 1966, 55-57, ACPSJ; and Anthony Seidl, "Planning for the Future," in *The Shape of Catholic Higher Education,* ed. Robert Hassenger (Chicago: University of Chicago Press, 1967), 337-48.

86. Paul C. Reinert, S.J., "Proposal for Reorganization of the Board of Trustees of St. Louis University and of the University's Legal Relationship to the Jesuit Community," 15 September 1966, "President's Report, Oct., 1966—March, 1967," Drawer 73, ACPSJ; and Schlereth, *The University of Notre Dame,* 221. See also Neil G. McCluskey, S.J., "The New Catholic College," *America,* 25 March 1967, 414-17.

87. Horace Mann League of the United States v. Board of Public Works, 242 Md. 645, *Atlantic Reporter* 220 A.2d. 51 (Court of Appeals of Maryland, 1966). See also "3 Church Schools Lose Public Funds," *New York Times,* 3 June 1966, 24; and McCluskey, "Board of Trustees of a Jesuit College or University," 57-58, ACPSJ.

88. "Church Colleges Lose an Aid Test," *New York Times,* 15 November 1966, 1 and 30; minutes of JEA Commission on Colleges and Universities, Pittsburgh, 11-12 January 1969, 5-9, "JEA—1969," Drawer 79, ACPSJ. In Tilton v. Richardson (1971), the U.S. Supreme Court ruled that federal aid to church-related higher education was constitutional. For a recent discussion of this case, see Joseph R. Preville, "Catholic Colleges and Supreme Court: An Historical Review of Tilton v. Richardson," *Journal of Church and State* 30 (Spring 1988): 291-307.

89. "Proceedings of the JEA Commission on Colleges and Universities," Los Angeles, 13-15 January 1967, ACPSJ; idem, Minneapolis, 13-14 January 1968, "JEA—1968," Drawer 79, ACPSJ. See also Francis Gallagher, "Observations Arising from the Horace Mann Case," *National Catholic Educational Association Bulletin* 63 (August 1966): 232-38; and Robert Drinan, S.J., "The Challenge to Catholic Educators in the Maryland Case," *National Catholic Educational Association Bulletin* 63 (May 1967): 3-7.

90. Burns, "Failures of Our Higher Schools," 636; Maher to Rooney, 11 June 1939 and Rooney to Maher, 13 July 1939, "Corr. w. Fr. Maher, 1937-1942," Box 20, JEA Collection, ABC. See also McCormick, "The Lay Instructor in the Catholic College," 142-55; and Poetker, "The Place of the Layman in Jesuit Schools," 14-15.

91. Matthew Germing, S.J., provincial of the Missouri Province, to Wlodimir Ledochowski, S.J., superior general of the Society of Jesus, 3 January 1930, "Letters to Fr. Gen.," AMPSJ; and [William Agnew, S.J.] president of Creighton to Matthew Germing, S.J., [late 1929], ibid.

92. Cloud to Thomas M. Knapp, S.J., 5 October 1929, "Ledochowski and SLU Reaction," ASLU; and Thomas E. Curley, "Robert I. Gannon, President of Fordham University, 1936-49: A Jesuit Educator" (Ph.D. dissertation, New York University, 1974), 115-24.

93. At least a few clerics had called for better salaries and benefits for lay teachers in the 1920s and 1930s, but the serious financial problems plaguing Catholic higher education during these years precluded much improvement. For instance, see reports of the Inter-Province Committee on Studies, 1924 and 1926, Drawer 73, ACPSJ; and *National Catholic Educational Association Bulletin* 33 (November 1936): 113.

94. "Report of the Committee on Insurance and Annuities," *National Catholic Educational Association Bulletin* 44 (August 1947): 214-20; Edward B. Rooney, S.J., "Report of the Executive Director, 1948," *Jesuit Educational Quarterly* 11 (June 1948): 9; and "Report of the Committee on Faculty Welfare," *National Catholic Educational Association Bulletin* 51 (August 1954): 208-11; and James J. Maguire, "A Family Affair," 172-73.

95. Minutes of meeting of the presidents and deans of the graduate schools of the central regional unit of the Jesuit Educational Association, Loyola University, Chicago,

21 November 1952, 8, "Grad Schools: Other Provinces' Meetings," Drawer 8, ACPSJ; Edward B. Rooney, S.J. to American Jesuit provincials, 29 September 1954, "JEA Correspondence, 1948-1955," Drawer 74, ACPSJ.

96. A. A. Lemieux, S.J., "Relations of Jesuits and Lay Faculties in Jesuit Universities and Colleges," in "Proceedings of the JEA Conference of Presidents," Boston College, 10-11 January 1960, 28-32, Drawer 77, ACPSJ; and James F. Maguire, S.J., "The Role of the Layman in Jesuit Colleges and Universities of the United States," in "Proceedings of the JEA Commission of Presidents of Jesuit Colleges and Universities," University of Santa Clara, 17-20 August 1964, 124-25, ACPSJ.

97. Minutes of Jesuit provincials' meeting, Buffalo, 2-4 October 1964, Drawer 85, ACPSJ; Reinert, "The Responsibility of American Catholic Higher Education in Meeting National Needs," 137-38; Ellis to Neil McCluskey, S.J., 16 November 1965, cited in McCluskey, "Board of Trustees of a Jesuit College or University," 55.

98. Leonard Buder, "Notre Dame Will Grant Laymen Greater Voice in Setting Policy," *New York Times*, 20 January 1967, 40; idem, "Jesuits Giving Up Control of St. Louis U.," *New York Times*, 22 January 1967, 1 and 56; FitzGerald, *The Governance of Jesuit Colleges*, 197-202; and Schlereth, *The University of Notre Dame*, 221.

5

Catholics and Educational Expansion after 1945

Catholic colleges and universities in the United States increased rapidly in number, size, and programs from 1945 to the late 1960s. Yet the causes of this growth and its relationship to the upward mobility and cultural assimilation of American Catholics remain obscure. Moreover, while Catholics as a group have advanced socially and economically in the last four decades, the Catholic system of higher education has not achieved comparable gains in quality and status, despite favorable conditions. An analysis of Catholic life and educational development between 1945 and 1970 isolates key reasons for the expansion of Catholic colleges and universities during these years, and it also helps explain the continued failure of Catholicism to build a network of postsecondary institutions exerting wide influence in American academic circles.

Changes in Catholic culture and American higher education after World War II shaped the evolution of Catholic colleges and universities during the postwar decades. Before 1945, American Catholics lagged well behind Jews and most Protestant denominations in social and economic standing. While aligning themselves with Roosevelt and the Democratic Party in the 1930s had improved the image and political status of Catholics, members of the Catholic Church still remained politically underrepresented in the early 1940s. In 1943, Catholics held only 13% of the seats in Congress (59 in the House and

10 in the Senate), though they made up approximately one-quarter of the American population.[1]

But starting in the late 1940s, Catholics gradually moved into the mainstream of American life, rising in income, political power, and social position. World War II increased contact between Protestants and Catholics, reducing barriers on both sides and fostering mutual acceptance. More important, Catholics after 1945 benefited from the cumulative effects of the G.I. Bill, the growth of labor unions, higher wages won by collective bargaining, and an expanding economy. Roper and Gallup polls in 1964 reported that Catholics outranked Protestants economically, findings confirmed by data compiled by Andrew Greeley in the early 1970s.[2]

The election of John Kennedy as the first Catholic president of the United States confirmed the arrival of Catholics in American politics and society. By 1977, one-third of state governors belonged to the Catholic Church, a notable change since 1930 when none was a Catholic. Furthermore, every Congress since 1960 has had at least one hundred Catholics in the House and Senate. A study of the 101st Congress elected in November 1988 showed that 120 representatives and nineteen senators were members of the Catholic Church, giving Catholics more seats in the national government than warranted by their percentage of the American population.[3]

As Catholics progressed in secular society, Catholicism flourished as a largely distinct, cohesive religious subculture until the mid-1960s. Between 1940 and 1960, membership in the American Catholic Church doubled to 42,000,000, partly the result of immigration and conversions to the Catholic faith but mainly due to natural increase. Though the move toward secularism accelerated in the United States and the rest of the Western world in the immediate postwar decades, most American Catholics remained firm in their religious beliefs and exercises. According to national polls conducted by the University of Michigan Survey Research Center in 1957, 81% of Catholic men and 88% of Catholic women surveyed reported that they attended church regularly or often, compared with 53% of Protestant males and 69% of Protestant females.[4] The vast majority of Catholics adhered to such religious practices as abstaining from meat on Fridays, and they accepted the spiritual authority of the pope and other clerical leaders. Much of their social life revolved around parish and parochial school events, activities reinforcing Catholic identity and values.[5]

But the conservative, relatively closed world of American Catholicism changed radically under the impact of the Second Vatican Council (1962-1965) and the general upheaval in American culture during the 1960s. The majority of bishops present at Vatican II approved decrees mandating sweeping reforms in the Catholic Church, and they also urged an end to defensiveness and isolation from contemporary society. In addition, student protests, racial violence, and the Vietnam War disrupted wider society. Such cultural and religious changes eroded the previous unity characterizing Catholic life in the United States. Catholics frequently found themselves caught up in controversies over liturgy, birth control, and ecclesiastical authority.

The turmoil within Catholicism generated doubts about the long-standing Catholic commitment to a separate educational network. Though acknowledging the need for certain kinds of Catholic schools, Mary Perkins Ryan in her 1964 book *Are Parochial Schools the Answer?* questioned whether "there should be a Catholic school *system*, maintained as part of the very structure of the Church." Leonard Swidler declared in an article published in *Commonweal* in 1965 that "It seems to me that the time has arrived to raise the question whether the Catholic Church in the United States as an institution, ought to start a massive withdrawal from the *business* of higher education." By the late 1960s, all levels of Catholic education clearly suffered from a crisis in purpose as well as from severe financial problems.[6]

Like Catholicism, American higher education changed greatly after 1945, affected most powerfully by surging enrollment and extensive financial support from the federal government. When World War II ended, the nation's colleges and universities registered fewer than 1,000,000 students; but by 1947, the total had soared to 2,300,000, far beyond predictions. Attendance grew steadily in succeeding years, reaching nearly 8,000,000 in 1970 and requiring construction of numerous classrooms, libraries, and residence halls. The 286,000 doctoral degrees earned in American higher education between 1948 and 1970 more than tripled the total earned during the previous eighty-seven years.[7]

Veterans taking advantage of the G.I. Bill accounted for much of the early jump in college registration. But enrollment growth after 1950 stemmed from changed perceptions and expectations of higher education. More Americans recognized the economic value of college degrees, prompting higher percentages of the 18-21 age group to attend college. Also, some educators wanted postsecondary institutions to perform a less elitist, more egalitarian function in national life. The President's Commission on Higher Education, appointed by President Truman in 1946, declared the following year that colleges and universities should not consider themselves "merely the instrument for producing an intellectual elite; they must become the means by which every citizen, youth, and adult is enabled and encouraged to carry his education, formal and informal, as far as his native capacities permit."

Furthermore, the public increasingly expected colleges and universities to provide the training and technology needed by business, industry, and the armed forces, especially during the Cold War and after Russia successfully launched its Sputnik satellite in 1957.[8]

But without massive federal aid, American colleges and universities could never have accommodated postwar demand for education. The institutions themselves lacked the necessary financial resources to fund needed programs and construction; and many educators sought assistance from federal sources. Large-scale government aid to higher education actually began during World War II with research contracts. It continued afterwards with the G.I. Bill and transferral of government-surplus buildings to schools for use as classrooms and housing. Counting educational benefits to veterans, federal expenditures for higher education in the 1947 fiscal year amounted to $2.5 billion, one-half of the total income of American colleges and universities that year. Lobbying for federal support of postsecondary education intensified after the Truman Commission recommended in 1947 and 1948 that the national government appropriate money for scholarships, fellowships, and additional facilities in public colleges and universities. Eventually, such legislation as the College Housing Act of 1950, the National Defense Education Act of 1958, and the Higher Education Act of 1965 provided billions of dollars for student aid, research, and new buildings.[9]

Not all educators immediately endorsed the growing federal role in American higher education. Though not advocating a halt to existing programs, a commission established by the Association of American Universities declared in 1952 that "it is time to stop the drift to *new forms* of federal subsidy." Their position reflected the fears of some officials in private colleges and universities that government control would follow federal aid; consequently, they preferred that additional funds come from nongovernment sources. But rising student numbers, inadequate institutional resources, and growing concern about educational quality during the 1950s and 1960s eroded such opposition; and institutions became dependent on federal support.[10]

Amid the changing educational, religious, and social context of American society following World War II, colleges and universities in the United States became larger and more complex, rising nearly 800% in enrollment between 1945 and 1970. The Catholic segment of American higher education grew at a slower rate; the number of students in Catholic postsecondary institutions rose from approximately 92,000 in the 1944-1945 academic year to 220,000 three years later and to 430,000 by 1970, an increase of 430%. For instance, St. Bonaventure, a school operated by the Franciscan order near Buffalo,

New York, registered fewer than 300 students in September 1945; but two years later its enrollment totaled more than 1,700. The student body at Boston College swelled from 2,000 in 1945 to 11,000 twenty-five years later.[11]

Besides the expansion among existing schools, the Catholic post-secondary educational network added forty-one senior colleges and twenty junior colleges for lay students between 1945 and 1967. New Catholic institutions opened in such places as Dallas, Houston, San Diego, Syracuse, and Wheeling, cities previously unserved by Catholic higher education. In addition, Catholic religious orders of men and women founded fifty-one schools (seventeen four-year colleges and thirty-four junior colleges) after 1950 for the training of their own members.[12]

Graduate education also assumed new prominence in Catholic schools after 1945 as master's programs became common and production of Ph.D.s increased. Boston College admitted its first doctoral students in 1953; and by 1967, it offered degrees in twenty fields. Notre Dame expanded its areas of Ph.D. research from seven in 1944 to fifteen in 1960 to twenty-four in 1982. Just as American higher education as a whole conferred most (81%) of its doctorates after World War II, so did the Catholic colleges and universities. Of the 10,892 doctorates awarded by Catholic universities through 1970, 80% (8,439) were granted after 1948.[13]

Various educational, religious-cultural, social, and economic causes accounted for the expansion of Catholic higher education after World War II. First, members of Catholic ethnic groups increasingly sought collegiate training after 1945, creating pressure on Catholic colleges and universities to admit more students and to add new programs. In 1940, an estimated 300,000 Catholic students attended American institutions of higher learning; forty years later, they totaled approximately three million.[14] The percentage of Catholics in the 17-25 age group enrolled in college rose from 19% during the 1930s to 45% in the 1960s, 2% above the national average. By the time of the Vietnam War, 59% of college-age Irish Catholics attended postsecondary institutions, a higher rate than any Gentile group in American culture except Scandinavian Protestants, with whom they were tied. The educational levels of German, Polish, and Italian Catholics during the late 1960s also exceeded the national norm, while Catholics of Slavic origin fell only 1% below it.[15]

Unless they responded favorably to the educational desires of their clientele, Catholic educators realized that they risked alienating local support vital to the development of Catholic higher education. For example, Jesuit college and university deans from the Midwest and

South acknowledged in 1953 that if their institutions refused to admit more freshmen, they faced a growing public relations problem. Moreover, these officials warned, "It is a fact that when the public makes demands, we must try to meet the demands, or be in danger of going out of existence." Edward Rooney, S.J., head of the Jesuit Educational Association, stressed in discussions with the Jesuit superior general in 1954 and 1955 that a strict no-growth policy "would sound rather callous on our part" and "seems untenable."[16]

Catholic educational leaders also recognized that if their institutions did not offer courses of the type and quality desired by Catholic students, more Catholics would enroll in non-Catholic schools. Registration of Catholics at secular colleges and universities grew steadily after World War II, increasing from approximately 140,000 in 1940 to 300,000 in 1950, and to 920,000 in 1967. Nearly 4,000 Catholics attended Columbia University in 1964, approximately 25% of the total enrollment; and by 1970, Catholics constituted 18% of the freshman class at Princeton, compared with 7% in the mid-1920s.[17]

A second factor in postwar Catholic educational expansion resulted from concerns about protecting Catholic faith and culture. Before the 1960s, many Catholics viewed secular schools with deep suspicion, regarding them as hostile to Catholic religious beliefs and cultural values. Clashes over aid to parochial schools and the danger of communism during the late 1940s and early 1950s confirmed negative feelings toward non-Catholic America and increased Catholic defensiveness. Consequently, numerous Catholic students wanting collegiate training but anxious to maintain their ethnic and religious heritage sought the reassuring social and academic atmosphere of Catholic colleges and universities.[18]

Between 1945 and 1960, Catholic educators commonly discouraged Catholics from attending secular schools, urging instead attendance at Catholic institutions. Asked in 1946 to recommend American universities suitable for graduates of a Catholic high school in Hong Kong, a Jesuit administrator in the California Province responded that he would not advise any Catholic to attend non-Catholic higher education. He warned that "The great majority of professors [in secular institutions] are materialists, or at best indifferentists," adding that Newman Clubs were admitted failures. Catholic high school personnel in the 1950s often declined to write letters of recommendation for their graduates applying to non-Catholic institutions, and a few Catholic schools even refused to send student transcripts to secular colleges and universities.[19]

Furthermore, officials in Catholic elementary and secondary schools commonly expected Catholic higher education to provide "Catholic-minded" teachers and administrators for their institutions.

A 1950 study of Catholic educational needs reported that to accommodate enrollment increases projected for the coming decade, Catholic grammar and high schools required almost 50,000 additional teachers. But as George Rock, dean of the graduate school at Catholic University, emphasized in 1953, Catholic graduate programs did not currently train enough classroom instructors even though "they know that the education of Catholic teachers, both religious and lay, is inherent in their purpose in order to maintain and to improve the whole Catholic educational program."[20]

To meet the rising demand for higher education under Catholic auspices and to strengthen Catholicism, lay Catholics, pastors, and bishops frequently urged that Catholic postsecondary institutions expand, especially in sections of the country lacking Catholic colleges and universities. Francis M. Crowley, dean of the school of education at Fordham, judged in 1949 that "The zeal of the Catholic laity in the cause of Catholic education has never been greater," noting that they had petitioned for parish schools, high schools, and colleges. In 1946, Archbishop John McNicholas of Cincinnati requested that Xavier University introduce graduate work.[21] Edward Rooney, S.J. reported to the superior general of the Jesuit order in 1954 that American Jesuits were under heavy pressure from the hierarchy and Catholic laity, especially alumni of Jesuit institutions, to increase enrollment.[22]

Responding to these desires for a Catholic educational environment and for teachers sympathetic to Catholic values, administrators in Catholic higher education increased the size and scope of their schools. They admitted more students on the undergraduate level, and a number established graduate programs in history, psychology, philosophy, social work, and biology because they thought degree work in these disciplines at non-Catholic institutions endangered the faith of Catholics. For example, American Jesuit provincials in 1958 approved guidelines for development of quality doctoral education in Jesuit universities; one of the criteria specified that fields chosen should be those "in which a student could encounter danger if not taught somewhere at the preeminent level under Catholic auspices." Representatives of Jesuit graduate schools acknowledged in 1952 that their institutions introduced graduate programs partially to supply trained, "Catholic-minded" teachers for Catholic schools, a further reflection of Catholic religious and cultural concerns.[23]

Meeting the rising demand for higher education among Catholics and providing an academic atmosphere sympathetic to Catholicism figured prominently among motives for expansion in Catholic higher education after 1945. But other considerations also promoted institutional growth. First, educational and religious leaders in the Catholic

Church wanted Catholic colleges and universities to wield significant influence in American society, especially in academic circles. To achieve their goal, they concluded that the changing conditions in contemporary higher education, particularly trends toward larger schools and extensive degree programs, required Catholic postsecondary institutions to increase enrollment and to become involved in graduate education, especially on the doctoral level.[24]

Numerous Catholic educational leaders believed that institutional growth would enhance the prestige of Catholic higher education in American academic culture. Though certainly not true for all, some Catholic educators tended to equate size and graduate studies with influence; consequently, they favored starting new schools, raising enrollment, and introducing graduate education. Edward Fitzpatrick, editor of the *Catholic School Journal*, noted in a 1950 editorial that a drive for recognition in academic circles explained much of the recent increase in the number of Catholic colleges and universities. Jesuit educational leaders acknowledged in the 1950s that their schools began offering graduate degrees partially to achieve status and to compete for students with secular colleges and universities.[25] Reflective of Catholic attitudes, a 1958 policy statement concerning graduate education in Jesuit universities declared that "to exercise intellectual leadership at the highest level, an institution must offer Doctorate work."[26]

Educational expansion also offered the possibility of communicating Catholic ideas more widely, thus extending Catholic influence in society. Fostering a social, political, and intellectual environment guided by Catholic teachings and moral values had always been an integral part of the Catholic educational commitment. But such an apostolic or religious focus became a higher priority within the Catholic Church after World War II, as secularism spread in Western civilization and the ideological conflict between democracy and communism deepened in intensity. James Murray, a Catholic member of the United States Senate, declared in a speech at the 1948 convention of the National Catholic Educational Association that Catholic education faced the challenge of "balancing the scales in favor of democracy." A year later, Jesuit theologian John Courtney Murray asserted that "the Catholic college and university today ought to be the point of departure for a missionary effort out into the thickening secularist intellectual and spiritual milieu."[27]

Such views about disseminating Catholic social theory and moral teachings encouraged the spread of Catholic higher education. Edward Rooney, S.J. stressed to his superior general in 1955 that future leaders of society would attend not only traditional liberal arts colleges but also schools stressing scientific research and professional studies.

Therefore, "If the Church is to be true to its mission, and exercise its influence on society, it must be found on all these educational fronts, for from every one of them inroads are being made into Catholic life." Jesuit college and university presidents insisted in 1964 that curtailing expansion in their institutions "would definitely inhibit the much needed growth and influence of the Jesuit educational apostolate for the Church in America."[28]

In particular, key educational officials within Catholicism emphasized the importance of developing quality Catholic graduate education. They realized the growing power of universities and academic research in shaping modern culture, and they wanted the Catholic Church to contribute to intellectual progress and to benefit from it. Robert Henle, S.J., dean of the graduate school and later academic vice-president at St. Louis University, argued in the mid-1950s that outstanding Catholic graduate schools "would bring Catholic intellectual life into the main stream of our culture as a powerful influence."[29]

In addition, some Catholic educators in the 1960s felt that the changing environment in American higher education compelled them to expand their schools, especially on the graduate level. Prominent educational figures issued warnings about the problems confronting liberal arts colleges. David Riesman told a meeting of Catholic college and university presidents in 1963 that traditional four-year institutions would face a crisis recruiting quality professors and students in the next ten years. Lacking graduate divisions, these schools would find it almost impossible to attract promising Ph.D.s to their faculties; and superior students would shun places with weak faculty. Agreeing with Riesman's assessment, Michael Walsh, S.J., president of Boston College, advised those attending the 1965 National Catholic Educational Association convention that "Today it seems impossible, or at least extremely difficult, to build strong undergraduate departments in arts and sciences unless one offers graduate programs and, in at least some areas, doctoral programs."[30]

Financial considerations supplied a fourth motive for the spread of Catholic higher education after 1945. The Depression and accompanying enrollment reductions had weakened many American colleges and universities, and certain Catholic institutions had barely survived. For example, Marquette University narrowly escaped bankruptcy in 1932; and the University of Detroit defaulted on $3.5 million in loans in 1933. St. Mary's College in Moraga, California suspended payment to its bondholders in 1934 and was sold at auction in 1937.[31]

World War II created further financial problems for higher education since military manpower needs drastically diminished the pool of potential students, thus reducing enrollment and income. Liberal arts and business students in the Jesuit segment of Catholic higher education decreased by 50% between 1940 and 1943. In January 1943, only ninety-one registered for classes at the University of Santa Clara, compared with 697 in September 1940.[32]

Consequently, despite problems in providing suitable faculty, classrooms, and living quarters for new students, many administrators on Catholic campuses welcomed the educational surge after 1945 because the additional tuition revenue enabled schools to reduce indebtedness and to make needed improvements. The University of Detroit allowed its attendance to climb from 1,800 in 1944 to 9,600 in 1948; and in 1950, it repaid the last of the debts it had refinanced in the 1930s. Hugh Duce, S.J., director of education for the California Province of the Society of Jesus, remarked in 1951 that "The postwar boom has permitted our institutions to make noted advances in admission policies, library expenditures, retirement funds for faculty members, personnel services for the students, the hiring of better prepared teachers, the establishment of more respectable salaries, etc."[33]

But even after reaching some degree of fiscal and academic health by the early 1950s, few Catholic colleges and universities could afford to cut enrollment. Lacking sizable endowments, they required large numbers of students to pay the higher operating costs resulting from their recently expanded facilities and staffs. Furthermore, increasing enrollment became a relatively easy way in subsequent years for many Catholic postsecondary schools to obtain money needed for new construction and faculty. Admitting more students to meet rising costs also allowed these institutions to maintain low tuition rates and thus enabled more Catholics to attend college. John P. Leary, S.J., president of Gonzaga University in Spokane, expressed concern in 1964 that schools which chose to remain small, "especially in the face of greater demands and almost inflationary salaries," would find it difficult to satisfy their clientele and to generate sufficient revenue.[34]

Some Catholic educational officials judged that offering graduate programs would enhance the economic health of their schools. The presidents and graduate school deans of Jesuit colleges and universities in the Midwest and South noted in 1952 that "In many instances public financial support is closely related to the offerings of our institutions on the graduate level." Certain Catholic educators also thought that initiation of graduate courses would attract more students and generate additional revenue. With foundations and the federal government more willing during the 1950s and 1960s to fund graduate education, many administrators in Catholic higher education chose to introduce or increase graduate programs, anxious to win support from federal and philanthropic sources. They felt that few schools without graduate divisions received such grants.[35]

The change in Catholic attitudes toward federal aid to higher education decisively influenced the postwar growth of Catholic colleges and universities, enabling schools to obtain funds for new construction and research. Before the 1930s, many Catholic educational and religious leaders strongly opposed federal aid to schools and creation of a national department of education, fearing that federal control and loss of institutional autonomy would result. They also maintained that responsibility for education rested with the various states.[36]

But the Depression, New Deal policies, and experiences with military training programs during World War II led to a major change in the Catholic viewpoint on the proper role of government in education. With states unable to resolve economic problems and private relief funds largely depleted, Catholic officials generally agreed that the desperate circumstances of the 1930s required federal intervention, and they praised legislation providing for social assistance programs, public works projects, and labor reforms. Roosevelt's skillful cultivation of Catholic support through federal appointments and contacts with Catholic prelates like Cardinal George Mundelein of Chicago further reduced Catholic fears of government power. Moreover, federal emergency assistance to students ($93,000,000 between 1935 and 1943) boosted enrollment and provided urgently needed revenue for numerous Catholic colleges and universities.[37]

By the early 1940s, various Catholic leaders favored federal aid to education, provided it did not entail federal control. Resistance diminished further during World War II. Government contracts to train army and navy personnel enabled many Catholic colleges and universities to survive the war years, and more Catholic educators realized that acceptance of federal funds did not lessen the autonomy of their institutions.[38]

After 1945 a growing number of Catholic leaders aggressively sought financial aid from the government, fully aware that the Catholic community alone could not finance the increasing social, educational, and religious expectations placed on Catholic schools. When the Truman Commission recommended in 1948 that the federal government confine its assistance to publicly controlled institutions of higher learning, Catholic officials and certain others from private institutions objected strenuously. They argued that service to the public rather than public control should be the criterion for aid.[39] Catholics campaigned unsuccessfully in 1949 and 1950 for passage of congressional legislation providing states with federal money to improve education and granting states the option of allocating these funds to private schools, including parochial institutions.[40]

But influenced by national defense concerns and the need to accommodate the rising college population, Congress passed legislation in the next two decades providing government loans and grants to both public and private colleges and universities. The availability of federal aid and the willingness of Catholic schools to accept it permitted Catholic higher education to expand dramatically and to move toward its goals of serving Catholics and increasing Catholic influence in American society. Like other American institutions of higher learning, Catholic schools obtained millions of dollars from the federal government to build residence halls, laboratories, cafeterias, and classroom buildings. Larger Catholic institutions also secured research contracts which helped pay higher operating costs. An advisor to the provincial of the Missouri Province of the Jesuit order reported to his Roman superiors in 1964 that "the University [St. Louis] will not be able in the future to maintain all of its operations unless there are more and more subsidies from the Federal Government." During 1967 alone, Catholic higher education received $125,000,000 in federal grants and contracts, not counting repayable loans.[41]

The postwar boom in Catholic higher education yielded significant benefits. First, it fostered the rise of lay faculty and administrators in Catholic colleges and universities since demand for personnel far exceeded the supply of clergy and religious. Also, the growth of Catholic postsecondary schools enabled numerous members of the Catholic Church and other Americans to receive collegiate, graduate, and professional training, helping them to advance socially and economically. For example, 78% of the lawyers, 87% of the dentists, and 40% of the physicians working in Omaha in 1980 had obtained their degrees from Creighton University. According to a 1984 report, two of every five attorneys and one of four medical doctors in the St. Louis metropolitan area had studied at St. Louis University. Of the one hundred Catholics in the U.S. House of Representatives in 1973-1974, 40% attended Catholic colleges and universities; 20% of them received all of their higher education in Catholic schools.[42]

Furthermore, because of expansion, more Catholics obtained academic instruction in a Catholic context, enriching many of them religiously and personally and, as a result, contributing to the vitality of Catholic life in the United States. At their best, Catholic colleges and universities fostered intellectual inquiry in an atmosphere characterized by faith, shared values, and a sense of community. Many students graduated from them with a better grasp of Catholic teachings and with a deeper religious commitment. In addition, Catholic higher education helped raise the social and academic expectations of Catholics, fostering self-criticism and reform within American Catholicism. During the 1960s, Catholic campuses became influential centers for change within the Catholic Church, particularly concerning such issues as liturgy, authority, and birth control.[43]

Catholic institutions of higher learning also served as "incubators" and agents of inculturation for Catholics. They offered an environment which strengthened Catholic cultural and religious identity while broadening perspectives and building confidence. Many of their students received the encouragement needed to move away from a rigid, defensive Catholicism toward an openness to the dominant secular society.[44]

In addition, Catholic higher education made academic gains after 1945 as many Catholic colleges and universities seized opportunities to upgrade their curricula, faculty, endowment, and facilities. By 1960, 87% of Catholic institutions of higher learning fulfilled the standards of regional accrediting associations compared to 76% in 1938. Between 1945 and 1982, the number of Phi Beta Kappa chapters on Catholic campuses increased from two to twelve.[45]

The percentage of faculty in Catholic postsecondary institutions with doctoral and professional degrees increased significantly between 1945 and 1980. For instance, in 1946, a maximum of 29% of full-time teachers at Holy Cross, 38% at the College of St. Catherine, 35% at DePaul, and 33% at the University of San Francisco held Ph.D. degrees. In 1980, these schools reported the following percentages of full-time faculty with doctorates: Holy Cross, 81%; College of St. Catherine, 48%; DePaul, 65%; and USF, 69%.[46]

But even though improved, Catholic higher education generally remains undistinguished in American intellectual culture, despite nearly four decades of effort and expenditure of millions of dollars. While many Catholic colleges and universities offer at least an adequate undergraduate education, few possess national reputations for academic excellence, and none ranks among elite institutions in graduate programs, research, and professional scholarship.

Recent investigations have spotlighted the low intellectual prestige of Catholic higher education. In 1982, the Conference Board of Associated Research Councils conducted an evaluation of American research-doctorate programs in the humanities, engineering, and mathematical, physical, biological, social, and behavioral sciences.[47] Of seventy-four departments in Catholic schools included in the study, only five (mathematics, chemistry, chemical engineering, and philosophy at Notre Dame and biochemistry at St. Louis University) received above average ratings. The most highly regarded Catholic university (Notre Dame) fell into the average category, and Catholic University, the priority higher educational institution of the Catholic hierarchy in the United States, ranked among the lowest one-sixth of American universities involved in doctoral education.[48]

Faculty of contemporary Catholic colleges and universities have fared poorly in competition for grants and fellowships. Only twenty-one of 716 Fulbright scholarships awarded in 1983 for teaching and research in foreign countries went to professors at Catholic institutions. Representatives from Catholic postsecondary institutions received two of 283 Guggenheim fellowships presented in 1984. The National Endowment for the Humanities granted just four of 439 awards during the 1983 fiscal year to individuals involved in Catholic higher education.[49]

Various reasons have been offered in the past thirty years for the inferior academic status of Catholic higher education in the United States. In 1955, John Tracy Ellis attributed the problem to the effects of anti-Catholic prejudice, poverty, lack of an intellectual tradition among many Catholic immigrants, poor training of clerical leaders, and over-expansion. Speaking in 1966, Paul Reinert, S.J., a veteran administrator in Jesuit higher education, emphasized that "the over-riding problem of Jesuit colleges and universities is the fact that they are under-financed." That same year, Catholic educational officials responding to a survey by the National Catholic Educational Association named inadequate financial support as the primary pressure on their institutions. Andrew Greeley asserted in a 1983 article that the poor academic reputation of Catholic universities stemmed from anti-intellectual attitudes among Catholic clergy and the hierarchy, particularly among members of the religious orders administering various schools.[50]

Yet while insightful and sometimes provocative, none of the preceding statements of Ellis and others, either singly or together, adequately accounts for the disappointing academic progress of Catholic colleges and universities since 1945. After World War II, the Catholic Church no longer had to devote a major portion of its resources to meeting the needs of millions of immigrants or con-tending with massive religious discrimination, in contrast to earlier decades. By the early 1960s, many Catholics had entered the main-stream of American society.

Recent studies have also persuasively established that the academic accomplishments of Catholics since the late 1950s compare favorably with the performance of other Americans, refuting suggestions that Catholic culture did not provide the climate necessary for scholastic success. Before World War II, Catholics had lagged badly in economic and educational achievement, and some analysts attributed the lack of Catholic intellectual attainment, especially in science, to the religious beliefs and attitudes of Catholics.[51] For instance, Harvey Lehman and Paul Witty commented in an article published in 1931 that "The conspicuous dearth of scientists among the Catholics suggests that the tenets of that Church are not consonant with scientific endeavor." In the late 1950s, Jesuit theologian Gustave Weigel and Thomas O'Dea, a lay sociologist teaching at Fordham, judged that the other-worldly values of Catholics and concerns about defending the Catholic faith produced a crippling anti-intellectualism among some Catholics.[52] But a major shift in Catholic educational achievement and aspirations occurred after 1945. By the late 1960s, Catholics were as likely as other Americans to attend college, begin graduate work, and pursue academic careers.[53]

The educational mobility of individual Catholics, along with their social and economic gains, makes the slow advance of Catholic higher education even more inexplicable. A bias against intellectual activities has plagued Catholic higher education at various times since World War II; but in the last twenty years the policies and actions of most Catholic educators, particularly in leading Catholic schools, contradict the charge of widespread anti-intellectualism among them. Besides adopting rationales committing their institutions to intellectual excellence, they have raised standards for hiring, stressed the importance of scholarly production for tenure, and increased institutional support for research.[54]

Undeniably, Catholic higher education has suffered from inadequate finances and overexpansion. In 1964, Georgetown, Notre Dame, and St. Louis were the only Catholic schools ranking among the one hundred best endowed postsecondary institutions in the United States. Because of their meager reserve funds, Catholic colleges and universities have had to depend mainly on tuition revenue, preventing them from setting standards too high lest they end up with insufficient enrollment. But despite serious financial problems, Catholic educational and religious leaders did not control expansion and concentrate on fewer institutions, another puzzling aspect of the evolution of Catholic higher education in the postwar period.[55]

A reappraisal of the postwar expansion in Catholic higher education, especially in light of unresolved questions and previous analyses, suggests that Catholicism failed to develop top-ranked colleges and universities for three main reasons. First, the persistent localism long prevalent in American Catholic culture, particularly among Catholic educators, stalled attempts to limit institutional growth, discouraged cooperation among schools, and frustrated effective national planning and evaluation, measures essential to improving the quality and reputation of Catholic higher learning. During much of the twentieth century, Catholic life and organizational structures centered around local social units such as the family, parish, or diocese, partly a legacy of immigration and poverty but also resulting from ethnic ties and concerns to safeguard Catholic faith and culture. Catholic colleges and universities were founded primarily to meet the religious and educational needs of a particular community of Catholics. Catholic schools traditionally operated with a strong local orientation, almost all of them relying heavily on Catholics in their immediate area for students and financial support.

Different religious orders conducted most Catholic postsecondary institutions, making united action additionally difficult. From their earliest days, Catholic colleges and universities operated independently of one another and the American hierarchy, never as part of a coordinated system. Preferring autonomy, most Catholic schools resisted Catholic University's moves to control American Catholic education before World War II. Cardinal George Mundelein's grand plan in the early 1920s to form all Catholic colleges and universities in his archdiocese into the Catholic University of Chicago failed in large part because the various religious orders involved preferred to maintain the autonomy of their institutions.[56]

Such traditions, needs, and perspectives within Catholicism and Catholic higher education promoted widespread, often unilateral, educational expansion after World War II. The leaders of Catholic colleges and universities commonly increased enrollment and introduced new programs to meet local demand; and they usually gave insufficient consideration to the national and long-term consequences of their decisions. Joseph Zuercher, S.J., provincial of the Missouri Province of the Jesuit order, lamented to Vincent McCormick, S.J., assistant to the Jesuit superior general for the United States, in 1947 that "You have no idea how difficult it is to 'sit on the lid' and keep these Rectors [presidents] from expanding in every direction. It would not be so bad if the Rectors forewarned you of their expansive ideas, but very often they proceed to such a point that it is next to impossible to stop them."[57]

Wasteful expansion and duplication particularly occurred on the graduate level. Between 1940 and 1980, the number of Catholic universities engaged in doctoral education rose from nine to twenty-one, and the total of Ph.D. programs increased from eighty-two to at least 160. Eight Catholic institutions in 1970 offered doctorates in history, nine in English and biology, ten in chemistry, and eleven in philosophy. In

1981, Georgetown and Catholic University, both located in Washington, D.C., competed against each other in five doctoral areas (biology, chemistry, history, modern languages, and philosophy); and though only ninety miles apart and operated by the same religious order, Marquette and Loyola University of Chicago each offered doctorates in chemistry, education, English, history, and philosophy.[58]

The prodigal development of Catholic higher education after World War II provoked severe criticisms from certain Catholic educational and religious leaders. A 1950 editorial in the *Catholic School Journal* protested that "we [Catholic educators] dilute our present service and even our future service by the almost senseless multiplication of Catholic institutions of higher learning." In 1955, Ellis denounced the duplication of Catholic graduate programs as "our betrayal of one another," and he said it resulted in "a perpetuation of mediocrity and the draining away from each other of the strength that is necessary if really superior achievements are to be attained." Paul Reinert, S.J. warned at the NCEA annual meeting in 1964 that the unplanned, excessive spread of Catholic colleges threatened the survival of all Catholic liberal arts institutions.[59]

Various Catholic officials between 1945 and 1970 called on Catholic colleges and universities to restrict expansion and to commit themselves to regional and national cooperation, especially in graduate education.[60] American Jesuits considered specific proposals for joint efforts in higher education. Convinced that Jesuit schools must cooperate to achieve educational distinction and to influence American academic culture, John Janssens, S.J., superior general of the Jesuit order, urged in 1948 that Jesuit universities in the United States pool their graduate resources and offer "high-level, excellently staffed and equipped graduate schools in philosophy in one university, in physical sciences in another, in political science in a third, in history and languages, etc. in still another."[61]

Similarly, Raymond Schoder, S.J., a classics professor at Loyola University in Chicago, suggested in 1956 that American Jesuits concentrate fifteen or twenty top Jesuit scholars in the humanities at one university, arguing that together such individuals could command national attention. Seeking to expand Catholic influence in American culture, Robert Henle, S.J. advocated in 1964 that American Jesuits work together to develop a few "university centers," institutions containing a substantial number of undergraduate and professional schools but especially committed to research, scholarship, and graduate programs of the highest quality.[62]

But the allegiance of so many Catholics to local educational institutions and communities stymied attempts to coordinate the development of Catholic higher education. Jesuit educational and religious leaders deemed Janssens' plan for cooperation "unfeasible and undesirable" because of the local obligations of their schools, the needs of their clientele, and the present complete independence of Jesuit provinces.[63] Also, many supporters of smaller Catholic colleges and universities feared that institutional cooperation would harm their schools, especially by depriving them of faculty and students. For example, though a longtime advocate of curriculum reform, graduate studies, and efficient administration, Hugh Duce, an influential Jesuit administrator in the California Province, maintained that schools should operate independently of each other. He became alarmed in the summer of 1954 about a proposal submitted to Janssens by a prominent American Jesuit calling for several Jesuit provinces to staff regional universities. Duce wrote Edward Rooney, "For heaven's sake, don't let that idea take root!" He added that such a plan would mean the death of Loyola University in Los Angeles, a school to which he had maintained close ties since serving as its president in the late 1930s. Moreover, Duce insisted that the concept of interprovince cooperation would not work because "No provincial is going to deprive himself of his best men to build up a university in another Province."[64]

The local loyalties of so many Catholic educators and their priority on freedom of action blocked the formation of external agencies with authority to plan development and build up quality in Catholic colleges and universities. Reflecting the wishes of its members, the National Catholic Educational Association had no supervisory function in Catholic higher education, though it provided a valuable forum for discussing educational trends and problems. The secretary of the NCEA Committee on Graduate Study reminded in 1953 that the Committee possessed no power to decide which schools should start graduate work nor to determine the fields they chose for concentration. Consequently, it was forced to rely on cooperation and discussion to give "some guidance and direction" to Catholic graduate education.[65]

Sentiment against centralized planning and control also prevailed in the Jesuit order. In 1962, a group of Jesuits representing every Jesuit province in the United States recommended the establishment of an administrative body to formulate educational policy for all provinces and to allocate specialized Jesuit manpower.[66] But even though supported by presidents of larger Jesuit colleges and universities, such an agency was never established. Besides conflicting with the interests of smaller Jesuit schools, it reduced the power of Jesuit provincials and leaders of the Jesuit Educational Association. Also, as Edward Rooney, S.J., a powerful opponent of the concept, pointed out, it proposed a degree of control over provinces and institutions similar to that found so objectionable when Daniel O'Connell, S.J. served as Commissarius of American Jesuit education between 1934 and 1937.[67]

By the early 1960s, the institutional leaders of Jesuit higher education, many of them educational entrepreneurs, clearly wanted to free themselves and their schools from any restraints imposed by the president of the JEA, province directors of education, and the American provincials. Arguing that the changing conditions and growing complexity in American higher education required greater institutional freedom, they gradually won support for their views, despite strenuous objections from Rooney and some of those responsible for province educational policies. In 1964, Jesuit superiors approved a major reorganization of the JEA, changing its previous supervisory function to one of offering advice and service to Jesuit colleges and universities. In succeeding years, Jesuit schools expanded even more according to local need and institutional resources, and they paid little attention to national planning and coordination. In doing so, they mirrored attitudes and conditions which helped prevent Catholicism from deriving maximum benefit from the considerable human and financial resources it devoted to higher education.[68]

Catholic higher education also failed to make greater academic progress in the postwar decades because its leaders and faculty often subordinated intellectual achievement to personal and institutional religious commitments. Such choices retarded development of quality educational programs and dampened interest in scholarship, the main criteria for status in American academic circles.

The expansion of Catholic colleges and universities between the 1940s and early 1960s clearly manifested a greater priority on pastoral concerns than on attaining academic excellence. Instead of focusing their efforts on improving existing institutions, Catholic educational and religious officials chose to spread scarce faculty and financial resources even thinner by founding new colleges and expanding current programs. Many of them felt obligated to meet the increasing demand for higher education in a Catholic context and to reduce the number of Catholics attending secular schools. Edward Rooney, S.J. told his superior general in 1955, "There is evidence that enemies of Catholic thought are striving to organize more and more state and even private resources to establish secular institutions on such a plane that they will dwarf Catholic educational institutions." In his judgment, the Catholic Church in America faced a crisis in education because it lacked sufficient facilities, making expansion imperative.[69]

But however praiseworthy such goals may have been from a religious perspective, they fostered a faulty approach to academics. For example, representatives of Jesuit graduate schools, recognizing the importance of doctoral studies in American higher education but also aware of local educational needs, proposed in 1953 that Jesuit universities commit themselves to two types of doctoral programs. The first would operate with a regional focus, providing "Catholic-minded teachers for Catholic colleges and to influence, by placement of our graduates, the non-Catholic institutions." It also would seek to produce "Catholic-minded scholars, scientists, and professional leaders." The second kind of doctorate work would aim for preeminent intellectual leadership on the national level, ranking with the best non-Catholic departments and producing first-class Catholic scholars.[70]

In effect, these officials called for ordinary and preeminent doctoral programs, perhaps the best possible approach at the time but not a plan to achieve intellectual distinction.[71] Rather than preeminence, the proposal resulted in debilitating competition and mediocre graduate education. In 1951, approximately forty departments in four Jesuit universities offered doctoral degrees. Within seven years, two more schools began granting doctorates, and the number of programs rose to sixty-seven. By 1967, eight Jesuit universities operated 134 doctoral programs with four schools competing against each other in such fields as economics, French, physics, psychology, and biochemistry, five in history and biology, and six in philosophy and chemistry.[72] In the 1982 evaluation of American graduate schools sponsored by the Conference Board of Associated Research Councils, only one department in a Jesuit university (biochemistry at St. Louis University) ranked average or above.[73]

Furthermore, until the late 1960s, most faculty and administrators involved in Catholic higher education emphasized teaching, student contact, and administrative needs. But while important, such priorities too often resulted in intellectual stagnation among many Catholic professors and their students. In addition, the focus on the classroom and communication of religious values almost guaranteed the neglect of research and scholarly writing, increasingly the route to distinction in American academic culture. A 1964 survey of attitudes among a representative group of male faculty in Catholic colleges and universities (267 professors from twenty-two institutions) reported that 80% preferred teaching but only 12.4% chose research; and 75% of the sample had little or no record of publication. In addition, many schools overburdened their professors with heavy teaching and institutional responsibilities, leaving little time or energy for scholarship. In their 1968 study of American higher education, *The Academic Revolution*, Christopher Jencks and David Riesman pointed out that "a strong tradition of pastoral concern for the moral and personal well-being of students" still prevailed among many faculty on Catholic campuses.

Joseph Fisher, S.J., provincial of the Missouri Province of the Jesuit order, told his superiors in 1960 that "Many of our men who have the best potential for scholarship are tied up with administrative work in our schools."[74]

In some instances, these preferences for teaching and association with students, especially in the 1940s and 1950s, reflected anti-intellectual attitudes and behavior. But to a decisive degree, the emphasis on classroom instruction and pastoral work among many in Catholic colleges and universities did not stem from opposition to academic excellence or unfamiliarity with trends in contemporary education. Rather, its roots lay in the explicit religious commitments and goals of Catholic higher education. According to Catholic educational theory, collegiate training should enrich students personally and spiritually, not concentrate solely on intellectual development. Therefore, in addition to academic knowledge, Catholic postsecondary institutions seek to transmit Catholic traditions, values, and principles, hoping to influence their students and the wider community.

This broader concept of education's purpose produced educational priorities different from the academic mainstream. The policies of Catholic colleges and universities stressed the importance of communication and personal influence. Moreover, they fostered a faculty culture which encouraged involvement with students and quality teaching but which did not sufficiently urge research and scholarship.

The religious convictions or sympathies of faculty and administrators in Catholic higher education also encouraged subordination of scholarship and academic status to teaching and spiritual concerns. Historically, most of the teaching and administrative personnel in Catholic colleges and universities have been members of the Catholic Church or, if non-Catholics, individuals with at least some orientation toward spiritual values. Studies of faculties in American institutions of higher learning have noted that scholarly production and religious commitment vary inversely and that "stronger degrees of one tend to be accompanied by weaker degrees of the other." Jencks and Riesman commented in 1968 that the low publication rates among Catholic faculty suggest "that it is hard to maximize both piety and scholarship simultaneously."[75]

Moreover, in his analysis of surveys of 60,000 college and university teachers sponsored in 1969 by the Carnegie Foundation, Stephen Steinberg discovered that professors with strong religious beliefs published less frequently than their peers who reported minimal or no connections with religion. Only 30% of Jewish faculty reported that they did not have any professional publications during the previous two years; but for Protestants, the figure was 55% and for Catholics 59%. Also, those with stronger religious convictions were less likely to think of themselves as intellectuals and more likely to stress teaching over research. Moreover, a higher proportion of faculty with strong religious commitments maintained that institutions should be as concerned about students' personal values as about their intellectual development.[76]

As Steinberg cautions, his findings do not indicate that religious beliefs preclude scholarly achievement. But they do suggest that commitments to religion inhibit scholarship and academic excellence. Considered with other evidence, they help explain the failure of Catholic higher education to make greater advances toward quality and status after 1945.

Besides the burdens of localism and an inadequate commitment to intellectual excellence, efforts to improve Catholic colleges and universities after 1945 suffered from a lack of effective national leadership. To achieve institutional cooperation and to link religious commitment and academic quality, Catholic colleges and universities needed the services of gifted leaders. They especially required individuals with a broad vision of needs and opportunities, the intelligence to analyze contemporary conditions correctly and to devise appropriate responses, and then the energy, courage, and diplomacy to build the broad consensus necessary to implement their plans.

Though a few schools like Boston College, Notre Dame, and St. Louis received such leadership, Catholic higher education as a whole did not. Certain Catholic educational and religious officials recognized the defects hindering development of academically strong Catholic institutions, and they periodically issued calls for consolidation and coordination. But their criticisms failed to elicit widespread action or significant support from those with power and responsibility in American Catholicism and Catholic higher education.

Many bishops encouraged expansion of Catholic colleges and universities in their diocese or archdiocese to meet the demand for Catholic higher education, paying little attention to regional or national approaches. Few of them used their position to encourage development of Catholic higher education known for academic rigor and wielding significant influence in American academic culture. Superiors in the religious communities conducting most of Catholic higher education seldom used their authority to eliminate wasteful competition among their own schools and those of other religious orders. Too often, these officials lacked a clear educational vision; consequently, they often became paralyzed by competing demands or resorted to compromise solutions that left basic problems unresolved. Without the catalyst of strong and sustained leadership, individual Catholics advocating cooperation and quality in Catholic higher education could not overcome the inertia, fragmentation, and rivalries besetting Catholic postsecondary institutions and their sponsoring religious orders.[77]

The actions and changing viewpoints of Edward Rooney and John Janssens, key architects of Jesuit educational policy between 1945 and 1965, illustrated the vacillation, present-mindedness, and limited vision so often plaguing Catholic higher education during the postwar years. Rooney frequently recommended between 1945 and the early 1950s that American Jesuits concentrate on existing institutions, and he proposed that they consider "some consolidation" in graduate and professional fields.[78] Starting in 1947, Janssens repeatedly stressed the need to curtail expansion and to pool resources so that Jesuit colleges and universities could strengthen themselves academically and grow in status. When a group of American Jesuit educators reported in 1952 that national cooperation among Jesuit schools was not feasible, he expressed sharp disagreement, declaring that if decisions regarding growth were left to local presidents, institutions would expand indefinitely.[79]

But Rooney and Janssens sympathized with desires for Catholic higher education and felt that Jesuits were obliged to respond. Both equivocated about institutional growth, and eventually they sacrificed long-term academic goals to present needs. For instance, even though officially opposed to expansion, Janssens approved the foundation of three Jesuit colleges between 1947 and 1954, responding to petitions from local bishops and lay Catholics. In 1953, Rooney endorsed requests from Boston College to begin offering Ph.D. degrees in history, economics, and education. When questioned by Janssens about his recommendation, he replied that the proposals would meet desires for Catholic education and strengthen Boston College. Furthermore, he maintained that such doctoral programs posed no danger of duplication, an inexplicable statement since Fordham, Loyola of Chicago, and St. Louis already conferred doctorates in the three fields.[80]

The crucial shift in Jesuit policy concerning institutional growth occurred in the mid-1950s. To meet requests from American Jesuits for guidelines concerning expansion, Rooney suggested in a lengthy memorandum sent to Janssens in February 1955 that Jesuit schools in the United States be permitted to "accept as many students as are clearly capable of profiting by the education we wish to give, and for whom we can provide the teaching and physical facilities necessary to give that education." Greatly influenced by Rooney, American Jesuit provincials, and the increasing demand for higher education among

Catholics in America, Janssens accepted Rooney's vague standard. In doing so, he unleashed powerful expansionist forces that soon dominated Jesuit higher education and ruled out cooperation for academic excellence.[81]

In their remaining years as Jesuit leaders, Janssens and Rooney never adopted consistent positions concerning the development of Jesuit schools, reflecting the general indecision among Catholic educators in the United States. Each encouraged national cooperation in graduate education but also approved numerous proposals for new departments and programs, some of them duplicating courses in other Jesuit institutions. Worried in part about overexpansion, Janssens in 1958 appointed "inspectors" to evaluate the religious and academic character of American Jesuit universities. Yet he continued to grant greater autonomy to Jesuit colleges and universities, giving them virtual independence from Jesuit superiors in 1964.[82]

In contrast, Rooney grew more troubled about excessive and unplanned growth, concerns about Catholic higher education shared by others in the 1960s.[83] He gradually became a sharp critic of increasing enrollments and new programs. In August 1964 he asked Janssens, "Is it not time to call a moratorium on expanding out and work more at expanding in depth?" But without leaders committed to national cooperation, comprehensive planning, and academic quality, Catholic educators could not halt expansion nor could they focus on raising standards.[84]

The rapid development of Catholic higher education between 1945 and 1970 reflected the rising economic, social, and educational aspirations of American Catholics as well as persistent concerns within Catholicism about maintaining Catholic faith and culture. Institutional financial problems, desires for prestige and influence, and the availability of federal aid further encouraged Catholic educators to expand their schools. In addition, the strong ties between Catholic postsecondary institutions and their local communities plus the decentralized system of government in the Catholic Church also created favorable conditions for expansion. Because they increased enrollment and added new programs, Catholic colleges and universities provided collegiate, graduate, and professional training for many Catholics, greatly assisting their upward mobility and cultural assimilation.

But while Catholics commonly rose in economic and social status after 1945, only a few Catholic higher educational institutions exceeded the general improvement in American higher education and advanced significantly in academic reputation. The pervasive localism in Catholic society, especially among Catholic educators, fostered a focus on current needs and opportunities rather than on long-range planning.

It also prevented the concentration of educational and financial resources necessary to develop quality institutions. Instead, Catholic colleges and universities maintained their autonomy and engaged in wasteful competition. Furthermore, Catholic higher education did not make greater academic progress after World War II because many involved in it gave preference to teaching and pastoral concerns rather than to academic goals, particularly scholarship. It also lacked leaders committed to the work of developing a network of distinguished Catholic colleges and universities. That task still remains for American Catholics.

Notes

1. Hadley Cantril, "Educational and Economic Composition of Religious Groups: An Analysis of Poll Data," *American Journal of Sociology* 48 (March 1943): 574-79; Liston Pope, "Religion and Class Structure," *Annals of the American Academy of Political and Social Science* 256 (March 1948): 85-91; Flynn, *American Catholics & the Roosevelt Presidency*, ix-xi; and Ellis, *American Catholics and the Intellectual Life*, 29.

2. O'Brien, *The Renewal of American Catholicism*, 6; Noval D. Glenn and Ruth Hyland, "Religious Preference and Worldly Success: Some Evidence from National Surveys," *American Sociological Review* 32 (February 1967): 73-85; Greeley, *The American Catholic*, 43-47 and 53-67.

3. Mary Hanna, *Catholics and American Politics* (Cambridge: Harvard University Press, 1979), 48-49; Hennesey, *American Catholics*, 314; Moore, *Will America Become Catholic?*, 233; and "Record Number of Women, Blacks in Congress," *Congressional Quarterly Weekly Report* 46 (12 November 1988): 3295.

4. Bernard Lazerwitz, "Some Factors Associated with Variations in Church Attendance," *Social Forces* 39 (May 1961): 303. For other surveys of Catholic religiosity, see Bernard Lazerwitz, "A Comparison of Major United States Religious Groups," *Journal of the American Statistical Association* 56 (September 1961): 569-79; and Andrew M. Greeley, "Some Information on the Present Situation of American Catholics," *Social Order* 13 (April 1963): 9-24.

5. Hennesey, *American Catholics*, 283-88; and McAvoy, *A History of the Catholic Church in the United States*, 440-48.

6. Mary Perkins Ryan, *Are Parochial Schools the Answer?* (New York: Holt, Rinehart & Winston, 1964), 174; and Leonard Swidler, "Catholic Colleges: A Modest Proposal," *Commonweal*, 29 January 1965, 559. See also Buetow, *Of Singular Benefit*, 284-94; "A Report on the Problems of the Disaffection of Young Jesuits for Our Current Educational Apostolate," *Woodstock Letters* 98 (Winter 1969): 113-29; and M.A. Fitzsimons, "The Catholic University: Problems and Prospects," *Notre Dame Journal of Education* 4 (Fall 1973): 250-57.

7. Garland G. Parker, *The Enrollment Explosion* (New York: School and Society Books, 1971), 37-40; David D. Henry, *Challenges Past, Challenges Present* (San Francisco: Jossey-Bass Publishers, 1975), 59-63 and 101; and W. Todd Furniss, ed., *American Universities and Colleges* (Washington, D.C.: American Council on Education, 1973), 1773.

8. Oscar and Mary Handlin, *The American College and American Culture* (New York: McGraw-Hill Book Company, 1970), 71-74; and President's Commission on Higher Education, *Higher Education for American Democracy*, 6 vols. (Washington, D.C.: Government Printing Office, 1947), vol. 1: *Establishing the Goals*, 101.

9. President's Commission on Higher Education, vol. 5: *Financing Higher Education*, 44-63; and Brubacher and Rudy, *Higher Education in Transition*, 230-37.

10. The Report of the Commission on Financing Higher Education, *Nature and Needs of Higher Education* (New York: Columbia University Press, 1952), 163; and Henry, *Challenges Past, Challenges Present*, 73-75.

11. *The Official Catholic Directory*, 1945, 1948, and 1970; Mark V. Angelo, O.F.M., *The History of St. Bonaventure University* (St. Bonaventure, N.Y.: Franciscan Institute, 1961), 170-73; "Enrollment, 1945-1946, Jesuit Colleges and Universities," *Jesuit Educational Quarterly* 8 (January 1946): 180a; Furniss, ed., *American Universities and Colleges*, 1973, 711-13.

12. Greeley, *From Backwater to Mainstream*, 6-7; Allan P. Farrell, S.J., "Enrollment in Catholic universities and men's colleges [sic], 1947-1948," *America*, 31 January 1948, 485-86; and Farrell, "Catholic colleges for women [sic]: 1947-1948," *America*, 3 April 1948, xvi-xx.

13. John Janssens, S.J. to Edward Rooney, S.J., 7 February 1953, "Correspondence with Fr. General and Fr. Assistant," Box 36, JEA Collection, ABC; "Graduate Programs at Jesuit Colleges and Universities," 1 May 1967, ACPSJ; Crocker, *The Student Guide to Catholic Colleges and Universities*, 465; Philip S. Moore, C.S.C., "Academic Development, University of Notre Dame: Past, Present, and Future," 1960, 139 (mimeographed); and Furniss, ed., *American Universities and Colleges*, 1973, 1773-79.

14. *Catholic Colleges and Schools in the United States*, 1942, 10; and Evans, *The Newman Movement*, ix and 55. For additional data on Catholic college attendance, see Martin W. Davis, *The Sister as Campus Minister* (Washington, D.C.: Center for Applied Research in the Apostolate, 1970), 1-14.

15. Greeley, *The American Catholic*, 43-47; and Philip Gleason, "Immigration and American Catholic Higher Education," in *American Education and the European Immigrant: 1840-1940*, ed. Bernard J. Weiss (Urbana: University of Illinois, 1982), 165.

16. Minutes, annual meeting of deans of the Missouri, Chicago, and New Orleans Provinces, St. Louis University, 28-29 November 1953, Drawer "III. Ed. Sec.," AMPSJ; Rooney to American provincials, 29 September 1954, 3-4, "JEA Correspondence (1948-1955)," Drawer 74, ACPSJ; and Rooney to Janssens, 5 February 1955, Rooney memoranda, vol. 2, JEA Collection, ABC.

17. Evans, *The Newman Movement*, 55, 99, and 131; Abdon Lewis, F.S.C., "The Traditional Four-Year Catholic College: Problems and Prospects," *National Catholic Educational Association Bulletin* 62 (August 1965): 180; and Synnott, *The Half-Opened Door*, 177 and 214.

18. For representative Catholic judgments of secular higher education, see Avery R. Dulles, S.J., "Catholics in Secular Colleges," *Catholic Mind* 49 (September 1951): 559-62; Jack Lucal, "The Case for a Catholic College," reprint from the *Georgetown College Journal*, [1954?], "Catholic Educational Philosophy," Drawer 7, ACPSJ; and Hennesey, *American Catholics*, 287 and 294-300.

19. Hugh Duce, S.J. to Albert Cooney, S.J., 4 May 1946, "Education, #114," Drawer 74, ACPSJ; Gerard F. Knoepful, S.J., guidance counselor, Xavier High School, New York City, to Hugh Duce, S.J., 20 January 1954, "Presidents' Meeting, 1954," Drawer 9, ACPSJ; Lewis, "The Traditional Four-Year College," 180.

20. Edward Rooney, S.J. to John Janssens, S.J., 5 February 1955, Rooney memoranda, vol. 2, JEA Collection, ABC; and George D. Rock, "Some Challenges Facing Catholic Graduate Education in the Next Half-Century," *National Catholic Educational Association Bulletin* 50 (August 1953): 205.

21. Francis M. Crowley, "Catholic Education in 1948," *Catholic School Journal* 49 (January 1949): 1-3; and "Report of the Meetings of the Commission on Graduate Schools of the Jesuit Educational Association Held at Saint Louis University, December 6-7, 1952 and Loyola University, Chicago, February 7, 1953," 3, "Graduate Depts. and Regulations," Drawer 8, ACPSJ. See also Allan P. Farrell, S.J. and Matthew J. Fitzsimons, S.J., "A Study of Jesuit Education," 344-45, ACPSJ (mimeographed).

22. Rooney to American provincials, 29 September 1954, "JEA Correspondence (1948-1955)," Drawer 74, ACPSJ; Rooney to Janssens, 3 February 1955, "Corr. with Fr. General," Box 36, JEA Collection, ABC; and idem, 5 February 1955, ABC.

23. "Report," JEA Commission on Graduate Schools, 6-7 December 1952 and 7 February 1953, 2, "Graduate Depts. and Regulations," Drawer 8, ACPSJ; and "Principles and Policies Governing Graduate Programs in Jesuit Institutions," 1958, 1 and 13, ACPSJ. See also Edward J. Drummond, S.J., "The Graduate School and Its Responsibility to the Community," *National Catholic Educational Association Bulletin* 44 (August 1947): 284-91; and FitzGerald, *The Governance of Jesuit Colleges*, 141-43.

24. For a sense of the pressures on Catholic higher education after 1945, see Power, *Catholic Higher Education in America*, 403-6; and Gleason, "A Historical Perspective," 48-51.

25. Edward Fitzpatrick, "Mass Education and Education Dilution," *Catholic School Journal* 50 (April 1950): 116; minutes, meeting of the presidents and deans of the graduate schools of the eastern region of the JEA, 19 December 1952, "Grad Schools," Drawer 8, ACPSJ; minutes, meeting of the presidents and deans of the graduate schools of the central region of the JEA, 21 November 1952, ibid.; and "Report," JEA Commission on Graduate Schools, 6-7 December 1952 and 7 February 1953, 2, "Graduate Depts. and Regulations," Drawer 8, ACPSJ.

26. "Principles and Policies Governing Graduate Programs in Jesuit Institutions," 1958, 7, ACPSJ.

27. James E. Murray, "Christian Education for Democracy," *National Catholic Educational Association Bulletin* 45 (August 1948): 70; and John Courtney Murray, S.J., "Reversing the Secularist Drift," *Thought* 49 (March 1949): 40-41. See also Robert Henle, S.J., "The Future Challenge to Catholic Education," *National Catholic Educational Association Bulletin* 45 (August 1948): 275-86.

28. Rooney to Janssens, 5 February 1955, 7, Rooney memoranda, vol. 2, JEA Collection, ABC; and "Statement of the Presidents of Jesuit Colleges and Universities Regarding the Development of Jesuit Higher Education," in "Proceedings of Jesuit Educational Association Commission of Presidents of Jesuit Colleges and Universities," University of Santa Clara, 17-20 August 1964, 140, ACPSJ.

29. Robert J. Henle, S.J., "The Catholic Graduate School," n.d. [1954?], 6, "JEA Grad. Commission," Drawer 3, Barnett Papers, AMU. See also Leo R. Ward, C.S.C., *Blueprint for a Catholic University* (St. Louis: B. Herder Book Company, 1949), 3-20, 89-110, and 251-72; John P. O'Brien, C.S.V., "Some Observations on the Formation of Catholic Scholars," *National Catholic Educational Association Bulletin* 48 (August 1951): 200; and Donald McDonald, ed., *Catholics in Conversation* (Philadelphia: J.B. Lippincott Company, 1960), 257-73.

30. William C. De Vane, "A Time and Place for Liberal Education," *Bulletin of the Association of American Colleges* (May 1964): 198; Lewis, "The Traditional Four-Year Catholic College," 177-84; and Walsh, "Catholic Universities—Problems and Prospects," 163.

31. Samuel Horine, S.J., provincial of the Missouri Province, to Zacheus Maher, S.J., provincial of the California Province, 25 June 1932, "Education #204," Drawer 75, ACPSJ; Hamilton, *The Story of Marquette University*, 281-84; Muller, *The University of Detroit*, 172 and 175; and Ronald E. Isetti, F.S.C., *Called to the Pacific: A History of the Christian Brothers of the San Francisco District, 1868-1944* (Moraga, Calif.: St. Mary's College of California, 1979), 339-45.

32. For enrollment statistics, see *Jesuit Educational Quarterly* 3 (December 1940), 4 (December 1941), and 6 (January 1944); and McKevitt, *The University of Santa Clara*, 261.

33. Muller, *The University of Detroit*, 244-46; and Duce to Edward B. Rooney, S.J., 22 February 1951, "1951-1952 JEA Ex. Comm.," Drawer 73, ACPSJ.

34. "Minutes of the Annual Meeting of the Deans of the Chicago, Missouri, and New Orleans Provinces," St. Louis University, 28-29 November 1953, 3, Drawer "III. Ed. Sec.," AMPSJ; and John P. Leary, S.J., "The Medium Sized Jesuit University and Growth," in "Proceedings, Jesuit Educational Association, Commission of Presidents of Jesuit Colleges and Universities," University of Santa Clara, 17-20 August 1964, 73, ACPSJ.

35. Minutes, meeting of the presidents and deans of the graduate schools of the central region of the JEA, Loyola University, Chicago, 21 November 1952, "Graduate Schools," Drawer 8, ACPSJ; Paul Reinert, S.J., "Finances," *National Catholic Educational Association Bulletin* 49 (August 1952): 189; Gannon, *Up to the Present*, 100 and 264-65.

36. For Catholic opinion on the government's role in education, see Plough, "Catholic Colleges and the Catholic Educational Association," 452-63, 469-77, and 492; Joseph M. Piet, S.J., provincial of the California Province to Charles F. Carroll, S.J., 21 March 1930, "Old Correspondence-Interprovince Committee," ACPSJ; minutes of meeting of Midwestern Jesuit college and university deans, Chicago, 9 April 1937, "JEA-Deans' meetings," Drawer 3, Barnett Papers, AMU; and Edward Rooney, S.J., personal memorandum of meeting of National Catholic Educational Association advisory committee, Philadelphia, 12 January 1939, "Office of President," Box 20, JEA Collection, ABC.

37. David J. O'Brien, *American Catholics and Social Reform* (New York: Oxford University Press, 1968), 212-15; Flynn, *American Catholics & the Roosevelt Presidency 1932-1936*, 36-50 and 74-87; Richard G. Axt, *The Federal Government and Financing Higher Education* (New York: Columbia University Press, 1945), 79-81; and Hamilton, *The Story of Marquette University*, 286-88.

38. Minutes of meeting of Jesuit deans, California Province, University of Santa Clara, 29 July 1941, "Education #108," Drawer 75, ACPSJ; minutes of JEA Executive Committee meeting, Loyola University, Chicago, 5-7 November 1943, "Education #10," Drawer 74, ACPSJ; McAvoy, *A History of the Catholic Church in the United States*, 446; and McKevitt, *The University of Santa Clara*, 261-63.

39. See in particular the statement of dissent filed by the two Catholic members of the commission, Monsignor Frederick Hochwalt and Martin R.P. McGuire, *Higher Education for American Democracy*, vol. 5: *Financing Higher Education*, 65-68. See also Byron S. Hollingshead, "Colleges of Freedom," *Association of American Colleges Bulletin* 35 (March 1949): 62-73; and Allan P. Farrell, S.J., ed., *Whither American Education* (pamphlet) (New York: America Press, 1948), 73-77.

40. Philip A. Grant, "Catholic Congressmen, Cardinal Spellman, Eleanor Roosevelt, and the 1949-1950 Federal Aid to Education Controversy," *Records of the American Catholic Historical Society of Philadelphia* 90 (March-December 1979): 3-13.

41. Brubacher and Rudy, *Higher Education in Transition*, 232-37; Robert Drinan, S.J., "Catholic Colleges and the Academic Facilities Bill of 1963," *National Catholic Educational Association Bulletin* 60 (August 1964): 155-62; excerpts from consultors' reports to Fr. General returned to the Missouri Province, 1 April 1964, AMPSJ; and Neil McCluskey, S.J., "The Governance," in *The Catholic University: A Modern Appraisal*, 153.

42. Creighton University, "Challenge for Century II," 1980; St. Louis University, "Resources for the Future," 1984; and Hanna, *Catholics and American Politics*, 48-50.

43. For observations on the impact of Catholic colleges and universities, see Alice Gallin, O.S.U., "The Contribution of Religious Commitment to Education," *Catholic Mind* 76 (March 1978): 9-25; Andrew M. Greeley, "The Changing Scene in Catholic Higher Education," in *Education and Acculturation in Modern Urban Society*, ed. Ernest V. Anderson and Walter B. Kolesnick (Detroit: University of Detroit Press, 1965), 58-59; and Hennesey, *American Catholics*, 321-23 and 327-29.

44. Timothy S. Healy, S.J., "A Rationale for Catholic Higher Education," *National Catholic Educational Association Bulletin* 64 (August 1967): 64; and Greeley, "The Changing

Scene in Catholic Higher Education," 66-75. See also Greeley, *From Backwater to Mainstream*, 78-81.

45. Robert Hassenger, "College and Catholics: An Introduction," in *The Shape of Catholic Higher Education*, 6; *Catholic Colleges and Schools in the United States*, 1938, 33; and Phi Beta Kappa Foundation, "Institutions Sheltering Phi Beta Kappa Chapters, Triennium 1982-1985." PBK awarded chapters to the following Catholic institutions in the years indicated: College of St. Catherine (1938), Catholic University (1941), Fordham (1962), Georgetown (1965), St. Louis University (1968), Notre Dame (1968), Boston College (1971), Manhattan (1971), Marquette (1971), Trinity (1971), Holy Cross (1974), Santa Clara (1977), Villanova (1986), and the University of Dallas (1989).

46. For data on faculty with doctorates, see entries for each institution in A.J. Brumbaugh, ed., *American Universities and Colleges* (Washington, D.C.: American Council on Education, 1948); and *American Universities and Colleges* (New York: Walter de Gruyter, Inc., 1983).

47. Conference Board of Associated Research Councils, *An Assessment of Research-Doctorate Programs in the United States*, 5 vols. (Washington, D.C.: National Academy Press, 1982).

48. Though relatively strong in the fields of history, philosophy, psychology, and physics, Catholic University ranked the lowest of Catholic universities in the disciplines of political science, chemistry, sociology, microbiology, English, and French. For comments on the academic ratings of Catholic universities, see Andrew M. Greeley, "Why Catholic higher learning is lower [sic]," *National Catholic Reporter*, 23 September 1983, 1-6 and 18.

49. See data reported by John Tracy Ellis, "Catholic Intellectual Life: 1984," *America*, 6 October 1984, 179. In 1955-1956, faculty from Catholic colleges and universities received eight of 461 Fulbright scholarships for foreign study and teaching; see "Catholics in the Fulbright Program," *America*, 28 January 1956, 469.

50. Ellis, *American Catholics and the Intellectual Life*; Paul Reinert, S.J., "In Response to Father Greeley," *Jesuit Educational Quarterly* 29 (October 1966): 124-25; National Catholic Educational Association, "A Working Paper: The Future Development of Catholic Institutions of Higher Education," 15 September 1966, ACPSJ; and Greeley, "Why Catholic higher learning is lower" [sic], 5.

51. For a summary of criticisms, see Greeley, *The American Catholic*, 69-73.

52. Lehman and Witty, "Scientific Eminence and Church Membership," 549; Gustave Weigel, S.J., "American Catholic Intellectualism: A Theologian's Reflections," *Review of Politics* 19 (July 1957): 65-89; and O'Dea, *American Catholic Dilemma*, 29-68.

53. Greeley, *The American Catholic*, 73-89; R.L. Schnell and Patricia T. Rooke, "Intellectualism, Educational Achievement, and American Catholicism: A Reconsideration of a Controversy, 1955-1975," *Canadian Review of American Studies* 8 (Spring 1977): 66-76; and Andrew M. Greeley, "Catholic Intellectual Life," *America*, 24 November 1984, 335.

54. See such documents as the "Land O'Lakes Statement: The Nature of the Contemporary Catholic University," in *The Catholic University: A Modern Appraisal*, 336-41; Hesburgh, "The Changing Face of Catholic Higher Education," 54-60; University of Santa Clara, "Goals and Guidelines," 1 February 1979; and University of Notre Dame, "A Report on Priorities and Commitments for Excellence at the University of Notre Dame," 30 November 1982, Office of the Provost.

55. Jencks and Riesman, *The Academic Revolution*, 349. See also Alexander W. Astin and John L. Holland, "The Distribution of 'Wealth' in Higher Education," *College and University* 37 (Winter 1962): 113-25.

56. Plough, "Catholic Colleges and the Catholic Educational Association," 164-65, 274-81, 380-84, and 489-503; James W. Sanders, *The Education of an Urban Minority: Catholics in Chicago, 1833-1965* (New York: Oxford University Press, 1977), 175-76; and

Kantowicz, *Corporation Sole*, 107-8.

57. Zuercher to McCormick, 2 March 1947, "Fr. Gen.-Am. Ass't Corr., 1946-59," Section VI, AMPSJ.

58. "Report of the Committee on Graduate Studies," *National Catholic Educational Association Bulletin* 38 (August 1941): 183; Crocker, *The Student Guide to Catholic Colleges and Universities*, 454-66; and Furniss, ed., *American Universities and Colleges*, 1970, 1784-1803.

59. Fitzpatrick, "Mass Education and Education Dilution," 116; Ellis, *American Catholics and the Intellectual Life*, 44; and Reinert, "The Responsibility of American Catholic Higher Education in Meeting National Needs," 136. See also Wilson, "Catholic College Education, 1900-1950," 122-23; and William T. Mulloy, "Catholic Higher Education Looks Ahead," *National Catholic Educational Association Bulletin* 50 (August 1953): 200.

60. Roy J. Deferrari, "Cooperation in Catholic Higher Education," *National Catholic Educational Association Bulletin* 42 (February 1946): 13-26; Meng, "American Thought: Contributions of Catholic Thought and Thinkers," 119; Archbishop Paul J. Hallinan, "The Responsibility of Catholic Higher Education," *National Catholic Educational Association Bulletin* 60 (August 1963): 149-52; Paul Reinert, S.J., "Toward Renewal: The Development of Catholic Higher Education," *National Catholic Educational Association Bulletin* 64 (August 1967): 74-78. Catholic educators in the 1980s have exhibited scant awareness of these earlier calls for limitations on growth and commitment to institutional cooperation, nor have they been inclined to reduce duplication of facilities and programs.

61. Janssens to Leo Sullivan, S.J., provincial of the Chicago Province, 20 April 1948, ACPSJ. Edward Rooney, head of the JEA, had proposed this consolidation plan at the JEA's annual meeting in 1948; see his "Report of the Executive Director, 1948," *Jesuit Educational Quarterly* 11 (June 1948): 6-7.

62. Schoder to Edward Rooney, S.J., excerpt of letter dated 30 May 1956, in minutes of the JEA Executive Committee meeting, Marquette University, 17-19 April 1957, Drawer 73, ACPSJ; and Robert J. Henle, S.J., "Jesuit Education: Expansion or Strategic Development," in "Proceedings, Jesuit Educational Association, Commission of Presidents of Jesuit Colleges and Universities," Santa Clara, 17-20 August 1964, 55-56, ACPSJ.

63. Minutes of meeting of the deans of Jesuit graduate schools, New York, 12 January 1949, "JEA meetings—Grad. Schools," Drawer 77, ACPSJ; minutes of JEA Executive Committee meeting, Kansas City, 9-11 April 1952, Drawer 73, ACPSJ; responses from the JEA Board of Governors [provincials], 9 May 1952, "Graduate Depts. and Regulations," Drawer 8, ACPSJ; and "Report," JEA Commission on Graduate Schools, 6-7 December 1952 and 7 February 1953, "Graduate Depts. and Regulations," Drawer 8, ACPSJ.

64. "Proceedings," JEA Commission of Jesuit Presidents, 1964, 15-19, ACPSJ; minutes of provincials' meeting, Canisius College, Buffalo, 26-28 March 1965, 9, ACPSJ; and Duce to Rooney, 23 July 1954, "Corr. with Prefect Generals," Box 20, JEA Collection, ABC.

65. Philip S. Moore, C.S.C., "Report of the Committee on Graduate Study," *National Catholic Educational Association Bulletin* 50 (August 1953): 162.

66. "Proceedings of [Jesuit Educational Association] Workshop on the Role of Philosophy and Theology as Academic Disciplines and Their Integration with the Moral, Religious and Spiritual Life of the Jesuit College Student," Loyola University, Los Angeles, 6-14 August 1962, vol. 5, 430, ACPSJ.

67. See "Proceedings," JEA Commission on Colleges and Universities, St. Louis, 15 April 1963, Drawer 77, ACPSJ; and Edward Rooney, S.J., "Interim Report of President to the Board of Governors, 1963," Drawer 73, ACPSJ.

68. For a summary of the presidents' efforts for complete autonomy and the subsequent development of Jesuit higher education, see FitzGerald, *The Governance of Jesuit Colleges*, 167-88 and 209-20.

69. Rooney to Janssens, 5 February 1955, Rooney memoranda, vol. 2, JEA Collection, ABC; Weigel, "American Catholic Intellectualism," 82. See also James F. Maguire, S.J., "High Admissions Standards and Our Apostolic Mission," in "Proceedings of Conference of Presidents of Jesuit Colleges and Universities, Georgetown University," 3-4 January 1958, Appendix H, 40-41, Drawer 77, ACPSJ.

70. "Report," JEA Commission on Graduate Schools, 6-7 December 1952 and 7 February 1953, 11 and 14, "Graduate Depts. and Regulations," Drawer 8, ACPSJ. For the revised version of this proposal and the list of fields chosen for preeminence, see "Principles and Policies Governing Graduate Programs in Jesuit Institutions," 1958, ACPSJ.

71. During the drafting of the proposal, one of the officials present (Henry Casper, S.J., dean of the graduate school at Creighton) expressed doubts about the plan. He questioned whether American Jesuits could build preeminent doctoral departments while at the same time expending manpower and money to develop less rigorous Ph.D. programs oriented to regional needs. See the second part of the report's first draft, 9 December 1952, 5, "JEA Grad. Commission—1950-1959," Drawer 3, Barnett Papers, AMU.

72. "Minutes of the meeting of the presidents and deans of the graduate schools of the central regional unit of the JEA," Loyola University, Chicago, 21 November 1953, 7, "Grad Schools," Drawer 8, ACPSJ; Farrell and Fitzsimons, "A Study of Jesuit Education," 376, ACPSJ; and "Graduate Programs at Jesuit Colleges and Universities, May 1, 1967," ACPSJ.

73. See Conference Board, *An Assessment of Research-Doctorate Programs: Biological Sciences*.

74. Donovan, *The Academic Man in the Catholic College*, 121 and 152; Arthur North, S.J., "Why Is the American Catholic Graduate School Failing to Develop Catholic Intellectualism?" *National Catholic Educational Association Bulletin* 53 (August 1956): 184-89; Jencks and Riesman, *The Academic Revolution*, 373; and Fisher to Janssens, 29 May 1960, "Letters to Fr. Gen., 1952-60," AMPSJ.

75. Steinberg, *The Academic Melting Pot*: 165; and Jencks and Riesman, *The Academic Revolution*, 373, fn. 64. See also Donald McDonald, ed., *Catholics in Conversation* (Philadephia: J.B. Lippincott Company, 1960), 249-50.

76. Steinberg, *The Academic Melting Pot*, 146-52 and 161-66.

77. For criticisms of Catholic educational leadership, see Ellis, "American Catholics and the Intellectual Life—Some Reactions," *National Catholic Educational Association Bulletin* 53 (August 1956): 107-8; Meng, "American Thought: Contributions of Catholic Thought and Thinkers," ibid., 120; "The Future Development of Catholic Institutions of Higher Education," NCEA Working Paper, 1966, 7-16, ACPSJ; and Andrew M. Greeley, *The Changing Catholic College* (Chicago: Aldine Publishing Company, 1967), 144-50.

78. For a sampling of Rooney's educational views in this period, see "1945 President's Report," Drawer 73, ACPSJ; minutes of JEA Executive Committee meeting, Loyola University, Los Angeles, 24-26 March 1948, ibid.; "Report of the Executive Director, 1948," *Jesuit Educational Quarterly* 11 (June 1948): 7; and minutes of JEA Executive Committee meeting, Fordham University, 1-3 April 1953, 17, Drawer 73, ACPSJ.

79. For Janssens' views on American Jesuit education, see Janssens to Leopold J. Robinson, S.J., provincial of Oregon Province, 23 April 1947, 1947 provincials' meeting, ACPSJ; Janssens to Leo D. Sullivan, S.J., provincial of Chicago Province, 20 April 1948, 1948 provincials' meeting, ibid.; Janssens to Joseph D. O'Brien, S.J., provincial of the California Province, 1 April 1951, 1951 provincials' meeting, ibid.; Janssens to John J. McMahon, S.J., provincial of the New York Province, 25 April 1952, 1952 provincials' meeting, ibid.; Janssens to American provincials, 19 June 1952, "Corr. with Fr. Gen., 1945-60," Box 36, JEA Collection, ABC.

80. William F. Kelley, S.J., *The Jesuit Order and Higher Education in the United States, 1789-*

1966 (Milwaukee: Wisconsin Jesuit Province, 1966), 53; Janssens to Rooney, 7 February 1955 and Rooney to Janssens, 12 March 1953, "Corr. with Fr. Gen. and Fr. Ass't, 1945-1950," Box 36, JEA Collection, ABC; minutes, meeting of presidents and graduate school deans of JEA central region, 21 November 1952, "Grad Schools," Drawer 8, ACPSJ.

81. Rooney to Vincent McCormick, S.J., 27 July 1954, "Corr. with Fr. Ass't., 1947-1956," Box 36, JEA Collection, ABC; Rooney to American provincials, 29 September 1954, "JEA Correspondence, (1948-1955)," Drawer 74, ACPSJ; Rooney to Janssens, 5 February 1955, 7, Rooney memoranda, vol. 2, JEA Collection, ABC; and Janssens to Henry Schultheis, S.J., provincial of the Oregon Province, 14 April 1955, 1955 provincials' meeting, ACPSJ; and FitzGerald, *The Governance of Jesuit Colleges*, 102-4.

82. Janssens to Carroll O'Sullivan, S.J., provincial of the California Province, 25 November 1958, "Confidential memos—Rooney," Box 20, JEA Collection, ABC; Rooney to Janssens, 23 August 1963, Rooney memoranda, vol. 2, JEA Collection, ABC; and Janssens to American provincials, 22 June 1964, "JEA Const. Revision," File "III. Education Section," AMPSJ.

83. For example, see Robert F. Harvanek, S.J., "The Objectives of the American Jesuit University—A Dilemma," *Jesuit Educational Quarterly* 24 (June 1961): 69-87; Manning M. Pattillo, Jr., "The Danforth Report and Catholic Higher Education," *National Catholic Educational Association Bulletin* 63 (August 1966): 214-15; and Andrew M. Greeley, "The Problems of Jesuit Higher Education in the United States," *Jesuit Educational Quarterly* 29 (October 1966): 108-9.

84. "Proceedings of Conference of Jesuit University and College Presidents," Denver, 8-9 January 1961, 35, ACPSJ; Rooney to Harold Small, S.J., assistant to the Jesuit superior general for the United States, 17 January 1962, "Corr. with Fr. Ass't, 1957-1963," Box 36, JEA Collection, ABC; and Rooney to Janssens, 17 August 1964, "Rooney Corr. with Rome, Jan.-Nov., 1964," Box 35, JEA Collection, ABC.

6

Catholics, Higher Education, and the Future

The question of secularization concerns many supporters of Catholic colleges and universities today—quite understandably, given the historical record and the many changes in the size, scope, curriculum, personnel, and governance in Catholic postsecondary schools since 1945.[1] Moreover, Catholic higher education has not been immune from secularizing pressures and negative aspects of academic professionalism. But while loss of religious purpose and identity is a real possibility and some existing Catholic colleges and universities may merge, close, or become nonsectarian schools, it is not inevitable that the entire Catholic higher educational network will fade as a force in American religious and educational culture.

First of all, Catholic schools since 1900 have improved significantly in faculty, facilities, and academic quality, especially on the under-graduate level. Almost all Catholic colleges and universities currently operate with the full approval of regional accrediting organizations. Course offerings have been expanded to include extensive graduate, business, and professional programs. In addition, Catholic colleges and universities have developed programs to raise funds from government and foundation sources, alumni, and their local communities.

Furthermore, contemporary Catholic higher education still seeks to communicate Catholic intellectual and religious values. Though Catholic schools have revised their curricula in recent decades, they remain committed to the humanities and, in particular, to the study of philosophy and theology. For example, in 1985, the twenty-eight American Jesuit postsecondary institutions required an average of eight semester hours of philosophy and 7.5 credits in theology.[2] A strong case can be made that contemporary Catholic colleges and universities do a far superior job of teaching philosophy and theology than they did before 1940 and that they are less caught up in indoctrination and a defensive Catholicism.

Most Catholic colleges and universities also have the benefit of trustees and at least a solid core of administrators and faculty who are sympathetic with Catholicism and who greatly want to enhance the Catholic character of their schools. These individuals, including clergy, religious, lay Catholics, Protestants, and Jews, provide a sense of continuity and help assimilate newcomers into the particular cultures of Catholic schools. Their ideas, generosity, and zeal represent rich resources for Catholic postsecondary schools.

Clearly, Catholic higher education faces the future with definite academic and religious strengths. But to continue serving and affecting modern society in the twenty-first century, Catholic colleges and universities must confront two crucial challenges. First, they need to devise ways of attracting and retaining personnel committed to the religious and academic goals of Catholic education. Before the 1960s, schools could usually draw on lay Catholics and members of the sponsoring religious community to fill vacancies. But the number of priests, sisters, and brothers available for faculty and administrative positions in higher education will continue to decline; and finding lay applicants, especially Catholics, who are academically qualified and who are interested in furthering the religious dimensions of Catholic higher education has already become difficult.

Catholic higher education in the United States also urgently requires a coherent, convincing theory of education and articulate, persuasive proponents of it. Before World War II, Catholic colleges and universities in America had a clear and compelling sense of purpose: to protect the faith of Catholics and to make it possible for Catholics to obtain a college education. But today changes in American culture, higher education, and the Catholic Church have largely dissolved the former consensus regarding the nature, characteristics, and meaning of Catholic education. Some advances have been made with recent mission statements, but too often these documents remain unread and lifeless, despite their value and impressive rhetoric. Consequently, Catholic postsecondary schools suffer from a lack of vision; and as Proverbs 29:18 proclaims, "Where there is no vision, the people perish."

Enabling Catholic higher education to remain true to the Catholic intellectual and religious heritage and to influence American academic culture and wider society in the years ahead will require intelligence, courage, tenacity, and hope. In particular, those involved in Catholic colleges and universities must effectively combine academic professionalism and religious commitment. Doing so should lead to renewed vigor in the Catholic educational enterprise, and it should also contribute immensely to helping Catholics in the United States determine what it means to be both American and Catholic.

Notes

1. For a sampling of comments in recent years about the religious identity and future of Catholic higher education, see George A. Kelly, ed., *Why Should the Catholic University Survive?* (New York: St. John's University Press, 1973); Dougherty, et al., "The Secularization of Western Culture," 7-23; Edmund Pellegrino, "Catholic Universities and the Church's Intellectual Ministry: The Crises of Identity and Justification," *Thought* 57 (June 1982): 165-79; David Riesman, "Reflections on Catholic Colleges, Especially Jesuit Colleges," *Journal of General Education* 34 (Summer 1982): 106-9; William J. Parente, "Are Catholic Colleges Still Catholic?" *Current Issues in Catholic Higher Education* 6 (Summer 1985): 29-34; Michael J. Wreen, "'Catholic' Universities: Independent or Nonsectarian?" *Fidelity* 6 (March 1987): 13-15; Joseph A. O'Hare, S.J., "The Vatican and Catholic Universities," *America*, 27 May 1989, 503-5; and Kenneth Woodward, "The Order of Education: Have the Jesuit Lost Their Special Touch?" *Newsweek*, 19 June 1989, 59.

2. Parente, "Are Catholic Colleges Still Catholic?" 30-31.

Selected Bibliography

Archival Sources

Boston, Massachusetts. Archives of Boston College. Jesuit Educational Association Collection. Edward B. Rooney, S.J. Papers.

Los Gatos, California. Archives of the California Province of the Society of Jesus.

Milwaukee, Wisconsin. Archives of Marquette University. General Administration Files. Maximilian G. Barnett Papers.

Omaha, Nebraska. Archives of Creighton University.

St. Louis, Missouri. Archives of St. Louis University.

St. Louis, Missouri. Archives of the Missouri Province of the Society of Jesus. Jesuit Education Collection. Francis X. McMenamy, S.J. Papers.

St. Louis, Missouri. Archives of the Jesuit Community, St. Louis University. Jesuit Education Collection.

Santa Clara, California. Archives of Santa Clara University.

Directories

American Universities and Colleges, 1928-1983.

Biographical Dictionary of American Mayors, 1820-1980. Edited by Melvin G. Holli and Peter d'A. Jones. Westport, Conn.: Greenwood Press, 1981.

Biographical Directory of the American Congress, 1774-1971. Washington: Government Printing Office, 1974.

Dictionary of American Catholic Biography. Garden City, N.Y.: Doubleday and Company, 1984.

Dictionary of Catholic Biography. Garden City, N.Y.: Doubleday and Company, 1961.
Directory of Catholic Colleges and Schools, 1921-1950.
Directory of the Jesuit Educational Association, 1945 and 1947-1970.
Directory, Association of Jesuit Colleges and Universities, 1970-1985.
Educational Directory, Colleges and Universities, 1983-1984. Compiled by Susan G. Broyles and Rosa M. Fernandez. Washington, D.C.: National Center for Educational Statistics, 1984.
Official Guide to Catholic Educational Institutions and Religious Communities in the United States, 1959-1973.
The Student Guide to Catholic Colleges and Universities. Compiled by John R. Crocker, S.J. San Francisco: Harper & Row, Publishers, 1982.

Periodicals

Association of Catholic Colleges. *Report of the Annual Conferences,* 1899-1903.
Catholic Educational Association. *Report of the Proceedings,* 1904-1907.
Catholic Educational Association Bulletin, 1907-1969. [The word *National* was added to the title in 1927.]
Jesuit Educational Quarterly, 1938-1970.
Woodstock Letters, 1880-1938.

Books

Abell, Aaron I. *American Catholicism and Social Action: A Search for Social Justice, 1865-1950.* Garden City, N.Y.: Doubleday & Company, 1960.
Angelo, Mark V., O.F.M. *The History of St. Bonaventure University.* St. Bonaventure, N.Y.: Franciscan Institute, 1961.
Annarelli, James J. *Academic Freedom and Catholic Higher Education.* Westport, Conn: Greenwood Press, 1987.
Axt, Richard G. *The Federal Government and Financing Higher Education.* New York: Columbia University Press, 1945.
Banner, Lois W. *Women in Modern America: A Brief History.* New York: Harcourt Brace Jovanovich, 1974.
Bianchi, Eugene. *John XXIII and American Protestants.* Washington, D.C.: Corpus Books, 1968.
Birmingham, Stephen. *Real Lace, America's Irish Rich.* New York: Harper & Row, 1973.
Bennish, Lee J., S.J. *Continuity and Change: Xavier University 1831-1981.* Chicago: Loyola University Press, 1981.

Bledstein, Burton J. *The Culture of Professionalism: The Middle Class and the Development of Higher Education in America.* New York: W.W. Norton and Company, 1976.

Brady, Charles A. *The First Hundred Years: Canisius College 1870-1970.* Buffalo: Canisius College, 1969.

Browne, Henry J. *The Catholic Church and the Knights of Labor.* Washington, D.C.: Catholic University of America Press, 1949.

Brubacher, John S., and Willis Rudy. *Higher Education in Transition: A History of American Colleges and Universities, 1636-1976.* 3d ed. New York: Harper & Row Publishers, 1976.

Buetow, Harold. *Of Singular Benefit: The Story of Catholic Education in the United States.* New York: The Macmillan Company, 1970.

Burke, Colin E. *American Collegiate Populations: A Test of the Traditional View.* New York: New York University Press, 1982.

Callahan, Daniel. *The Mind of the Catholic Layman.* New York: Charles Scribner's Sons, 1963.

Carlen, Claudia, compiler. *The Papal Encyclicals 1903-1939.* Wilmington, N. C.: McGrath Publishing Company, 1981.

Commission on Financing Higher Education. *Nature and Needs of Higher Education.* New York: Columbia University Press, 1952.

Conference Board of Associated Research Councils. *An Assessment of Research-Doctorate Programs in the United States.* 5 vols. Washington, D.C.: National Academy Press, 1982.

Coogan, M. Jane, B.V.M. *The Price Of Our Heritage.* 2 vols. Dubuque: Mount Carmel Press, 1978.

Cross, Robert D. *The Emergence of Liberal Catholicism in America.* Cambridge: Harvard University Press, 1958.

Curry, Lerond. *Protestant-Catholic Relations in America, World War I through Vatican II.* Lexington, Ky.: University Press of Kentucky, 1972.

Datelines: Canisius College, 1870-1980. Buffalo: Canisius College, 1981.

Davis, Calvin O. *A History of the North Central Association of Colleges and Secondary Schools, 1895-1945.* Ann Arbor, Mich.: North Central Association, 1945.

Davis, Martin W. *The Sister as Campus Minister.* Washington, D.C.: Center for Applied Research in the Apostolate, 1970.

Deferrari, Roy J. *Memoirs of the Catholic University of America, 1918-1960.* Boston: Daughters of St. Paul, 1962.

_____., ed. *Essays on Catholic Education in the United States.* Washington, D.C.: Catholic University of America Press, 1942; reprint ed., Freeport, N.Y.: Books for Libraries Press, 1969.

_____., ed. *Vital Problems of Catholic Education in the United States.* Washington, D.C.: Catholic University of America Press, 1939.

Degler, Carl. *At Odds: Women and the Family in America from the Revolution to the Present.* New York: Oxford University Press, 1980.

Dohen, Dorothy. *Nationalism and American Catholicism.* New York: Sheed and Ward, 1967.

Dolan, Jay P. *The American Catholic Experience.* New York: Doubleday and Company, 1985.

_____. *The Immigrant Church: New York's Irish and German Catholics, 1815-1865.* Baltimore: Johns Hopkins University Press, 1975.

Donovan, John D. *The Academic Man in the Catholic College.* New York: Sheed and Ward, 1964.

Dunigan, David R., S.J. *A History of Boston College.* Milwaukee: Bruce Publishing Company, 1947.

Elliot, Orrin. *Stanford University: The First Twenty-Five Years.* Stanford: Stanford University Press, 1937.

Ellis, John Tracy. *American Catholicism.* 2d ed. Chicago: University of Chicago Press, 1969.

_____. *Catholic Bishops: A Memoir.* Wilmington, Del.: Michael Glazier, 1983.

_____. *American Catholics and the Intellectual Life.* Chicago: Heritage Foundation, 1956.

_____. *The Formative Years of the Catholic University of America.* Washington, D.C.: American Catholic Historical Association, 1946.

Evans, John Whitney. *The Newman Movement: Roman Catholics in American Higher Education, 1883-1971.* Notre Dame, Ind.: University of Notre Dame Press, 1980.

Faherty, William B., S.J. *Better the Dream: Saint Louis: University and Community.* St. Louis, n.p., 1968.

Feldman, Saul D. *Escape from the Doll's House: Women in Graduate and Professional School Education.* New York: McGraw-Hill Book Company, 1974.

FitzGerald, Paul A., S.J. *The Governance of Jesuit Colleges in the United States, 1920-1970.* Notre Dame, Ind.: University of Notre Dame Press, 1984.

Flynn, George Q. *American Catholics & the Roosevelt Presidency.* Lexington, Ky.: University of Kentucky Press, 1968.

Fogarty, Gerald P., S.J., ed. *Patterns of Episcopal Leadership.* New York: Macmillan Publishing Company, 1989.

_____. *The Vatican and the American Hierarchy from 1870 to 1965.* Wilmington, Del.: Michael Glazier, 1985.

Gannon, Robert I., S.J. *The Poor Old Liberal Arts.* New York: Farrar, Straus & Cudahy, 1961.

_____. *Up to the Present: The Story of Fordham.* Garden City, N.Y.: Doubleday & Company, 1967.

Gaustad, Edwin S. *Historical Atlas of Religion in America.* New York: Harper & Row, 1976.

Gavin, Donald P. *John Carroll University: A Century of Service.* Bowling Green, Ohio: Kent State University Press, 1985.

Greeley, Andrew M. *The American Catholic: A Social Portrait.* New York: Basic Books, 1977.

_____. *The Changing Catholic College.* Chicago: Aldine Publishing Company, 1967.

_____. *From Backwater to Mainstream: A Profile of Catholic Higher Education.* New York: McGraw-Hill Book Company, 1969.

Halsey, William M. *The Survival of American Innocence: Catholicism in an Era of Disillusionment, 1920-1940.* Notre Dame, Ind.: University of Notre Dame Press, 1980.

Hamilton, Raphael, S.J. *The Story of Marquette University.* Milwaukee: Marquette University Press, 1953.

Handlin, Oscar and Mary. *The American College and American Culture.* New York: McGraw-Hill Book Company, 1970.

Handy, Robert T. *A History of the Churches in the United States and Canada.* New York: Oxford University Press, 1976; paperback, 1979.

Hanna, Mary. *Catholics and American Politics.* Cambridge: Harvard University Press, 1979.

Harris, Seymour E. *A Statistical Portrait of Higher Education.* New York: McGraw-Hill Book Company, 1972.

Hatch, Nathan O., ed. *The Professions in American History.* Notre Dame, Ind.: University of Notre Dame Press, 1988.

Hennesey, James, S.J. *American Catholics: A History of the Roman Catholic Community in the United States.* New York: Oxford University Press, 1981.

Henry, David D. *Challenges Past, Challenges Present.* San Francisco: Jossey-Bass Publishers, 1975.

Hofstadter, Richard. *Academic Freedom in the Age of the College.* New York: Columbia University Press, 1955.

_____, and C. Dewitt Hardy. *The Development and Scope of Higher Education in the United States.* New York: Columbia University Press, 1952.

_____, and Walter Metzger. *The Development of Academic Freedom in the United States.* New York: Columbia University Press, 1955.

Hunt, John F., and Terrence R. Connelly. *The Responsibility of Dissent: The Church and Academic Freedom.* New York: Sheed and Ward, 1969.

Isetti, Ronald E., F.S.C. *Called to the Pacific: A History of the Christian Brothers of the San Francisco District, 1868-1944.* Moraga, Calif.: St. Mary's College of California, 1979.

Jencks, Christopher, and David Riesman. *The Academic Revolution.* Garden City, N.Y.: Doubleday & Company, 1968.

Kantowicz, Edward. *Corporation Sole: Cardinal Mundelein and Chicago Catholicism.* Notre Dame, Ind.: University of Notre Dame Press, 1983.

Kelley, William F., S.J. *The Jesuit Order and Higher Education in the United States, 1789-1966.* Milwaukee: Wisconsin Jesuit Province, 1966.

Kelly, George A., ed. *Why Should the Catholic University Survive?* New York: St. John's University Press, 1973.

Kessner, Thomas. *The Golden Door: Italian and Jewish Immigrant Mobility in New York City, 1880-1915.* New York: Oxford University Press, 1977.

Lannie, Vincent P. *Public Money and Parochial Education: Bishop Hughes, Governor Seward, and the New York School Controversy.* Cleveland: Case Western Reserve University Press, 1968.

Limbert, Paul Moyer. *Denominational Policies in the Support and Supervision of Higher Education.* New York: Teachers College Press, 1929.

Linkh, Richard M. *American Catholicism and European Immigrants, 1900-1924.* Staten Island, N.Y.: Center for Migration Studies, 1975.

Liptak, Delores, R.S.M. *Immigrants and Their Church.* New York: Macmillan Publishing Company, 1989.

McAvoy, Thomas T., C.S.C. *The Great Crisis in American Catholic History, 1895-1900.* Chicago: Henry Regnery Company, 1957.

_____. *A History of the Catholic Church in the United States.* Notre Dame, Ind.: University of Notre Dame Press, 1969.

McCluskey, Neil, S.J., ed. *The Catholic University: A Modern Appraisal.* Notre Dame, Ind.: University of Notre Dame Press, 1970.

McDonald, Donald, ed. *Catholics in Conversation.* Philadelphia: J.B. Lippincott Company, 1960.

McKevitt, Gerald, S.J. *The University of Santa Clara: A History.* Stanford, Calif.: Stanford University Press, 1979.

McShane, Joseph M., S.J. *"Sufficiently Radical": Catholicism, Progressivism, and the Bishops' Program of 1919.* Washington, D.C.: Catholic University of America Press, 1986.

Moore, Philip S., C.S.C. "Academic Development, University of Notre Dame: Past, Present, and Future." Notre Dame, 1960. [mimeographed]

Moore, John F. *Will America Become Catholic?* New York: Harper & Brothers, 1931.

Muller, Herman J., S.J. *The University of Detroit, 1877-1977.* Detroit: n.p., 1976.

Nelli, Humbert. *The Italians in Chicago 1880-1930: A Study in Ethnic Mobility.* New York: Oxford University Press, 1970.

Newcomer, Mabel. *A Century of Higher Education for American Women.* New York: Harper & Brothers, 1959.

Nolan, Hugh J., ed. *Pastoral Letters of the United States Catholic Bishops.* Vol. 1: 1792-1940. Washington, D.C.: United States Catholic Conference, 1984.

Oates, Mary J., ed. *Higher Education for Catholic Women: An Historical Anthology.* New York: Garland Publishing, 1987.

O'Brien, David J. *American Catholics and Social Reform.* New York: Oxford University Press, 1968.

_____. *The Renewal of American Catholicism.* New York: Oxford University Press, 1972; paperback ed., Paramus, N.J.: Paulist Press, 1974.

O'Connell, Marvin R. *John Ireland and the American Catholic Church.* St. Paul: Minnesota Historical Society Press, 1988.

O'Dea, Thomas F. *American Catholic Dilemma.* New York: Sheed and Ward, 1958; Mentor Omega Books, 1962.

Parsonage, Robert Rue, ed. *Church Related Higher Education: Perceptions and Perspectives.* Valley Forge: Judson Press, 1978.

Piehl, Mel. *Breaking Bread: The Catholic Worker and the Origins of Catholic Radicalism in America.* Philadelphia: Temple University Press, 1982.

Power, Edward. *A History of Catholic Higher Education in the United States.* Milwaukee: Bruce Publishing Company, 1958.

_____. *Catholic Higher Education in America: A History.* New York: Appleton-Century Crofts, 1972.

President's Commission on Higher Education. *Higher Education for American Democracy.* 6 vols. Washington, D.C.: Government Printing Office, 1947-1948.

Project One: The Jesuit Apostolate of Education in the United States. 6 vols. Washington, D.C.: Jesuit Conference, 1974-1975.

Reilly, Daniel F., O.P. *The School Controversy, 1891-1893.* Washington, D.C.: Catholic University of America Press, 1943; reprint ed., New York: Arno Press, 1969.

Ringenberg, William C. *The Christian College: A History of Protestant Higher Education in America.* Grand Rapids: Christian University Press, 1984.

Rischin, Moses. *The Promised City: New York Jews, 1870-1914.* Cambridge: Harvard University Press, 1962.

Rudolph, Frederick. *The American College and University, A History.* New York: Alfred A. Knopf, 1962.

Sanders, James. *The Education of an Urban Minority: Catholics in Chicago, 1833-1965.* Chicago: University of Chicago Press, 1977.

Scaglione, Aldo. *The Liberal Arts and the Jesuit College System*. Amsterdam/Philadelphia: John Benjamins Publishing Company, 1986.

Schlereth, Thomas J. *The University of Notre Dame: A Portrait of Its History and Campus*. Notre Dame: University of Notre Dame Press, 1976.

Schoenberg, Wilfred P., S.J. *Paths to the Northwest: A Jesuit History of the Oregon Province*. Chicago: Loyola University Press, 1982.

Selden, William K. *Accreditation: A Struggle over Standards in Higher Education*. New York: Harper & Brothers, 1960.

Shaw, Richard. *Dagger John: The Unquiet Life and Times of Archbishop John Hughes of New York*. New York: Paulist Press, 1977.

Solberg, Richard W., and Merton P. Strommen. *How Church-Related Are Church-Related Colleges?* New York: Division for Mission in North America, Lutheran Church, 1980.

Solomon, Barbara. *In the Company of Educated Women*. New Haven: Yale University Press, 1985.

Stansell, Harold L., S.J. *Regis: On the Crest of the West*. Denver: Regis Educational Corporation, 1977.

Steinberg, Stephen. *The Academic Melting Pot: Catholics and Jews in American Higher Education*. New York: McGraw-Hill Book Company, 1974.

Synnott, Marcia Graham. *The Half-Opened Door: Discrimination and Admissions at Harvard, Yale, and Princeton, 1900-1970*. Westport, Conn.: Greenwood Press, 1979.

Tewksbury, Donald G. *The Founding of American Colleges and Universities before the Civil War*. New York: Columbia University Press, 1932.

Thernstrom, Stephen. *The Other Bostonians: Poverty and Progress in the American Metropolis, 1880-1970*. Cambridge: Harvard University Press, 1973.

_____. *Poverty and Progress: Social Mobility in a Nineteenth Century City*. Cambridge: Harvard University Press, 1964.

Tyack, David B. *The One Best System: A History of American Urban Education*. Cambridge: Harvard University Press, 1974.

Veysey, Laurence R. *The Emergence of the American University*. Chicago: University of Chicago Press, 1965; Phoenix Books, 1974.

Ward, Leo R., C.S.C. *Blueprint for a Catholic University*. St. Louis: B. Herder Book Company, 1949.

Weber, Ralph E. *Notre Dame's John Zahm: American Catholic Apologist and Educator*. Notre Dame, Ind.: University of Notre Dame Press, 1961.

Whelan, James F., S.J., compiler. *Catholic Colleges of the United States of America 1952-1953*. New Orleans: Loyola University, 1954.

Woody, Thomas. *A History of Women's Education in the United States.* 2 vols. New York: Science Press, 1929.

Articles and Pamphlets

"Accredited Higher Institutions." *Educational Record* 1 (October 1920): 71-80.

Ament, William S. "Religion, Education, and Distinction." *School and Society* 26 (24 September 1927): 399-406.

Aquinas, Sr. Thomas, O.S.U. "Some Problems of the Catholic Women's College." *Catholic Educational Association Bulletin* 21 (November 1924): 271-77.

Astin, Alexander W., and John L. Holland. "The Distribution of 'Wealth' in Higher Education." *College and University* 37 (Winter 1962): 113-25.

Bannon, John F., S.J., and Elvis Patea. "Notes for an Academic History of Saint Louis University—Suggested by the Record of Degrees Awarded during Its 163 Years of Service." Office of University Registrar, St. Louis University, 1982.

Barbera, Mario, S.J. "Catholic Foundations in Secular Universities." *Woodstock Letters* 57 (1928): 14-32.

Bergin, William J., C.S.V. "The Conservation of Our Educational Resources." *Catholic Educational Association Bulletin* 14 (November 1917): 57-70.

Betts, John R. "Darwinism, Evolution, and American Catholic Thought, 1860-1900." *Catholic Historical Review* 45 (July 1959): 161-85.

Bocock, John P. "The Irish Conquest of Our Cities." *The Forum* 17 (April 1894): 186-95; reprinted in James B. Walsh, ed., *The Irish: America's Political Class.* New York: Arno Press, 1976.

Bonnette, Dennis. "The Doctrinal Crisis in Catholic Colleges and Universities and Its Effect upon Education." *Social Justice Review* 60 (November 1967): 220-36.

Bowen, Robert O. "The Lay Faculty on the Jesuit Campus." *Ramparts* 1 (March 1963): 16-20.

Brosnahan, Timothy, S.J. *President Eliot and Jesuit Colleges.* Boston: Review Publishing Company, n.d. [pamphlet]

_____. "The Carnegie Foundation for the Advancement of Teaching—Its Aims and Tendency." *Catholic Educational Association Bulletin* 8 (November 1911): 119-56.

Browne, Henry J. "Catholics and the AAUP." *Commonweal,* 5 October 1956, 10-12.

Buckley, Michael J., S.J. "The Catholic University as Pluralistic Forum." *Thought* 46 (June 1971): 200-212.

Bull, George, S.J. "The Function of the Catholic Graduate School." *Thought* 13 (September 1938): 364-80.

Burns, James, C.S.C. "Failures of Our Higher Schools." *Commonweal*, 3 November 1926, 634-36.

Burrowes, Alexander J., S.J. "Attitude of Catholics towards Higher Education." *Catholic Educational Association Bulletin* 16 (November 1919): 159-74.

Canavan, Francis, S.J. "Academic Revolution at St. John's." *America*, 7 August 1965, 136-40.

Cantril, Hadley. "Educational and Economic Composition of Religious Groups: An Analysis of Poll Data." *American Journal of Sociology* 14 (March 1943): 574-79.

Carr, Aidan M. "The Church on Coeducation." *Homiletic and Pastoral Review* 58 (September 1958): 1147-51.

Catherine, Sr. M. "The Higher Education of Women under Catholic Auspices." *Catholic Educational Association Bulletin* 21 (November 1921): 429-40.

"Catholics in the Fulbright Program." *America*, 28 January 1956, 469.

Conley, William. "The Lay Teacher in Catholic Education." *National Catholic Educational Association Bulletin* 59 (August 1962): 25-30.

Conway, Katherine E. "Woman Has No Vocation to Public Life." *Catholic World* 57 (August 1893): 677-81.

Cook, William. "A Comparative Study of Standardizing Agencies." *North Central Association Quarterly* 4 (December 1929): 377-455.

Cross, Robert D. "Origins of the Catholic Parochial Schools in America." *American Benedictine Review* 16 (June 1965): 194-209.

Crowley, Francis M. "American Catholic Universities." *Historical Records and Studies* 29 (1938): 79-106.

_____. "Catholic Education in 1948." *Catholic School Journal* 49 (January 1949): 1-3.

_____. "Catholic Education in the United States." In *The Official Catholic Yearbook, 1928*, 404-25.

_____. "Catholic Graduate Schools." *America*, 21 May 1932, 163-64.

_____. "Institutionalism in Higher Education." *America*, 18 June 1932, 257-58.

_____. "Only One Graduate School?" *America*, 11 June 1932, 234-35.

_____, compiler. *Why a Catholic College Education?* Washington, D.C.: Department of Education, National Catholic Welfare Conference, 1926. [pamphlet]

Curran, Emmett R., S.J. "Conservative Thought and Strategy in the School Controversy." *Notre Dame Journal of Education* 7 (Spring 1976): 44-62.

Dalcourt, Gerard J. "Lay Control of Catholic Colleges." *America*, 14

October 1967, 412-14.

Damann, Grace, R.S.C.J. "The American Catholic College for Women." In *Essays on Catholic Education in the United States,* 173-94. Edited by Roy J. Deferrari. Washington, D.C.: Catholic University of America Press, 1942; reprint ed., Freeport, N.Y.: Books for Libraries Press, 1969.

Deferrari, Roy J. "Are the Popes in Error?" *Commonweal,* 16 December 1931, 181-82.

_____. "Catholics and Graduate Study." *Commonweal,* 24 June 1931, 203-5.

_____. "Cooperation in Catholic Higher Education." *National Catholic Educational Association Bulletin* 42 (February 1946): 13-26.

Dinnerstein, Leonard. "Education and the Advancement of American Jews." In *American Education and the European Immigrant: 1840-1940,* 44-60. Edited by Bernard J. Weiss. Urbana: University of Illinois Press, 1982.

Dolan, Jay P. "American Catholicism and Modernity." *Cross Currents* 31 (Summer 1981): 150-62.

Donnelly, Eleanor C. "The Home Is Woman's Sphere." *Catholic World* 57 (August 1893): 677-81.

Donnelly, F.P., S.J. "Is the American College Doomed?" *American Ecclesiastical Review* 60 (April 1919): 359-65.

Dougherty, Jude P., Desmond Fitzgerald, Thomas Langan, and Kenneth Schmitz. "The Secularization of Western Culture and the Catholic College and University." *Current Issues in Catholic Higher Education* 2 (Summer 1981): 7-23.

Doyle, David Noel. "The Irish and Christian Churches in America." In *America and Ireland, 1776-1976: The America Identity and the Irish Connection,* 177-91. Edited by David Noel Doyle and Owen Dudley Edwards. Westport, Conn.: Greenwood Press, 1980.

Drinan, Robert, S.J. "Catholic Colleges and the Academic Facilities Bill of 1963." *National Catholic Educational Association Bulletin* 60 (August 1964): 155-62.

_____. "The Challenge to Catholic Educators in the Maryland Case." *National Catholic Educational Association Bulletin* 63 (May 1967): 3-7.

Drummond, Edward J. "The Graduate School and Its Responsibility to the Community." *National Catholic Educational Association Bulletin* 44 (August 1947): 284-91.

Dulles, Avery, S.J. "Catholics in Secular Colleges." *Catholic Mind* 49 (September 1951): 559-62.

Ellis, John Tracy. "American Catholics and the Intellectual Life-Some Reactions." *National Catholic Educational Association Bulletin* 53

(August 1956): 105-12.

_____. "Catholic Intellectual Life: 1984." *America*, 6 October 1984, 179-80.

_____. "The Formation of the American Priest: An Historical Perspective." In *The Catholic Priest in the United States: Historical Investigations*, 3-110. Edited by John Tracy Ellis. Collegeville, Minn.: Saint John's University Press, 1971.

Evans, John Whitney. "John LaFarge, *America*, and the Newman Movement." *Catholic Historical Review* 65 (October 1978): 614-43.

Everett, Ruth. "Jesuit Educators and Modern Colleges." *The Arena* 23 (1900): 647-53.

Fagan, James P., S.J. "Meeting of the N.E.A. at Chicago." *Woodstock Letters* 29 (1900): 123-36.

Farrell, John J. "The Catholic Chaplain at the Secular University." *Catholic Educational Association Bulletin* 4 (1907): 150-63.

"F.L." "Dangers of Secular Universities." *Catholic Mind* 14 (22 August 1916): 423-33.

Fitzpatrick, Edward A. "Mass Education and Education Dilution." *Catholic School Journal* 50 (April 1950): 116.

_____. "Theology of Education in the Encyclical on Xian Education." *National Catholic Educational Association Bulletin* 44 (February 1948): 6-26.

Fitzsimons, M.A. "The Catholic University: Problems and Prospects." *Notre Dame Journal of Education* 4 (Fall 1973): 250-57.

Fitzsimons, Matthew J., S.J. "The Instructio, 1934-1949." *Jesuit Educational Quarterly* 12 (October 1949): 69-78.

Gallagher, Francis. "Observations Arising from the Horace Mann Case." *National Catholic Educational Association Bulletin* 63 (August 1966): 232-38.

Gallin, Alice, O.S.U. "The Contribution of Religious Commitment to Education." *Catholic Mind* 76 (March 1978): 9-25.

Gannon, Michael V. "Before and After Modernism: The Intellectual Isolation of the American Priest." In *The Catholic Priest in the United States: Historical Investigations*, 293-383. Edited by John Tracy Ellis. Collegeville, Minn.: Saint John's University Press, 1971.

Gleason, Philip. "Academic Freedom: Survey, Retrospect, and Prospects." *National Catholic Educational Association Bulletin* 64 (November 1967): 67-73.

_____. "American Catholic Higher Education: A Historical Perspective." In *The Shape of Catholic Higher Education*, 15-53. Edited by Robert Hassenger. Chicago: University of Chicago Press, 1967.

_____. "Immigration and American Catholic Intellectual Life." *Review of Politics* 26 (April 1964): 147-73.

Glenn, Noval D., and Ruth Hyland. "Religious Preference and Worldly Success: Some Evidence from National Surveys." *American Sociological Review* 32 (February 1967): 73-85.

Grant, Philip A. "Catholic Congressmen, Cardinal Spellman, Eleanor Roosevelt, and the 1949-1950 Federal Aid to Education Controversy." *Records of the American Catholic Historical Society of Philadelphia* 90 (March-December 1979): 3-13.

Greeley, Andrew M. "Catholic Intellectual Life." *America*, 24 November 1984, 335.

_____. "The Changing Scene in Catholic Higher Education." In *Education and Acculturation in Modern Urban Society*, 57-78. Edited by Ernest V. Anderson and Walter B. Kolesnick. Detroit: University of Detroit Press, 1965.

_____. "Myths and Fads in Catholic Higher Education." *America*, 11 November 1957, 422-25.

_____. "The Problems of Jesuit Higher Education in the United States." *Jesuit Educational Quarterly* 29 (October 1966): 102-20.

_____. "Some Information on the Present Situation of American Catholics." *Social Order* 13 (April 1963): 9-24.

_____. "Why Catholic higher learning is lower [*sic*]." *National Catholic Reporter*, 23 September 1983, 1-6 and 18.

Hall, G. Stanley. "The Question of Coeducation." *Munsey's Magazine* 34 (February 1906): 588-92.

Hallinan, Paul J. "The Responsibility of Catholic Higher Education." *National Catholic Educational Association Bulletin* 60 (August 1963): 145-52.

Harvanek, Robert F., S.J. "The Objectives of the American Jesuit University—A Dilemma." *Jesuit Educational Quarterly* 24 (June 1961): 69-87.

Hassenger, Robert. "Catholic Colleges and Universities after the Second 100 Years." In *Catholics/U.S.A.*, 171-226. Edited by William T. Liu and Nathaniel J. Pallone. New York: John Wiley & Sons, 1970.

_____. "College and Catholics: An Introduction." In *The Shape of Catholic Higher Education*, 3-13. Edited by Robert Hassenger. Chicago: University of Chicago Press, 1967.

Haun, Julius. "The Contribution of the College and University Department of the National Catholic Educational Association to the Growth and Development of Catholic Higher Education in the Past Fifty Years." *National Catholic Educational Association Bulletin* 50 (August 1953): 172-73.

Hayes, Carleton J.H. "A Call for Intellectual Leaders." *Catholic Mind* 20 (22 July 1922): 261-75.

Hayes, Ralph L. "The Problem of Teacher Certification." *Catholic Educational Association Bulletin* 19 (November 1922): 362-69.

Healy, Timothy S., S.J. "A Rationale for Catholic Higher Education." *National Catholic Educational Association Bulletin* 64 (August 1967): 63-67.

Henle, Robert, S.J. "The Future Challenge to Catholic Education." *National Catholic Educational Association Bulletin* 45 (August 1948): 275-86.

Herzfeld, Karl F. "Scientific Research and Religion." *Commonweal*, 20 March 1929, 560-62.

Hesburgh, Theodore, C.S.C. "The Changing Face of Catholic Higher Education." *National Catholic Educational Association Bulletin* 66 (August 1969): 54-60.

[Heuser, H.J.]. "Compulsory Education in the United States." *American Ecclesiastical Review* 3 (December 1890): 420-35.

Higgins, Edward A., S.J. "The American State and Private School." *Catholic World* 53 (July 1891): 521-37.

Hinrichs, Gerard. "Faculty Participation in the Government of Catholic Colleges and Universities." *American Association of University Professors Bulletin* 50 (December 1964): 336-42.

"Historical Notes: Father Joseph Havens Richards' Notes on Georgetown and the Catholic University." *Woodstock Letters* 83 (February 1954): 77-101.

Huntington, Ellsworth, and Leon F. Whitney. "Religion and 'Who's Who.'" *American Mercury* 12 (August 1927): 438-43.

Hutchins, Robert, and William J. McGucken, S.J. "The Integrating Principle of Catholic Higher Education." *College Newsletter, Midwest Regional Unit, N.C.E.A.*, May 1937, 1 and 4.

Ireland, John. "The Mission of Catholics in America." In *The Church and Modern Society*, 49-83. Chicago: D.H. McClurg Co., 1897.

_____. "State Schools and Parish Schools—Is Union between Them Possible?" In *The Journal of Proceedings and Addresses of the National Education Association, 1890*, 179-85. Topeka: Kansas Publishing House, 1890.

Jordan, David Starr. "The Question of Coeducation." *Munsey's Magazine* 34 (March 1906): 683-88.

Judd, Charles H. "List of Approved Colleges and Universities in the North Central Association of Colleges and Secondary Schools for 1913." In *School Review Monographs*, vol. 4, 1-32. Chicago: University of Chicago Press, 1913.

Kean, Helen E. "History of Women in Jesuit Colleges." In *Proceedings of the Jesuit Education Association Workshop for Jesuit Student*

Personnel Programs and Services, 88-110. Regis College, Denver, 18-30 July 1965.

Kearns, Francis E. "Handkerchief Heads and Clerical Collars." *Ramparts* 2 (Winter 1964): 18-24.

Kenneally, James J. "Eve, Mary and the Historians: American Catholicism and Women." *Horizons* 3 (Fall 1976): 187-202.

Kernan, Thomas P. "The Catholic Layman in Higher Education." *Catholic World* 71 (June 1900): 381-85.

Lackner, Joseph H., S.M. "Bishop Ignatius Horstmann and the School Controversy of the 1890s." *Catholic Historical Review* 75 (January 1989): 73-90.

"Land O'Lakes Statement: The Nature of the Contemporary Catholic University." In *The Catholic University: A Modern Appraisal*, 336-41. Edited by Neil McCluskey, S.J. Notre Dame, Ind.: University of Notre Dame Press, 1970.

Lazerson, Marvin. "Understanding Catholic Educational History." *History of Education Quarterly* 16 (Fall 1977): 297-317.

Lazerwitz, Bernard. "A Comparison of Major United States Religious Groups." *Journal of the American Statistical Association* 56 (September 1961): 569-79.

————. "Some Factors Associated with Variations in Church Attendance." *Social Forces* 39 (May 1961): 301-9.

Leader, Robert. "How the Landscape Has Changed." *Notre Dame Magazine* 13 (Spring 1984): 22-25.

Lehman, Harvey C., and Paul A. Witty. "Scientific Eminence and Church Membership." *Scientific Monthly* 33 (December 1931): 544-49.

Lewis, Abdon, F.S.C. "The Traditional Four-Year Catholic College: Problems and Prospects." *National Catholic Educational Association Bulletin* 62 (August 1965): 177-84.

Lischka, Charles N. "The Attendance of Catholic Students at Non-Catholic Colleges and Universities." *Catholic Educational Association Bulletin* 22 (November 1925): 101-8.

McAvoy, Thomas T., C.S.C. "The Catholic Minority after the Americanist Controversy, 1899-1917: A Survey." *Review of Politics* 21 (January 1959): 53-82.

————. "Notre Dame 1919-1922: The Burns Revolution." *Review of Politics* 25 (October 1963): 431-50.

————. "Public Schools vs. Catholic Schools and James McMaster." *Review of Politics* 28 (January 1966): 19-46.

McCluskey, Neil G. "The New Catholic College." *America*, 25 March 1967, 414-17.

McCormick, John F., S.J. "The Lay Instructor in the Catholic College." *National Catholic Educational Association Bulletin* 25 (August 1928): 142-55.

McDannell, Colleen. "Catholic Domesticity, 1860-1960." In *American Catholic Women: A Historical Exploration*, 48-80. Edited by Karen Kennelly, C.S.J. New York: Macmillan Publishing Company, 1989.

McGrath, Earl J., and Gerald E. Dupont, S.S.E. *The Future Governance of Catholic Higher Education in the United States*. Summer 1967, n.p. [pamphlet]

MacGregor, R.R. "The Catholic Lay Professor." *America*, 12 September 1925, 513-14.

McGucken, William J., S.J. "Should We Have Coeducation in Catholic Colleges and University?" *Thought* 13 (December 1938): 537-40.

_____. "The White Steed and Education." *Thought* 14 (September 1939): 358-64.

McGuire, Martin R.P. "Catholic Education and the Graduate School." In *Vital Problems of Catholic Education in the United States*, 108-26. Edited by Roy J. Deferrari. Washington, D.C.: Catholic University of America Press, 1939.

McKeown, Elizabeth. "The National Bishops' Conference: An Analysis of Its Origins." *Catholic Historical Review* 66 (October 1980): 565-83.

Maguire, James J. "A Family Affair." *Commonweal*, 10 November 1961, 171-73.

Mallon, Wilfred, S.J. "Faculty Ranks, Tenure, and Academic Freedom." *National Catholic Educational Association Bulletin* 39 (August 1942): 177-94.

Maynard, Theodore. "The Lay Professor Again." *Commonweal*, 17 May 1935, 64-66.

Meade, Francis L., C.M. "Academic Freedom in Catholic Education." *National Catholic Educational Association Bulletin* 35 (August 1938): 109-14.

Meng, John J. "American Thought: Contributions of Catholic Thought and Thinkers." *National Catholic Educational Association Bulletin* 53 (August 1956): 113-20.

Miller, William. "American Historians and the Business Elite." *Journal of Economic History* 9 (November 1949): 184-208.

Misiak, Henryk. "Catholic Participation in the History of Psychology in America." *Historical Records and Studies* 49 (1962): 15-23.

Molanphy, C. "Catholic Colleges." *Commonweal*, 23 September 1925, 481-82.

Mulloy, William T. "Catholic Higher Education Looks Ahead." *National Catholic Educational Association Bulletin* 50 (August 1953): 199-204.

Muntsch, Albert, S.J. "Coeducation from a Catholic Standpoint." *Catholic Educational Association Bulletin* 13 (November 1916): 352-66.

Murray, James E. "Christian Education for Democracy." *National Catholic Educational Association Bulletin* 45 (August 1948): 60-70.

Murray, John Courtney, S.J. "Reversing the Secularist Drift." *Thought* 49 (March 1949): 36-46.

Noonan, Herbert, S.J. "The Need of Jesuit Universities." *Woodstock Letters* 54 (1925): 238-48.

North, Arthur, S.J. "Why Is the American Catholic Graduate School Failing to Develop Catholic Intellectualism?" *National Catholic Educational Association Bulletin* 53 (August 1956): 184-89.

Nuesse, C. Joseph. "Undergraduate Education at the Catholic University of America: The First Decades, 1889-1930." *U.S. Catholic Historian* 7 (Fall 1988): 429-51.

Nutting, Willis D. "Catholic Higher Education in America." *New Blackfriars* 32 (July 1951): 341-44.

Oates, Mary J., C.S.J. "Catholic Laywomen in the Labor Force, 1850-1950." In *American Catholic Women: A Historical Exploration*, 81-124. Edited by Karen Kennelly, C.S.J. New York: Macmillan Publishing Company, 1989.

_____. "The Development of Catholic Colleges for Women, 1895-1960." *U.S. Catholic Historian* 7 (Fall 1988): 413-28.

_____. "Learning to Teach: The Professional Preparation of Massachusetts Parochial School Faculty, 1870-1940." Working Paper Series 10, no. 2 (Fall 1981). Cushwa Center for the Study of American Catholicism, University of Notre Dame.

O'Brien, John P., C.S.V. "Some Observations on the Formation of Catholic Scholars." *National Catholic Educational Association Bulletin* 48 (August 1951): 199-202.

O'Dea, Thomas F. "The Role of the Intellectual in the Catholic Tradition." *Daedalus* 101 (Spring 1972): 151-89.

O'Hara, Charles M., S.J. "The Expanse of American Jesuit Education." *Jesuit Educational Quarterly* 2 (June 1939): 14-18.

O'Hare, Joseph A., S.J. "The Vatican and Catholic Universities," *America*, 27 May 1989, 503-5.

Opportunities for Foreign Students at Catholic Colleges and Universities in the United States. Washington, D.C.: National Catholic Welfare Conference, 1921. [pamphlet]

"Panel on Coeducation and Education of Women." *National Catholic Educational Association Bulletin* 51 (August 1954): 284-304.

Parente, William J. "Are Catholic Colleges Still Catholic?" *Current Issues in Catholic Higher Education* 6 (Summer 1985): 29-34.

Parker, Garland G. "50 Years of Collegiate Enrollments: 1919-20 to

1969-70." *School and Society* 98 (January 1970): 148-59.

Pattillo, Manning M., Jr. "The Danforth Report and Catholic Higher Education." *National Catholic Educational Association Bulletin* 63 (August 1966): 214-22.

Pellegrino, Edmund. "Catholic Universities and the Church's Intellectual Ministry: The Crises of Identity and Justification." *Thought* 57 (June 1982): 165-72.

Perlmutter, Oscar. "The Lay Professor." *Commonweal*, 11 April 1958, 31-34.

Peterson, Charles E., Jr. "The Church-Related College: Whence before Whether." In *The Contribution of the Church-Related College to the Public Good*, 3-41. Edited by Samuel H. Magill. Washington, D.C.: Association of American Colleges, 1970.

Poetker, Albert H., S.J. "The Place of the Layman in Jesuit Schools." *Jesuit Educational Quarterly* 9 (June 1946): 12-19.

Pope, Liston. "Religion and Class Structure." *Annals of the American Academy of Political and Social Science* 256 (March 1948): 85-91.

Preville, Joseph R. "Catholic Colleges and the Supreme Court: The Case of 'Tilton v. Richardson'." *Journal of Church and State* 30 (Spring 1988): 297-307.

Pritchett, Henry S. "The Relations of Christian Denominations to Colleges." *Educational Review* 36 (October 1908): 217-41.

"Record Number of Women, Blacks in Congress." *Congressional Quarterly Weekly Report*, 46 (12 November 1988): 3293-94.

Reinert, Paul C., S.J. "First Meeting of a Board." *Jesuit Educational Quarterly* 30 (October 1967): 112-17.

_____. "The Imperatives Determining the Future of Jesuit Higher Education." *Jesuit Educational Quarterly* 32 (October 1969): 65-80.

_____. "In Response to Father Greeley." *Jesuit Educational Quarterly* 29 (October 1966): 121-29.

_____. "The Responsibility of American Catholic Higher Education in Meeting National Needs." *National Catholic Educational Association Bulletin* 60 (August 1964): 137-42.

_____. "Toward Renewal: The Development of Catholic Higher Education." *National Catholic Educational Association Bulletin* 64 (August 1967): 74-78.

Reisman, David. "Reflections on Catholic Colleges, Especially Jesuit Colleges." *Journal of General Education* 34 (Summer 1982): 106-19.

Reiss, Paul J. "Faculty and Administration: The Jesuit-Lay Character." *Jesuit Educational Quarterly* 32 (October 1969): 99-116.

"Report of the Committee on Financial Standards for Catholic Institutions." *North Central Association Quarterly* 5 (September 1930): 191-92.

"Report of the Committee on Graduate Instruction." *Educational Record* 15 (April 1934): 192-234.

"Report on the Attendance at Catholic Colleges and Universities in the United States." *Catholic Educational Association Bulletin* 12 (August 1916): 5-17.

"A Report on the Problems of the Disaffection of Young Jesuits for Our Current Educational Apostolate." *Woodstock Letters* 98 (Winter 1969): 116-29.

Rice, Charles [pseud.]. "The Plight of the professor [sic]." *America*, 8 September 1951, 543-44 and 548.

Rock, George D. "Some Challenges Facing Catholic Graduate Education in the Next Half-Century." *National Catholic Educational Association Bulletin* 50 (August 1953): 205-8.

Rooney, Edward B., S.J. "The Philosophy of Academic Freedom." In *A Philosophical Symposium on American Catholic Education*, 116-28. Edited by Hunter Guthrie, S.J. and Gerald G. Walsh, S.J. New York: Fordham University Press, 1941.

Ross, J. Elliot, C.S.P. "Catholics in Non-Catholic Colleges." *Religious Education* 21 (August 1926): 399-405.

Ryan, James H. "The Catholic University of America: Focus of National Catholic Influence." *American Ecclesiastical Review* 85 (July 1931): 25-39.

_____. "Foundations of Culture." *Commonweal*, 30 April 1930, 729-31.

Sanchez, José M. "Cardinal Glennon and Academic Freedom at Saint Louis University: The Fleischer Case Revisited." *Gateway Heritage* 8 (Winter 1987-88): 2-11.

Schnell, R.L., and Patricia T. Rooke. "Intellectualism, Educational Achievement, American Catholicism: A Reconsideration of a Controversy, 1955-1975." *Canadian Review of American Studies* 8 (Spring 1977): 66-76.

Schwitalla, Alphonse, S.J. "Graduate Study in Catholic Colleges and Universities." *National Catholic Educational Association Bulletin* 28 (November 1931): 83-110.

Semper, I.J. "The Church and Higher Education for Girls." *Catholic Educational Review* 29 (April 1931): 215-25.

Shelley, Thomas J. "The Oregon School Case and the National Catholic Welfare Conference." *Catholic Historical Review* 75 (July 1989): 439-57.

Sherman, Thomas Ewing, S.J. "Higher Education of Catholic Women." *Report of the Proceedings and Addresses of the Third Annual Meeting of the Catholic Educational Association*, Cleveland, Ohio, 9-12 July 1906, 90-98.

Shuster, George N. "Have We Any Scholars?" *America*, 15 August 1925, 418-19.

"63 Are Designated Graduate Schools." *New York Times*, 2 April 1934, 18.

Smith, Thurber M., S.J. "At Variance with Fr. Bull." *Thought* 13 (December 1938): 638-43.

Smith, Timothy L. "Immigrant Social Aspirations and American Education, 1880-1930." *American Quarterly* 21 (Fall 1969): 523-43.

Spalding, John Lancaster. "The Higher Education." In *Means and Ends of Education*, 181-232. Chicago: A.C. McClurg and Co., 1897.

Stamm, Martin J. "The Emerging Guardianship of American Catholic Higher Education." *Occasional Papers on Catholic Higher Education* 5 (Summer 1979): 25-29.

_____. "Evaluating Presidential Leadership: A Case Study in Redefining Sponsorship." *Current Issues in Catholic Higher Education* 4 (Winter 1984): 28-36.

_____. "The Laicization of Corporate Governance of Twentieth Century American Catholic Higher Education." *Records of the American Catholic Historical Society of Philadelphia* 94 (March-December 1983): 81-99.

Swidler, Leonard. "Catholic Colleges: A Modest Proposal." *Commonweal*, 29 January 1965, 559-62.

Walsh, Michael, S.J. "Catholic Universities—Problems and Prospects in the Changing Educational Scene." *National Catholic Educational Association Bulletin* 62 (August 1965): 159-65.

Weare, Eugene. "Laymen on a College Council." *America*, 22 February 1930, 475-76.

Wefle, Frederick J., S.J. "Functions of the Advisory Board of Trustees." *Jesuit Educational Quarterly* 18 (October 1955): 87-99.

Weigel, Gustave, S.J. "American Catholic Intellectualism: A Theologian's Reflections." *Review of Politics* 19 (July 1957): 65-89.

Wein, Roberta. "Women's Colleges and Domesticity, 1875-1918." *History of Education Quarterly* 14 (Spring 1974): 31-47.

Weiss, Bernard J. "Duquesne University and the Urban Ethnic." In *American Education and the European Immigrant*, 176-82. Edited by Bernard J. Weiss. Urbana: University of Illinois Press, 1982.

Welter, Barbara. "Anti-Intellectualism and the American Woman, 1800-1860." *Mid-America* 48 (1966): 258-70.

_____. "The Cult of True Womanhood: 1820-1860." *American Quarterly* 18 (Summer 1966): 151-74.

Wilson, Samuel Knox. "Catholic College Education, 1900-1950." *Catholic School Journal* 51 (April 1951): 121-23.

Woodward, Kenneth. "The Order of Education: Have the Jesuits Lost Their Special Touch?" *Newsweek*, 19 June 1989, 59.

Wreen, Michael J. "'Catholic' Universities: Independent or Nonsectarian?" *Fidelity* 6 (March 1987): 13-15.

Unpublished Materials

Arthur, David J. "The University of Notre Dame, 1919-1933: An Administrative History." Ph.D. dissertation, University of Michigan, 1973.

Bannon, John F., S.J. "The Department of History, Saint Louis University, 1925-1973." St. Louis University, 1980 (mimeographed).

Bernad, Miguel, S.J. "The Faculty of Arts in the Jesuit Colleges in the Eastern Part of the United States: Theory and Practice, 1782-1923." Ph.D. dissertation, Yale University, 1951.

Bernert, Roman, S.J. "A Study of the Responses of Jesuit Educators in Theory and Practice to the Transformation of Curricular Patterns in Popular Secondary Education between 1880 and 1920." Ph.D. dissertation, University of Wisconsin, 1963.

Bowler, Mary Mariella. "A History of Catholic Colleges for Women in the United States of America." Ph.D. dissertation, Catholic University of America, 1933.

Brill, Earl H. "Religion and the Rise of the University: A Study of the Secularization of American Higher Education, 1870-1910." Ph.D. dissertation, American University, 1969.

Curley, Thomas E. "Robert I. Gannon, President of Fordham University 1936-49: A Jesuit Educator." Ph.D. dissertation, New York University, 1974.

Gawrysiak, Kenneth J. "The Administration of Albert C. Fox, A Portrait of Educational Leadership." Ph.D. dissertation, Marquette University, 1973.

Goodchild, Lester F. "The Mission of the Catholic University in the Midwest, 1842-1980: A Comparative Case Study of the Effects of Strategic Policy Decisions upon the Mission of the University of Notre Dame, Loyola University of Chicago, and DePaul University." Ph.D. dissertation, University of Chicago, 1986.

Labaj, Joseph J., S.J. "The Development of the Department of Education at Saint Louis University, 1900-1942." M.A. thesis, St. Louis University, 1952.

Lucey, Gregory F., S.J. "The Meaning and Maintenance of Catholicity as a Distinctive Characteristic of American Catholic Higher Education: A Case Study." Ph.D. dissertation, University of Wisconsin-Madison, 1978.

Mallon, Wilfred M., S.J. "The Jesuit College: An Investigation into Factors Affecting the Efficiency of the Jesuit College in the Central States." Ph.D. dissertation, St. Louis University, 1932.

Maxwell, John C. "Should the Educations of Boys and Girls Differ? A Half Century of Debate—1870-1920." Ph.D. dissertation, University of Wisconsin, 1966.

Morrissey, Timothy H. "Archbishop John Ireland and the Faribault-Stillwater School Plan of the 1890s: A Reappraisal." Ph.D. dissertation, University of Notre Dame, 1975.

Plough, James H. "Catholic Colleges and the Catholic Educational Association: The Foundation and Early Years of the CEA, 1899-1919." Ph.D. dissertation, University of Notre Dame, 1967.

Salvaterra, David L. "The Apostolate of the Intellect: Development and Diffusion of an Academic Ethos among American Catholics in the Early Twentieth Century." Ph.D. dissertation, University of Notre Dame, 1983.

Schenk, John F., S.J. "The History of Coeducation in Catholic Colleges and Universities in the United States." M.A. thesis, St. Louis University, 1943.

Trindade, Armando. "Roman Catholic Worship at Stanford University: 1891-1971." Ph.D. dissertation, Stanford University, 1971.

Zimmerman, Joan Grace. "College Culture in the Midwest, 1890-1920." Ph.D. dissertation, University of Virginia, 1978.

Index